THE NEW 52

FUTURES END

VOLUME 1

THE NEW 52 FUTURES END

VOLUME 1

BRIAN **AZZARELLO** JEFF **LEMIRE**
DAN **JURGENS** KEITH **GIFFEN** writers

PATRICK **ZIRCHER** ETHAN **VAN SCIVER**
DAN **JURGENS** MARK **IRWIN**
JESÚS **MERINO** DAN **GREEN**
AARON **LOPRESTI** ART **THIBERT**
SCOT **EATON** DREW **GERACI**
GEORGES **JEANTY** CAM **SMITH** artists

KEITH **GIFFEN** art consultant

HI-FI colorist

CARLOS M. **MANGUAL** DEZI **SIENTY**
TAYLOR **ESPOSITO** DAVE **SHARPE** letterers

RYAN **SOOK** collection cover artist

SUPERMAN created by JERRY **SIEGEL** & JOE **SHUSTER**
By special arrangement with the Jerry Siegel family

THE NEW 52: FUTURES END VOLUME 1

DC Comics, 1700 Broadway, New York, NY 10019
A Warner Bros. Entertainment Company
Printed by RR Donnelley, Salem, VA, USA. 10/31/14. First Printing.

ISBN: 978-1-4012-5244-1

Certified Chain of Custody
20% Certified Forest Content,
80% Certified Sourcing
www.sfiprogram.org
SFI-01042
APPLIES TO TEXT STOCK ONLY

Library of Congress Cataloging-in-Publication Data is available.

SOOK

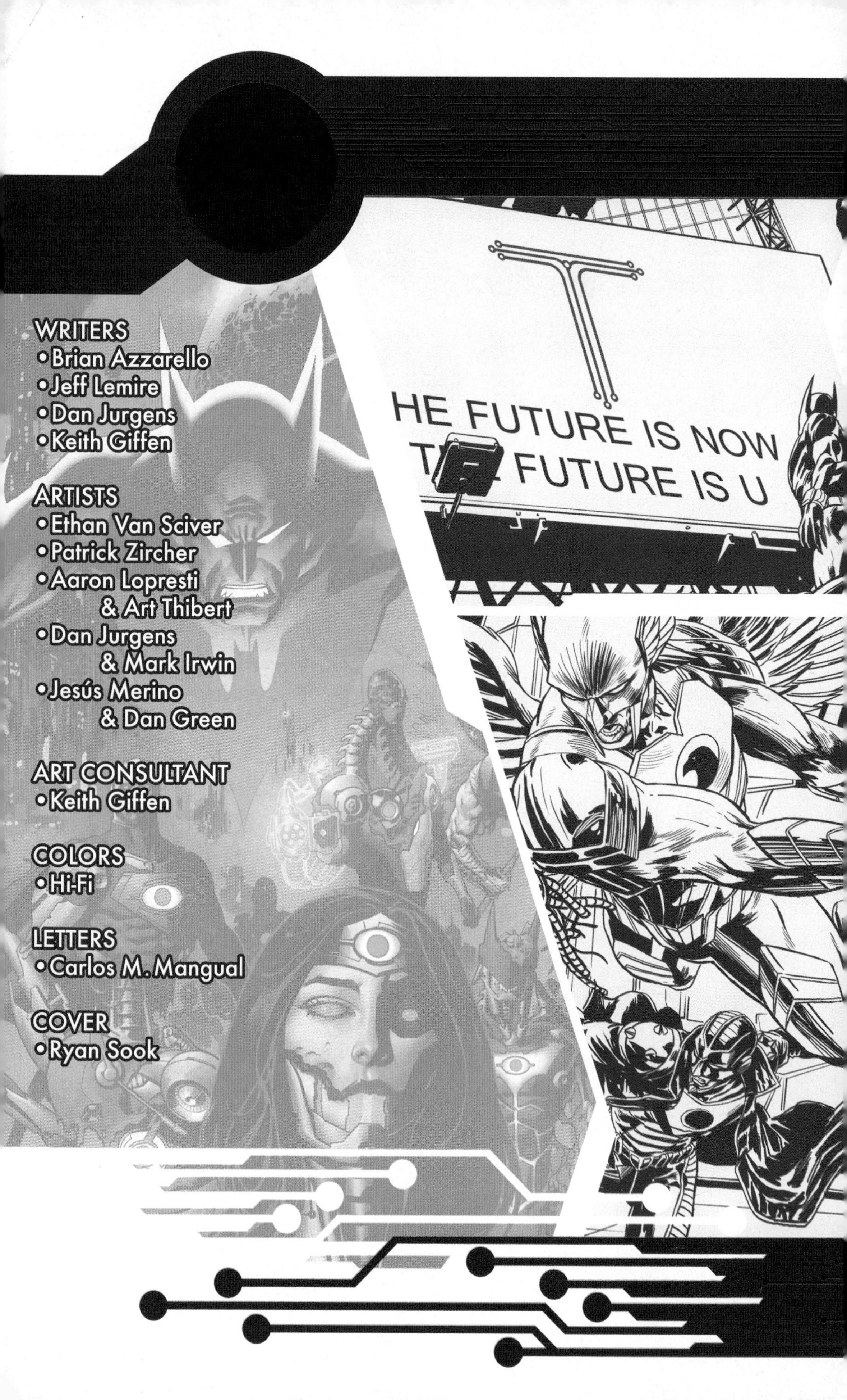

WRITERS
- Brian Azzarello
- Jeff Lemire
- Dan Jurgens
- Keith Giffen

ARTISTS
- Ethan Van Sciver
- Patrick Zircher
- Aaron Lopresti & Art Thibert
- Dan Jurgens & Mark Irwin
- Jesús Merino & Dan Green

ART CONSULTANT
- Keith Giffen

COLORS
- Hi-Fi

LETTERS
- Carlos M. Mangual

COVER
- Ryan Sook

NTRAL CITY.
RTY-FIVE YEARS FROM NOW.
CLOSE IT! CLOSE THE DAMN DOOR!
NOT YET! HE'S COMING!
CHOOM
THE TRANSMISSION FROM BUDAPEST SAID HE'S ON HIS WAY!
SORRY, CAPTAIN! --IF THE BUGS GET IN, WE'RE ALL DEAD!
--HOLD IT!
I-- I MADE IT.
SO TIRED...BEEN RUNNING ALL NIGHT.
DIDN'T YOU FIND ANYONE ELSE?
IT'S--IT'S BAD OUT THERE, LEONARD. NOT MUCH LEFT. BUT I ONLY COUNTED A FEW SMALL BUGS OUTSIDE.
THE DOOR SHOULD HOLD THEM UNTIL WE HAVE TIME TO--

THOOM
WHAT THE HELL IS THAT? I THOUGHT YOU SAID THERE WERE ONLY A FEW BUGS!?
I--I MUST HAVE BEEN FOLLOWED.
NON-ASSIMILATED UNITS DETECTED. TWO SUPER-HUMANS. THREAT LEVEL SEVENTY-EIGHT.
CHOOOM
EYE IS ALL. EYE IS ORDER...
ARRGHH!
DAMN IT! SAVE AS MANY AS YOU CAN!
TOO MANY!
WOUND FATAL. EYE-SEED PLANTED.
ARRRGHH0101-01010101!
JUST KEEP SHOOTING! I'VE GOT HAWK!

KZZT
--ENOUGH!! DIE ALREADY!!
ARRGH!
SHLUNK
LEONARD!!
--I--I--
--EYE SEE IT.
--KILL YOU! KILL EVERY LAST ONE OF YOU!
WON'T STOP RUNNING TILL YOU'RE ALL SCRAP METAL.
PANT--PANT-- PANT--
EYE IS ORDER. EYE IS ALL.
NO! NO!
STOP!

THIS ONE IS MINE.
F-FRANKENSTEIN?!
FLASH. YOU WERE ONCE A NOBLE WARRIOR... A FRIEND.
SO, I WILL GIVE YOU A CHOICE. YOU MAY JOIN BROTHER EYE FREELY, OR I WILL DESTROY YOU.
GO TO HELL, YOU MONSTER.
HRRN... VERY WELL.
C-CANARY?! WHAT HAVE YOU DONE TO HER?
BROTHER EYE SHOWED ME THE WAY.
I HAVE MADE HER A PART OF ME. WELL... NOT ALL OF HER...
...JUST HER LOVELY VOICE.
AARRRGGGHHHH!

I ONCE WAS A MONSTER, BUT NOW I AM SO MUCH MORE.
I USED TO WALK THIS WORLD ALONE, BUT NOW I AM OF THE MANY...NOW I AM PART OF BROTHER EYE.
I ONCE THOUGHT MY FLESH WAS DEAD, UNHOLY...BUT NOW I SEE THAT IT IS ALL FLESH THAT IS EVIL.
IT MUST BE PURGED. THE WORLD MUST BE CLEANSED.
THESE ARE THE LAST DAYS.
...THIS IS THE END.

METROPOLIS.
WE'RE ALMOST THERE.
ONCE WE'RE UP TOP, WE'LL DISTRACT THE CYBORGS, SO **GRIFTER** AND **AMETHYST** CAN SHUT DOWN THE **FIRESTORM BATTERY.**

AT LEAST WE WON'T BE IN A SEWER. ANOTHER MINUTE DOWN HERE AND I'LL PASS OUT.
AT LEAST IT'S SAFE.
FROM THE **EYE**, MAYBE. BUT THE SMELL IS JUST AS LETHAL!

THIS IS IT, JAIME.
READY TO GO?
...YEAH.

REGRETS?
ONLY ONE, JOHN.

I WISH WE WERE MORE THAN A DIVERSIONARY TACTIC.
SECTOR ZERO BREACHED.
TARGET ASSAILANTS FOR IMMEDIATE ASSIMILATION. THREAT LEVEL NINETY-NINE.
EYE IS ORDER. EYE IS ALL.

HIT 'EM HARD! WE DON'T HAVE MUCH TIME!
SUBJECT IDENTIFIED AS BLUE BEETLE. ASSIMILATION PROTOCOL INITIATED.

WHA--?
EYE-SEEDS INSERTED. ASSIMILATION UNDER WAY.

NO--!
TARGET ONE ASSIMILATED.

JAIME!

HANG ON! IF MY RING CAN--
RUN BEFORE0101 01010101!

TARGET TWO IDENTIFIED AS A GREEN LANTERN.

CLARK?!

WHEN YOU WENT MISSING, WE FEARED THE WORST.
BUT SEEING YOU LIKE THIS...

SKOWWW
NO... YOU AREN'T *SUPERMAN!*
HE'S *DEAD!*

ASSIMILATION INITIATED.

HIGH VALUE TARGET.
MARKED FOR PRIORITY ALPHA ASSIMILATION.

PROBLEMS, COLE?
TO GO UNDETECTED, WE NEEDED A LONGER DIVERSION, AMETHYST. NOW...
IT IS WHAT IT IS. WE GO AS PLANNED.
STAY FOCUSED, GRIFTER. ONCE YOU DISCONNECT FIRESTORM, BROTHER EYE WON'T BE ABLE TO POWER ITS SATELLITE AND CONTROL THE OTHER HEROES.

THOSE BUGS AREN'T HEROES, BATMAN--NOT ANYMORE. THE HEROES ARE DEAD.
THEN DON'T LET THEM HAVE DIED IN VAIN.
YOU TWO ARE HUMANITY'S LAST HOPE.

WITH ZERO CHANCE OF SURVIVING THE RADIATION.
I'LL DO WHAT I CAN TO PROTECT US, BUT WE'RE ALL EARTH HAS.

NOT ANYMORE.
EYE IS ORDER. EYE IS ALL.
GYAHH!

BY THE LORDS--!
GRIFTER? WHAT HAPPENED?
REPORT!

THEY GOT JOHN! THERE'S NO WAY WE'LL GET TO FIRESTORM!
TELL BRUCE--

"--WE FAILED."
SHRAKK!

WAYNE MANOR.
"THEY'VE FAILED. IT'S OVER."
"NOT IF IT'S NEVER BEGUN."
"IS THAT WHAT WE'RE USING TO JUSTIFY SENDING THEM ALL TO SLAUGHTER?"
...YES.
YOU KNOW WHAT'S AT STAKE. WHERE'S THIS COMING FROM?
THE ENDS JUSTIFY THE MEANS. IT'S A BIT TOO CLOSE TO BROTHER EYE'S LOGIC FOR COMFORT.
THINK WHAT YOU LIKE, AS LONG AS YOU DO WHAT NEEDS DOING.

I'M STILL HAVING A HARD TIME GETTING MY HEAD AROUND THIS. I MEAN, TIME TRAVEL?
YOU SURE YOU WON'T JUST VAPORIZE YOURSELF?
YES. MAYBE. I...WHY ARE YOU DOING THIS?

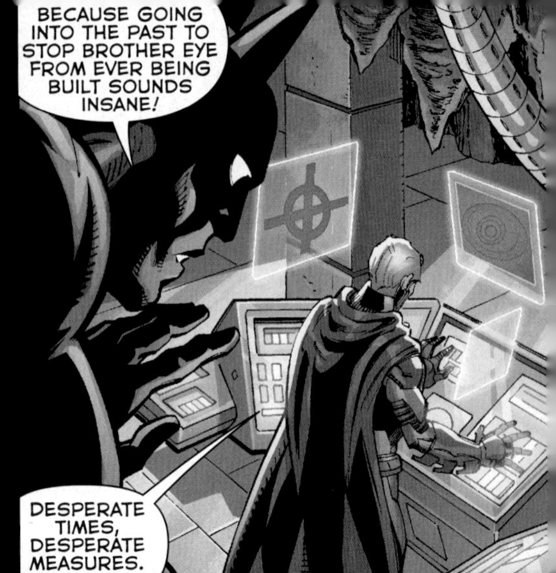
BECAUSE GOING INTO THE PAST TO STOP BROTHER EYE FROM EVER BEING BUILT SOUNDS INSANE!
DESPERATE TIMES, DESPERATE MEASURES.

I WON'T LIVE IN BROTHER EYE'S WORLD.
THEN YOU AND *MR. TERRIFIC* SHOULD NEVER HAVE HAD IT BUILT.

I'M DIVERTING POWER FROM THE SECURITY GRID TO THE TIME PORTAL DEVICE.
DIMINISHED SHIELDS WON'T HOLD THEM BACK. I NEED SIXTY SECONDS TO POWER UP--
WE'VE BEEN OVER THIS. IT'S WHY I'M HERE.

IF I SUCCEED, THIS WILL NEVER HAVE HAPPENED.
THEN STOP SAYING "IF."

CH-KOOOOM
RAK-KKKOOM
ROGUE TECH-CELL IN SECTOR TEN ACCESSED.
FINAL TARGETS ACQUIRED.
LETHAL FORCE ENABLED.
BATMAN!
FORTY-FIVE SECONDS!

FINAL TARGE-- -KZZZK-
BLOONT
FORTY SECONDS!
23 : 44
00004355031
0.00325 MTS
A.L.F.R.E.D.
NO PRESSURE! RIGHT?!
SQUARRRRRRK!
RAKKT

THUNK
SHK-LKKTCH
NO!
TH... THIRTY SEC... SEC...

BRUCE!
SKZZZZZZTTTZZZ
NO.
NO.
NO...
HANG ON...
WITH WHAT, TERRY?

TAKE IT.
I'M NOT TRAINED FOR TIME TRAVEL, BRUCE!
YOU *ARE* TRAINED BY ME-- UNDERSTOOD?
FATE IS UP TO YOU NOW.
STOP HELL FROM REACHING EARTH.
AND TERRY?
WHATEVER YOU DO, DON'T CONTACT ME IN THE PAST.
WHY?
BECAUSE NOT ONLY WON'T I BELIEVE YOUR STORY...
BUT I'LL STOP YOU.

CLARK, TOO. HE GETS INVOLVED, HE'LL JUST MUDDY THINGS UP.
I MEAN...
WE'RE TALKING ABOUT KILLING A MAN HERE.
I'LL GET IT DONE, BRUCE.
I KNOW.
BLAAM
ZZZKKKKT
OR YOU MIGHT BE VAPORIZED.
BOOM
THIS...
THIS IS NOT WHY I LIVED MY LIFE...
TO DIE LIKE THIS....

WHUMP

SMASH

A.L.F.R.E.D.?
MASTER TERRY.
COORDINATES.
SEARCHING NOW...
SCANNING...

OH, MY.
OH MY WHAT?
WE SEEM TO HAVE MISSED THE TARGET DATE.
TIMES SQUARE.
FIVE YEARS FROM NOW.
WHAT YOU'VE TRAVELED TO THE PAST TO PREVENT...
...IS ALREADY IN PLAY.
DAMN.
LexCo
CADMUS
The FAST Lane
S.T.A.R. LABORATORIES
GBS
THE REUNION
A BENEFIT FOR VETERANS
TERRIFITECH
FITECH

COOK

WRITERS
•Brian Azzarello
•Jeff Lemire
•Dan Jurgens
•Keith Giffen
ARTIST
•Patrick Zircher
ART CONSULTANT
•Keith Giffen
COLORS
•Hi-Fi
LETTERS
•Dezi Sienty
COVER
•Ryan Sook
POLICE
T

IVE YEARS FROM NOW...
SO NOW WHAT, A.L.F.R.E.D.?
"NOW" INDEED, AS THE NOW WE FIND OURSELVES IN IS NOT WHERE WE ARE MEANT TO BE.
INTERESTING... THEORETICALLY, THAT MIGHT BE WHAT NOW ETERNALLY IS.
WAS THE *REAL* ALFRED LIKE YOU?
REAL ALFRED. ARE YOU INSINUATING THAT I'M IMAGINARY?
NO...
...ANNOYING.

OH, I APOLOGIZE FOR ENGAGING IN CONVERSATION WHILE ACCESSING NETWORKS. I'LL BE QUIET WHILE I PINPOINT OUR--
--ALLOW ME. WE'RE SEVEN YEARS TOO LATE TO STOP MR.TERRIFIC'S CREATION OF BROTHER EYE, WHICH IS RESPONSIBLE FOR THE HELL OF A FUTURE WE CAME FROM.
NOT TO MENTION THE TIME BAND HAD ONLY ONE JUMP. MEANING WE'RE STUCK HERE.
THE FUTURE IS NOW
THE FUTURE IS U
THAT'S CORRECT, MASTER TERRY.
HOW'D YOU LET THAT HAPPEN?
I?--THE TIME BAND WAS CALIBRATED TO MASTER BRUCE'S... MASS.
YOU DON'T MEASURE UP.
YOU GET A REAL KICK OUT OF YOURSELF, DON'T YOU?
MASTER BRUCE PROGRAMMED ME.
THE KICKS ARE ALL HIS.
SO WHAT DO WE DO WITH THIS CYBORG THAT HITCHED A RIDE BACK WITH US?
GYAAAHH!

SMASH
A.L.F.R.E.D., YOU DIDN'T MENTION SHE WAS STILL ALIVE!
WHHRRR
THE FUTURE IS NOW
SMASH
WHY WOULD I? SHE'S NOT.
SHE SEEMS PRETTY ALIVE TO ME!
THAT IS AN INCORRECT ASSUMPTION. LIFE IS DEFINED BY BRAIN FUNCTION...
SZZZZKKKK
...AND NOW SHE'S NO LONGER FUNCTIONAL.

MASTER TERRY, YOU'RE INJURED.
I'LL LIVE. THOUGH... TECHNICALLY, I WON'T FOR, WHAT -- AT LEAST A FEW MORE YEARS?
WHICH IS FUNNY.
I DON'T UNDERSTAND.
WHAT?
LIFE AS FUNNY.
THAT'S BECAUSE BRUCE PROGRAMMED YOU.

THE HURON SYSTEM.
THE FARTHEST REACHES OF KNOWN SPACE.
E CARRIER.
OBILE HEADQUARTERS OF STORMWATCH.
"--WHAT JUST HAPPENED? ENGINEER, I NEED A SITREP--WHERE THE HELL ARE WE?!"
I'M NOT SURE, JACK. THE CARRIER HAS EEN PULLED OUT OF THE BLEED BY AN UNKNOWN ENERGY SOURCE.
PULLED OUT--?! HOW IS THAT POSSIBLE, ENGINEER?! WHO COULD REACH US WHILE WE'RE TRAVELING BETWEEN UNIVERSES?
HAWKMAN'S RIGHT, ANGIE. THE BLEED SITS OUTSIDE THIS DIMENSION. THERE IS NO WAY ANYONE COULD TOUCH US!

WHAT'S THE SHIP SAYING TO YOU, ANGIE?
I DON'T -- THE CARRIER IS TRYING TO SHUT ME OUT, JACK. IT'S LIKE MY NANITE BLOOD IS SUDDENLY SPEAKING A LANGUAGE THAT'S DIFFERENT FROM THE SHIP'S!
ARRRGH!!!...
ENGINEER
JACK HAWKSMOOR...LEADER OF STORMWATCH. YOUR TEAM HAS SECRETLY PROTECTED EARTH FROM ALIEN TREATS SINCE THE DARK AGES--BUT YOU ALWAYS KNEW THAT WAS ALL JUST PREPARATION FOR THE TRUE STORM...THE ULTIMATE THREAT...
WHAT THE HELL'S WRONG WITH THE ENGINEER, JACK?!
TH--THAT'S NOT ANGIE ANYMORE, MIDNIGHTER--
NO, JACK HAWKSMOOR. ANGELA SPICA, CODENAME: THE ENGINEER, IS GONE. AM THE STORM YOU WERE CREATED FOR. I AM HERE.
JACK, SOMETHING'S TAKING CONTROL OF THE CARRIER'S SELF-DEFENSE SYSTEMS!!
ARRRGHH0101-0101010!
ANGIE!

THE CARRIER'S TURNED AGAINST US, HAWKMAN!
SO HIT IT BACK, APOLLO!
ANGIE-- CAN YOU HEAR ME?
--JACK, MY BLOOD, JACK-- MY MACHINE BLOOD--
--IT WAS INSIDE OF ME--AN INTELLIGENCE SO BIG--SO IMMENSE--
APOLLO! SOMETHING OUT THERE IS DOING THIS! IT HAS TO BE--
I'M ON IT, JACK.
APOLLO...
WHAT IS IT?
JUST--BE CAREFUL. I HAVE A BAD FEELING ABOUT THIS ONE.
DON'T WORRY. IT'S ME.

JACK, I CAN'T SEE ANYTHING OUT OF THE--

--WAIT--

SUPERHUMAN DETECTED. POWER LEVEL 10.

THREAT LEVEL... PROCESSING...2.

RECOMMENDATION-- PROCEED WITH DESTRUCTION OF EXTRADIMENSIONAL STARCRAFT DESIGNATE: THE CARRIER.

APOLLO?

WHAT IS IT, APOLLO? OUR SENSORS HAVE JUST ***SHUT DOWN...*** WE ARE BLIND IN HERE!

MIDNIGHTER, JACK...I THINK I SEE IT--IT'S--OH GOD, IT'S--

AARRGHH!!!!

NO!

S--SOMETHING ELSE IS HAPPENING, JACK!

WHAT NOW, MERMAID?!

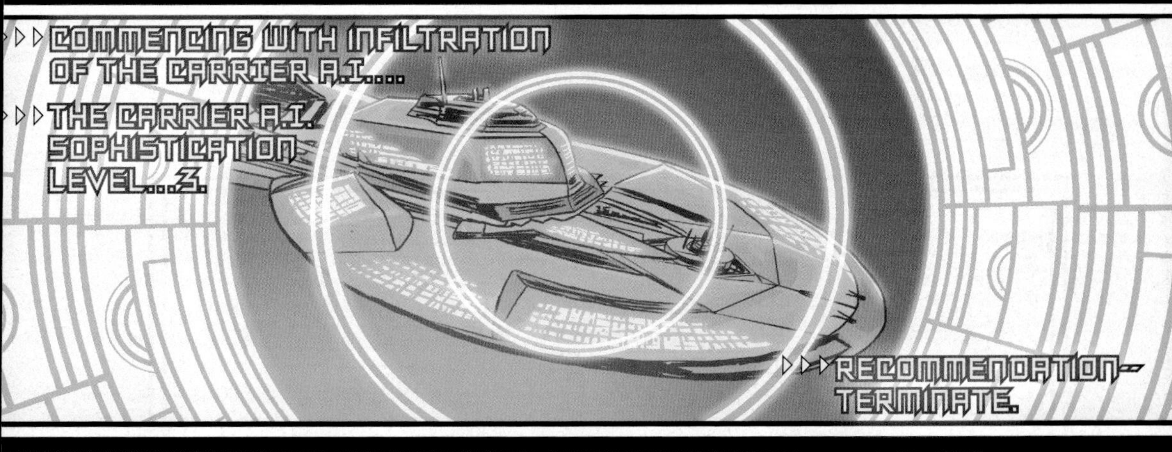

THOOOM
▷▷▷EARTH'S EARLY DETECTION SYSTEM CODENAMED: STORMWATCH DESTROYED.
▷▷▷PROCEED WITH PRIMARY OBJECTIVE... CHARTING COURSE TO TARGET PLANET DESIGNATE: EARTH.

CONOVER COVE, NORTH CAROLINA.
THEY CLUSTER.
THEY'RE LIKE US THAT WAY. SOCIAL. THEY GRAVITATE TOWARD EACH OTHER.
BEFORE THIS OP, I STUMBLED ACROSS AN ENTIRE FRAT HOUSE FULL OF THEM.
THE SIX NORMALS LIVING AMONG THEM DIDN'T HAVE A CLUE.

TRUTH IS, THEY'RE EVERY-WHERE. HIDING IN PLAIN SIGHT.

REMEMBER THAT MOVIE ABOUT PODS FROM OUTER SPACE POSSESSING PEOPLE?

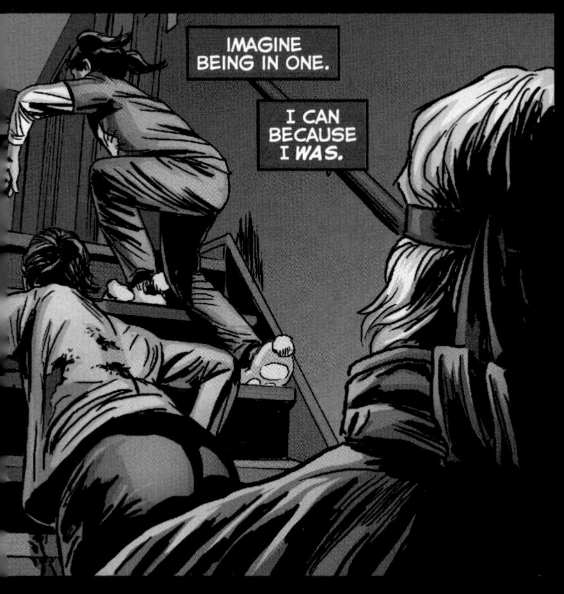
IMAGINE BEING IN ONE.
I CAN BECAUSE I *WAS.*

LUCKILY, I GOT OUT BEFORE I TURNED INTO ONE OF THESE POOR BASTARDS.

BUT NOT BEFORE I GOT STUCK WITH THE ABILITY TO SEE THROUGH THEIR LIES.

KLAK
KINDA IRONIC CONSIDERING I USED TO BE THE CON ARTIST...

NOW I'M A ONE-MAN ARMY AGAINST ANOTHER INVASION.

MOST PEOPLE THINK I'M CRAZY.
WHEN THE ALIENS PLAY IT OUT THIS LONG, EVEN I START TO WONDER.

GUESS THEY'RE HOPING TO GET ME DOUBTING, STRIKE WHILE I'M SECOND-GUESSING MYSELF.

NOT GONNA HAPPEN.
I'M NEVER WRONG.

COME ON... YOU KNOW YOU WANT TO...

THERE WE GO.

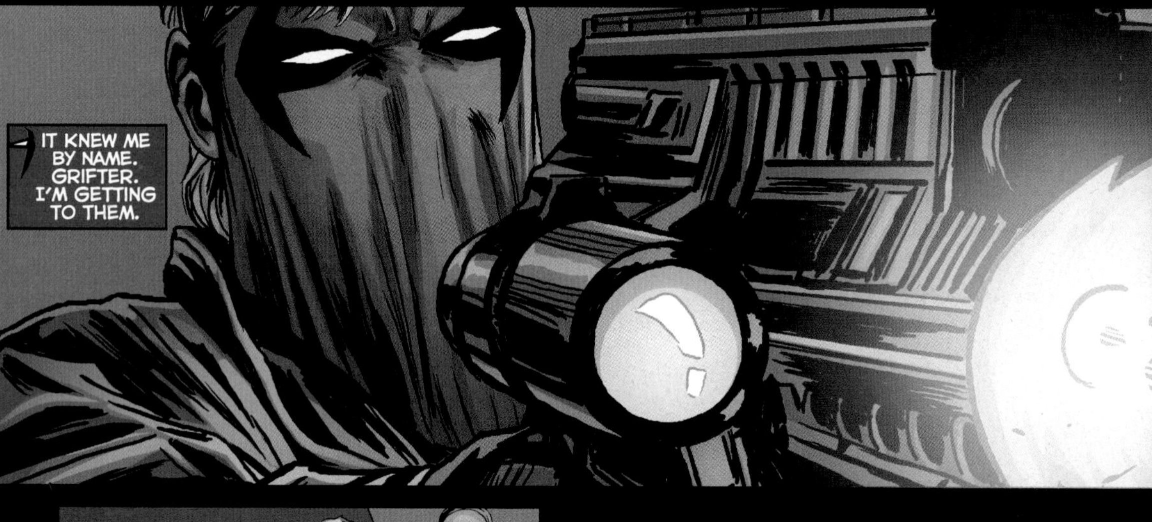
IT KNEW ME BY NAME. GRIFTER. I'M GETTING TO THEM.

THEY WALK AMONG US AND I WALK AMONG THEM.

BEST JOB *EVER.*

ORNINGSIDE HEIGHTS,
EW YORK CITY.

Open
Spot Hott
Spot Hott
RAYMOND?!
ANSWER YOUR DAMN PHONE!
THE FUTURE IS NOW
THE FUTURE IS U
Spring Fling at Spot Hott

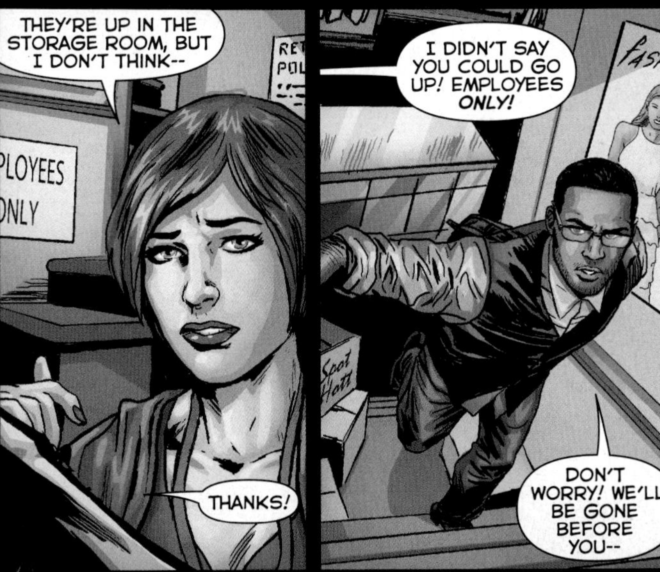

CAN'T YOU SEE I'M BUSY HERE, RUSCH?
BEAT IT!
I... UM...
WHY WEREN'T YOU ANSWERING YOUR PHONE?
Spot Hott
Spot Hott
DO YOU REALLY NEED ME TO EXPLAIN?
NO! WAIT! LISTEN TO ME!
I DO NOT NEED THIS.
HAPPY WITH YOURSELF?
WE GOT A DISTRESS CALL FROM OLIVER-- GREEN ARROW-- FORTY-FIVE MINUTES AGO. HE NEEDS US!
SO WE'LL BE LATE. HE'S A SUPERHERO. HE CAN TAKE CARE OF HIMSELF.
ONCE UPON A TIME, SO WERE WE.
BUT YOU CAN'T BE BOTHERED.
I DON'T DO 24/7. ESPECIALLY WHEN EMILY'S ON SPEED DIAL.
YOU DON'T CARE ABOUT HER!
I CARE ABOUT HAVING A GOOD TIME. YOU SHOULD TRY IT.
DON'T YOU TOUCH ME! I AM NOT--
TOO LATE.

I SHOULD GO INTO WITNESS PROTECTION TO STOP THIS.
SEATTLE--FAST AS YOU CAN.
OR KILL YOU. THAT'D WORK.
LOOK, OLIVER BROUGHT US INTO THE JUSTICE LEAGUE AFTER THE *WAR*. HE TRUSTS US MORE THAN ANYONE.
IF HE NEEDS OUR HELP, WE CAN'T LET HIM DOWN!
DO WE EVEN KNOW WHAT THE PROBLEM IS?
OLLIE'S PRETTY PROUD. IF HE FELT LIKE HE COULDN'T HANDLE IT ON HIS OWN, IT MUST BE *BAD.*
MAYBE SOMETHING NUCLEAR, THAT ONLY OUR POWERS CAN HANDLE.
HEAD FOR THE HARBOR. THAT WAS WHERE HE SIGNALED FROM.
AND *HOPE* HE WAS ABLE TO HANG ON WITHOUT US.
IS THAT A FIRE?
DAMN.
WHAT THE HELL--?
WHAT HAPPENED?!

I...
IT'S LIKE A WAR ZONE... ALL OVER AGAIN...
OLLIE'S LAB IS GONE!
LOOKS LIKE IT WAS GROUND ZERO FOR WHATEVER HAPPENED HERE!
CHANGE THE OXYGEN TO CARBON DIOXIDE AND PUT THE FIRE OUT.
THEN TAKE CARE OF THE PEOPLE!
OKAY, I SCREWED UP. I GET THAT.
SCREWING UP IS ALL YOU EVER DO.
FIRESTORM SHOULD BE A PRIORITY, BUT YOU GAVE UP ON THAT A LONG TIME AGO.
I'VE PAID MY DUES, RUSCH.
AND I DON'T NEED A NANNY.
WHAT YOU NEED IS A KICK IN THE ASS!
BECAUSE ALL YOU CARE ABOUT IS YOURSELF.
OH, MY GOD! THANK YOU!
GLAD I COULD HELP.
I THOUGHT WE WERE DEAD FOR SURE!
NOT WHEN I'M AROUND.
SURE. NOW YOU CARE!
YOUR HEAD--I GUESS THAT'S WHY THEY CALL YOU FIREHAIR.
FIRESTORM.

OVER HERE!
YOU HAVE TO HELP HIM!
PLEASE! YOU CAN'T LET HIM DIE!
COMING.
HE WAS TRYING TO HELP US!
BUT THEN THERE WAS ANOTHER EXPLOSION AND--!
MOVE BACK. THERE'S A BETTER WAY.
NOT HYDROGEN--
THANKS FOR THE TIP, GENIUS.
LIKE I WOULDN'T KNOW ENOUGH TO CHANGE IT TO HELIUM.
ARE YOU TALKING TO *ME?*
HOW LONG AGO DID THIS HAPPEN?
20, 25 MINUTES. I DID ALL I COULD...
I'M SURE YOU DID.
25 MINUTES?
IT CAN'T BE...
THERE HE IS!
NO!
THIS IS ON YOU, RAYMOND!
THIS IS *YOUR FAULT!*
YOUR SELFISHNESS CAUSED THIS!
BECAUSE OF *YOU*--

--GREEN ARROW IS DEAD!

SOOK

WRITERS
- Brian Azzarello
- Jeff Lemire
- Dan Jurgens
- Keith Giffen

PENCILLER
- Jesús Merino

INKER
- Dan Green

ART CONSULTANT
- Keith Giffen

COLORS
- Hi-Fi

LETTERS
- Carlos M. Mangual

COVER
- Ryan Sook

FIVE YEARS FROM NOW.
YOU HAVEN'T SAID A WORD SINCE WE LEFT NEW YORK.
GUILT EATING AWAY AT YOU?
GOT NUTHIN' TO SAY. IT ONLY ENCOURAGES YOU TO TALK MORE.
AND I'M TIRED OF LISTENING TO YOU.
THAT'S BECAUSE YOU KNOW I'M *RIGHT*, RAYMOND.
OLIVER QUEEN IS DEAD.
ALL BECAUSE *YOU* WERE TOO BUSY GETTING DOWN WITH ONE OF YOUR CONQUESTS.
OLIVER DIED BECAUSE HALF THE WATERFRONT BLEW UP.
NOT BECAUSE OF *ME.*
YEAH, BUT IT'S *YOUR* FAULT WE WERE *LATE.*
GREEN ARROW NEEDED *FIRESTORM'S* HELP AND WE DIDN'T SHOW. WHEN WE SEE ANIMAL MAN, THE FLASH AND THE REST, YOU HAVE TO OWN UP TO THAT.
WOULDJA GIVE IT A REST, JASON?
WE'RE HERE FOR A *FUNERAL.*

SO WHAT'S TRENDING RIGHT NOW?
UM...
THAT'S THE "NOT YOU" UM, ISN'T IT?
UM...
JESUS...
#RIPGREENARROW...
#NOSHOBATMAN...
#WHERESBATS?...
#ANOTHERONEBITESTHEDUST?
#GREENISTHENEWDEAD?
DAMN, PEOPLE ARE COLD.
YO, JEEVES-- WHAT GIVES? WE'RE GONNA BE LATE!
I'M SORRY, SIR--THE CROWDS.
CROWDS?
HOLD UP.

WATCH ME TREND.
MR. TERRIFIC!
MR. TERRIFIC!
WHAT DO YOU THINK OF THIS TURNOUT? DID YOU KNOW GREEN ARROW WAS THIS LOVED?
NOT WHILE HE WAS ALIVE.
THINK YOU ARE?
I DON'T PLAN TO FIND OUT.

YOU DON'T SEEM TOO BROKEN UP ABOUT GREEN ARROW'S DEATH.
HUH?
WHY WOULD YOU...

LOOK--IT WAS OLIVER QUEEN WHO INSPIRED ME TO "COME OUT."
HIS EXAMPLE SHOWED ME THAT TO BE A HERO, I DIDN'T NEED A SECRET IDENTITY HIDING BEHIND A MASK.
IT'S TRUE, WE DIDN'T ALWAYS SEE EYE TO EYE...

BUT I'M HERE TO PAY RESPECTS TO THAT MAN.
YOU DON'T THINK DONATING TEN MILLION DOLLARS TO THE QUEEN FOUNDATION AFTER HIS DEATH WAS ENOUGH?

QUESTION MY MOTIVES ALL YOU WANT, HATER, BUT MAKE NOTE OF THE GOOD ALL THAT MONEY DOES.
AND THAT'S ALL I HAVE TO SAY ABOUT THAT--

"THIS DAY'S NOT ABOUT ME."
YOU NEVER MISS A CHANCE, DO YOU, MICHAEL?
CHANCE? I PREFER TO CALL THEM OPPORTUNITIES, ARTHUR.
POLICE
ANY TIME WE GET TO ADDRESS THE PEOPLE DIRECTLY IS AN OPPORTUNITY.
AND YOU'RE WELCOME.
?
LOOK, I'M OUT THERE ACTUALLY TALKING-- MEANING TAKING THE HEAT.
BECAUSE OF ME, THE TRUST WITH THE PUBLIC AND THE HERO COMMUNITY ISN'T COMPLETELY ERODED.
PHNFF
YOU HAVE A PROBLEM WITH THE WAY I OPERATE-- I KNOW THAT.
SO KNOW I DON'T CARE.
AND THAT I KNOW ME TURNING DOWN A PLACE IN THE LEAGUE EATS YOU UP.

SOMEONE LIKE ME--TELLING THE JUSTICE LEAGUE, I DON'T NEED TO BE A PART OF YOU TO DO GOOD.
TO HELP.
TO FULFILL MY POTENTIAL...
AND THEN BE PROVEN RIGHT.
THAT'S WHAT BOTHERS YOU THE MOST, ISN'T IT?
THAT I ACTUALLY HAD THE NERVE TO GO IT ALONE.
THE LEAGUE HAS NEVER BEEN ANYTHING BUT SUPPORTIVE OF--
--YOU'RE IN THE LEAGUE, YOU TAKE A BACKSEAT TO YOURSELF.
I'M TOO DRIVEN TO DO THAT, ARTHUR.
HEH.
WE'RE LUCKY I'M NOT A VILLAIN.
WHY'S THAT?

NEW YORK CITY.
"BECAUSE ALL OF YOU, HERE TOGETHER? IT'S LIKE SHOOTING FISH IN A BARREL."
SO IT'S IN THERE?
NO, BROTHER EYE IS IN ORBIT, BUT IT WAS CREATED THERE.
THE SATELLITE HAS BEEN DARK SINCE JUST PRIOR TO THE WAR. PRESUMABLY RENDERED INOPERABLE BY THE INVADING ARMADA.
TERRIFITECH
ARE YOU KIDDING? WE CTUALLY LANDED IN THE WRONG TIME, RIGHT PLACE?
YOU'RE VERY DROLL, SIR.
NOW OUR MISSION IS TO MAKE SURE BROTHER EYE *STAYS* DARK.
THAT WOULD SEEM SO.
SO LET'S GET STARTED. WHAT'S THE SECURITY LIKE IN TERRIFITECH?
CLEVER. BUT PRIMITIVE. I WON'T HAVE A PROBLEM WITH IT.
AND WHAT ARE WE LOOKING FOR EXACTLY?
WHY, WHAT EVERY DETECTIVE CRAVES, MASTER TERRY...
CLUES.
I'M A *SOLDIER*-- POINT ME AND MY GUN IN THE RIGHT DIRECTION, A.L.F.R.E.D.
I'M NOT A *DETECTIVE.*
WHO
WE'LL WORK ON THAT.

LAMBERT

MOIRA QUE
SHELTER FOR HOMELESS Y
POLICE
POLICE

WHEN I FIRST MET OLIVER QUEEN-- GREEN ARROW-- I COULDN'T STAND HIM. I THOUGHT HE WAS AN ARROGANT, OVERPRIVILEGED BRAT.
MAN... WAS I WRONG.
THIS CROWD, ALL THE PEOPLE GATHERED HERE TODAY, ARE A TESTAMENT TO THE MAN OLIVER QUEEN WAS.
AND TO THE HERO THAT GREEN ARROW BECAME.
AS ANIMAL MAN, I WAS IN THE JUSTICE LEAGUE WITH GREEN ARROW. AND WHILE I COULDN'T STAND HIM AT FIRST, HE BECAME--HE WAS MY BEST FRIEND.
OUR ADVENTURES WITH THE LEAGUE TOOK US TO PLACES-- TO WORLDS--WE COULD NEVER EVEN HAVE DREAMED OF.
BUT NO MATTER HOW FAR WE TRAVELED, OLLIE'S HEART WAS ALWAYS RIGHT HERE. IN THE CITY HE DIED PROTECTING...
HIS HEART WAS IN THE STREETS...WITH HIS PEOPLE.

HE MAY HAVE BEEN BORN INTO WEALTH, BUT OLLIE ACTUALLY LOST HIS ENTIRE FORTUNE A FEW YEARS INTO HIS CAREER AS GREEN ARROW. BUT HE DIDN'T LET THAT KEEP HIM DOWN.
HE QUICKLY REBUILT THAT FORTUNE, AND HE USED IT, NOT FOR PERSONAL GAIN, BUT TO BUILD THIS SHELTER, ALONG WITH A HALF-DOZEN HOMELESS SHELTERS AND REHABILITATION CENTERS AROUND THE CITY.
HE USED HIS INGENUITY AND TECHNOLOGY TO CREATE FREE AND ACCESSIBLE RESOURCES FOR HIS CITY AND FOR PEOPLE ALL OVER THE WORLD.
NO MATTER WHAT HE DID, OR HOW MUCH HE GAVE BACK, OLLIE ALWAYS HAD HIS DETRACTORS.
THERE ARE MANY WHO SAY HE WASN'T A "REAL" SUPERHERO. THAT HE WAS JUST A RICH GUY WITH A BUNCH OF GIZMOS AND TRICK ARROWS.
WELL, THOSE PEOPLE CLEARLY DIDN'T KNOW OLIVER QUEEN.
WHEN APOKOLIPS CHASED THE SURVIVORS OF ANOTHER EARTH TO OUR OWN...OLLIE UNITED US.
NOT JUST DURING THE WAR. BUT, MORE IMPORTANTLY, AFTERWARDS, WHEN OUR DIFFERENCES THREATENED TO DIVIDE US.
TWO WORLDS ONE HUMANITY

HE HAD NO SUPER POWERS TO PROTECT HIM, NO INVULNERABILITY OR MAGICAL WEAPONS TO SHIELD HIM...BUT GREEN ARROW WAS THE FIRST ONE INTO THE FRAY.
"HE DID IT FOR HIS CITY.
"HE DID IT FOR HIS PEOPLE."
OLIVER QUEEN MAY HAVE STARTED OFF AS A SPOILED, ARROGANT BRAT. BUT HE DIED A MAN.
...WITH MORE HEART, MORE COMPASSION AND MORE DIGNITY THAN ANY OF US.
...THERE'S NO TRICK ARROW THAT CAN DO THAT.

CHARLOTTE, NC.
POLICE HQ.
...GOT BLOOD, SPENT SHELL CASINGS AND CLOTHING BUT NO BODIES.
HOW DO YOU FIGURE THAT?
I DON'T. YET.
CHECK OUT THEM PHOTOS. THE PLACE IS A CHARNEL HOUSE. THIS SMACKS OF *THEM.*
UM-HM.
JUST SAYIN'...IF IT'S WEIRD, ODDS ARE THERE'S A SUPER-HUMAN INVOLVED, RIGHT?
YOU HEARD OF THE GARRISON DISAPPEARANCE?
CAN'T SAY THAT I HAVE.
HE REALLY DISAPPEARED. LITERALLY! POOR GUY NEVER EVEN KNEW HE WAS A POTENTIAL.
KILLED HIMSELF. COULDN'T FIGURE OUT HOW TO TURN HIS POWERS OFF, SO HE TURNED HIMSELF OFF.
THERE'S THE PROBLEM RIGHT THERE. PEOPLE ONLY HEAR 'BOUT THE ONES THAT DRESS UP 'N' FLOUNCE AROUND IN PUBLIC.
DON'T YOU HAVE SOMEPLACE YOU HAVE TO BE? PLEASE?
FBI
FBI

THANK YOU. PLEASE CLOSE THE DOOR BEHIND YOU.
SLAM
TIK
AT LEAST THIS ONE DIDN'T ASK ME IF MY NAME IS REALLY *KING* FARADAY. I *HATE* IT WHEN THEY ASK THAT.
UNFORTUNATELY, NO. OUR "PERSON OF INTEREST" IS VERY GOOD AT WHAT HE DOES.
STILL, YOU'D THINK ONE OF HIS TARGETS WOULD SCRATCH HIM, DRAW BLOOD. IT WOULD CERTAINLY SIMPLIFY MATTERS...
NO, NO. NOTHING WE DON'T ALREADY KNOW. STILL, BETTER SAFE THAN SORRY.
NASTY THINGS, VIRUSES. THE CASE FILES SHOULD BE IRRETRIEVABLY CORRUPTED.
IT'S ALMOST TOO EASY. IT LOOKS LIKE A FLASH DRIVE SO IT MUST BE A FLASH DRIVE. SURPRISE!
YES, THEY DO, DON'T THEY? BUT THEN, DON'T WE *ALL* ACCEPT THE REALITY WITH WHICH WE'RE PRESENTED?

GET ME OUT OF HERE.
...FEDERAL STIFFS GIVE ME GAS. YOU SHOULD CHECK OUT THE ATTITUDE ON THAT ONE. WHY THE HELL THEY GOTTA SEND A FED DOWN?
WHAT? THEY AFRAID US YOKELS WILL MAKE A MESS OF--
YEAH, YEAH, WE SEE YOU, Y' PUFFED-UP--
SUNNUVA! YOU SEEING THI--
?!
NO. I HAVE NO INTEREST IN SEEING THE LOOKS ON THEIR FACES.
THE FORENSICS EVIDENCE AND ALL RECORDS REGARDING SUCH ARE DESTROYED. MISSION ACCOMPLISHED.
NO FUN? I SUPPOSE I'M NOT.
I'VE ALWAYS THOUGHT THAT A VIRTUE.
WELL, OF COURSE, YOU AGREE. IN ALL HONESTY, YOU'VE LITTLE CHOICE IN THE MATTER.
NOW BE A DEAR AND UPDATE ME ON GRIFTER'S WHERE-ABOUTS?
TAXI
TERRIFI
building
TAX

MOIRA Q
SHELTER FOR HOM
NOW, AFTER THAT MOVING TRIBUTE BY BUDDY BAKER, MORE POPULARLY KNOWN AS ANIMAL MAN...
...HE, FIRESTORM, ARSENAL, THE FLASH, ADAM STRANGE, AND THE ENIGMATIC MR. DIGGLE WILL HAND OVER OLIVER QUEEN'S BODY FOR ONE FINAL JOURNEY.
WE HAVEN'T SEEN AN ASSEMBLY LIKE THIS SINCE THE END OF THE WAR FOUR YEARS AGO--
ENOUGH. I CAN'T TAKE ANOTHER WORD.
LEAVE IT ON. I WANT TO WATCH IT.
THEY'RE HEROES!
THAT'S WHAT THEY WANT YOU TO THINK.
THEY'VE GOT THEIR SECRETS AND SKELETONS, JUST LIKE EVERYONE ELSE.
MORE, IN FACT.
ARE YOU FO REAL?
DESPITE EVERYTHING WE'VE BEEN THROUGH, THIS HASN'T GOTTEN ANY EASIER.
NEVER WILL WHEN IT'S A CLOSE FRIEND.
YEAH.

THE FACT THAT YOU ARE INCLUDED IN THIS --
--THAT YOU'RE ANYWHERE NEAR HERE--
--IS A LOAD OF CRAP!
WHOA.
LET ARSENAL RANT, RONNIE. DON'T TAKE THE BAIT.
GOT SOMETHING TO SAY, HARPER?
DAMN RIGHT I DO.
DON'T, RONNIE. NOT HERE.
OLLIE NEEDED YOU. YOU TOLD HIM YOU'D BE THERE.
HE COUNTED ON YOU, BUT YOU WERE AN HOUR LATE!
AFTER EVERYTHING YOU GUYS WENT THROUGH IN THE WAR...
I...I WAS BUSY WITH ANOTHER EMERGENCY.
I GOT THERE AS FAST AS I COULD.
NO. DO NOT LIE.
WE EXAMINED OUR JLA MEMBER ACKING DATA, CHECKED NERAL NEWS ACCOUNTS AND TRACKED YOUR POWER SIGNATURE, FIRESTORM.
YOU AND RUSCH DIDN'T MERGE UNTIL LONG AFTER THE CALL WENT OUT.
WAIT--! AFTER ALL I DID, EVERYTHING I LOST--
--YOU'RE SPYING ON ME?
RONNIE, THERE ARE CAMERAS EVERYWHERE.
DON'T.

ACCUSE ME OF BEING A LIAR AND WE'RE GONNA HAVE MAJOR TROUBLE, HARPER.
YOU ARE A LIAR! DIAL IT BACK!
YEAH.
I'M CALLING YOU A LIAR.
AS WELL AS A FRAUD--
--PHONY--
--AND COMPLETE AND TOTAL COWARD.
STOP IT. HAVE SOME RESPECT.
I COULD STEP IN...
FOR AN EVEN BIGGER DISPLAY? NO.
IF YOU'D BEEN ON TIME, OLIVER WOULD STILL BE ALIVE!
ONE MORE WORD AND I'M GONNA DROP YOU ON THE SPOT.
CHANGE BACK RIGHT NOW! PUL ME OUT OF THE MATRIX SO I CA APOLOGIZE!
YOU.
ARE GOING TO PUT ME DOWN?
NOT ON YOUR BEST DAY.
WHUD
LET ME OUT SO I CAN FIX THIS!

SHUT UP!
YOU AREN'T GOING ANYWHERE.
DON'T IGNORE ME!
I HAVE TO TELL THEM WHAT HAPPENED!
WHUH!
OH, MY GOD. YOU'RE--THIS IS A DISASTER. LET ME OUT!
NO.
YOU'RE DESTROYING EVERYTHING!
YOU CAN'T MAKE ME A PRISONER!
FREE ME!
I DON'T NEED THIS.
I DON'T NEED ANY OF YOU.
LET ME TALK TO THEM!
SO YOU CAN THROW ME UNDER THE BUS?
NOT NOW.
NOT EVER.
I... I CAN'T BELIEVE WHAT I JUST SAW!
KLIKT
SEE WHAT I MEAN?
JERKS.
EACH AND EVERY ONE OF 'EM.

THERE ARE NO WORDS LEFT.

I'M THE MOST SUCCESSFUL FREELANCE REPORTER ON THE PLANET. MY BLOG, **THE FAST LANE,** IS ONE OF THE MOST READ AND WELL-RESPECTED SOURCES OF NEWS **IN THE WORLD.**

YET...ON NIGHTS LIKE TONIGHT...I FEEL SPENT. I FEEL LIKE THERE ARE **NO WORDS LEFT.**

LOIS
...AND JUST LIKE THAT...THE REAL STORY STARTS TO SHOW ITSELF TO ME.
4238l6
1052010
LOIS, GO ALONE
TRUST NO ONE ELSE

CAM 19 22:15:03
22:13:48
CAM 19 22:14
SOOK

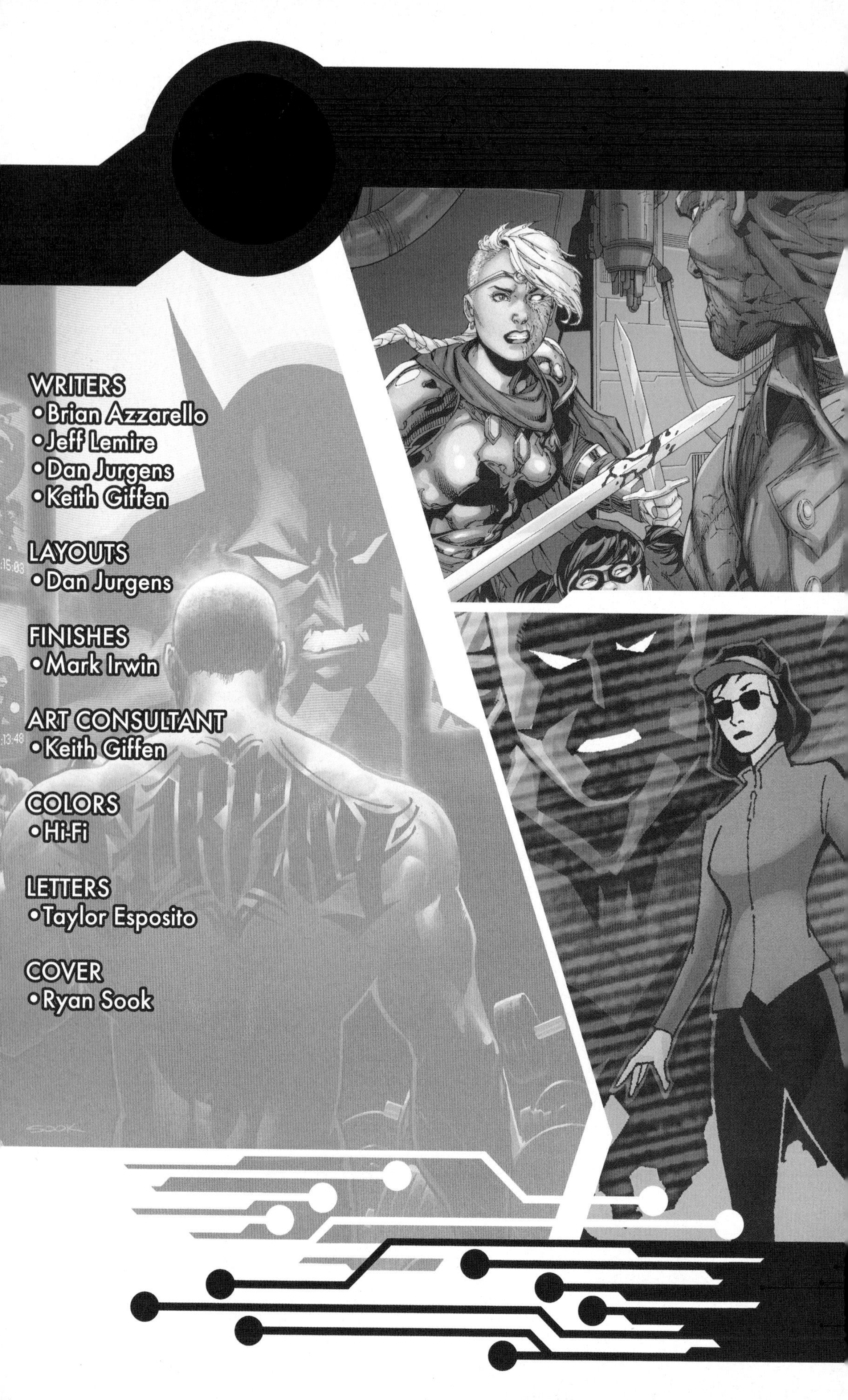
WRITERS
• Brian Azzarello
• Jeff Lemire
• Dan Jurgens
• Keith Giffen
LAYOUTS
• Dan Jurgens
FINISHES
• Mark Irwin
ART CONSULTANT
• Keith Giffen
COLORS
• Hi-Fi
LETTERS
• Taylor Esposito
COVER
• Ryan Sook
SOOK

GRISE FJORD, NUNAVUT, CANADA.
CRUNCH
CRUNCH
RRRRRRRRRR...

GRRAAARK
AH!

RRAAARRR

SCHUNK

YOU HAVE STRAYED TOO FAR FROM YOUR HOME AND YOUR TRIBE, YOUNG ONE...

THIS SAVAGE LAND IS NO PLACE FOR A BOY.

SLORP
WHAT KIND OF DEMONIC SPAWN STIRS IN THE BELLY OF THIS PROUD BEAST?
ARRRGH!
THIS IS NO DEMON... BUT A MACHINE!
KRENCH
BUT WHAT IS A MACHINE, OTHER THAN A DEMON MADE BY MAN'S OWN HAND?
WELL, LITTLE THING. YOU HAVE INVADED MY REFUGE AND MY HOME. AND I WISH YOU DID HAVE AN INFERNAL SOUL SOMEWHERE IN THAT METAL HUSK...

BUT INVADE YOU HAVE. TRESPASS YOU HAVE.

AND NOW S.H.A.D.E. WILL FEEL THE COLD STING OF FRANKENSTEIN'S BLADE.

CRUNCH CRUNCH CRUNCH

NEW YORK CITY.
FOR THE LOVE OF GOD, RONNIE.
I'M BEGGING YOU.
YOU'VE KEPT ME PRISONER IN THE FIRESTORM MATRIX FOR DAYS.
LET ME OUT.
PLEASE.
SO YOU CAN DO WHAT, JASON?
STAB ME IN THE BACK?
BETRAY ME?

YOU'RE ACCUSING ME OF BETRAYING YOU?
YOU'VE KEPT ME HERE SINCE OLIVER'S FUNERAL!
I WANT OUT!
SO YOU CAN LIE TO THE WORLD? TELL THEM I'M RESPONSIBLE FOR GREEN ARROW'S DEATH?
NO WAY.
I WON'T LET YOU TURN THE WORLD AGAINST ME.
I-- YOU--YOU CAN'T DO THIS TO ME!
HOW LONG ARE YOU GOING TO LEAVE ME HERE?
ANOTHER WEEK?
A MONTH?
PEOPLE HAVE GOT TO BE LOOKING FOR ME.
LIKE ALL THE HOTTIES YOU'VE BEEN-- OH, WAIT.
THEY DON'T EXIST.
IT'S FINALS WEEK!
I'LL LOSE MY SCHOLARSHIP! MY JOB WITH DR. YAMAZAKE!
YOU WERE MY FRIEND! HOW COULD YOU DO THIS?
YOU GAVE ME NO CHOICE.
THE BAD GUYS ARE RESPONSIBLE FOR ARROW'S DEATH. NOT ME.
YOU MADE US LATE.
I'VE SACRIFICED ENOUGH TO BE FIRESTORM!
I WANT A LIFE!
FOR FIRESTORM TO BECOME A REALITY, WE BOTH HAVE TO WANT IT.

JUST LIKE BOTH OF US HAVE TO WANT TO SEPARATE--

--IF RONNIE RAYMOND AND JASON RUSCH ARE GOING TO GO THEIR SEPARATE WAYS.

YOU THINK THAT BECAUSE YOU'RE THE "DRIVER" YOU GET TO DECIDE EVERYTHING, BUT-- WHAT ARE YOU LOOKING AT?

URGENT BUSINESS.

DON'T *IGNORE* ME!

YOU SAY THAT BEING A HERO TAKES PRECEDENCE.

I'M GIVING FIRESTORM TO THE WORLD 24/7. ISN'T THAT WHAT YOU WANT?

YOU KNOW THAT ISN'T WHAT I-- WHAT ARE YOU UP TO?

PEOPLE HANGING OUT ON A HOTEL ROOFTOP.

COULD BE TERRORISTS.

OR MORE INVADERS FROM EARTH 2.

CAN'T BE TOO CAREFUL.

OH, MY GOD! YOU'RE--

FIRESTORM.

BAD DAY TO TAN.

TRUE, BUT IT'S THE ONLY BREAK WE HAVE WHILE WE'RE IN TOWN.

WILL THIS HELP?

THAT'S *FANTASTIC!*

YOU ARE ***AWESOME!***

THIS CAN'T LAST.

EVENTUALLY, YOU'RE GOING TO LET ME GO.

HOW CAN WE REPAY YOU?

WELL...

AND WHEN YOU DO...

...I WILL KILL YOU.

CAMDEN, N.J.
HOW DID NO ONE SEE THIS COMING?
Mas Por to Bodega
I MEAN, IF GREEN ARROW HAD BEEN OUT THERE TAKING IT TO COMANCHES, I CAN SEE IT. BUT A BOW AND ARROWS? AGAINST WHAT'S ROAMING AROUND OUT THERE, LOOKING FOR A FIGHT?
MAKES ME LOOK LIKE I KNOW WHAT I'M DOING, AND I DIDN'T THINK THAT WAS POSSIBLE.
OLIVER QUEEN, NO LESS. TALK ABOUT TOO MUCH MONEY AND TOO LITTLE COMMON SENSE.
HELL, YOU DON'T SEE BRUCE WAYNE SLAPPING ON A MASK AND ROUGHING UP PERPS...AND HIS PARENTS WERE GUNNED DOWN RIGHT IN FRONT OF HIM.
STILL AT IT, AIN'T THEY? BAD ENOUGH TH' CABLE NEWS PUT US THROUGH 24/7 COVERAGE, NOW WE GOTTA READ ABOUT WHAT WE WAS FORCED T' WATCH.
THERE'S A NEW TREND OUT THERE. IT'S CALLED CHANGING THE CHANNEL. YOU MIGHT WANT TO LOOK INTO THAT.
SURE. PLAY TH' COMEDIAN WHILE OUR LIVES ARE TAKEN OVER BY E.T.s OR SUPERHUMANS OR WHATEVER.
IS THAT WHAT THEY'RE DOING?
JUST LOOKIT THAT ARROW GUY, SACRIFICED T' DRUM UP SYMPATHY SO THE REST CAN WORM THEIR WAY EVEN DEEPER INTO OUR WAY'A LIFE.
YOU LIVE IN CAMDEN AND YOU'RE WORRIED ABOUT YOUR WAY OF LIFE?
17.00

YEAH, SMART GUY. YOU JUST WAIT. SUPERMAN AND THAT WONDER WOMAN BEEN SHACKIN' UP TOGETHER. THEY DROP A KID, YOU WATCH HOW FAST THEY'LL CHILDPROOF TH' WHOLE DAMN WORLD T' MAKE SURE THEIR "PRECIOUS" IS SAFE FROM...FROM...

FROM LOW-INFORMATION TROGLODYTES WHO, AS IT TURNS OUT, REALLY ARE THAT STUPID?
YOU'LL SEE! JUST YOU WAIT 'N' SEE!

PROBLEM IS...I AGREE WITH HIM. NOT THAT I'D EVER GIVE HIS KIND THE SATISFACTION OF KNOWING THAT.
OPEN
NEVER CONSIDERED THE SUPERMAN/WONDER WOMAN SCENARIO HE LAID OUT, THOUGH. ODDS ARE IT CAME FROM ONE OF THE HATE BLOGS.

DAMN THINGS HAVE BEEN SPRINGING UP LIKE RAGWEED SINCE THE EARTH 2 WAR.
LIKE EXTRA-TERRESTRIALS WEREN'T BAD ENOUGH, NOW I'VE GOT TO KEEP AN EYE ON EARTH 2 DOPPELGANGERS.

AND, WOULDN'T YOU KNOW IT, I SEE THEM, TOO.
THAT MIGHT MEAN THAT MY LITTLE "TALENT" IS STILL EVOLVING. NOW THERE'S A PLEASANT THOUGHT.
TRUE

USED TO BE CONFINED TO SEEING DAEMONITES. MADE SENSE. THEY'RE THE ONES WHO ABDUCTED AND MESSED WITH ME, ONLY STANDS TO REASON I'D COME TO KNOW ONE WHEN I SEE ONE.

"HONEY," I'M HOME.

NOT FUNNY.

STILL TRYING TO KILL OUR GUEST?

IT'S FRUSTRATING'S WHAT IT IS!

I'M THE REAL ME

JUST SHOOT IT AND BE DONE WITH IT.
A BULLET ELIMINATES ONE. SINGULAR. I'M LOOKING FOR A DISPERSIBLE AGENT THAT WILL TAKE CARE OF THEM IN CLUSTERS. PLURAL.
AND YOU THINK DRAIN CLEANSER MIGHT BE THE ANSWER?

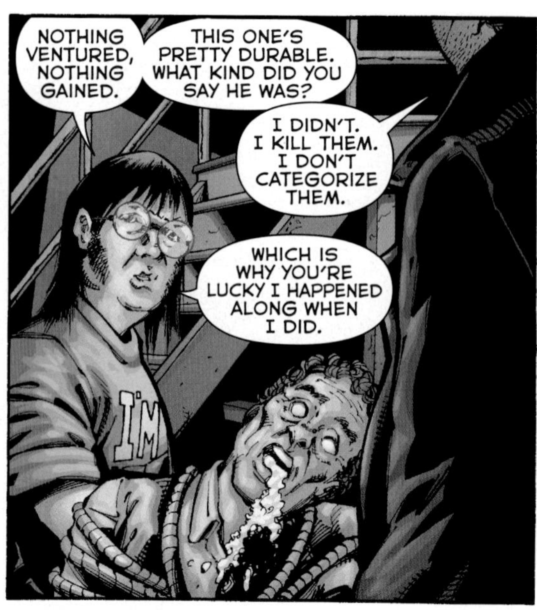
NOTHING VENTURED, NOTHING GAINED.
THIS ONE'S PRETTY DURABLE. WHAT KIND DID YOU SAY HE WAS?
I DIDN'T. I KILL THEM. I DON'T CATEGORIZE THEM.
WHICH IS WHY YOU'RE LUCKY I HAPPENED ALONG WHEN I DID.

"HAPPENED ALONG"? JUSTIN, YOUR PARENTS WERE ABOUT TO HELP THE DAEMONITES DO TO YOU WHAT HAD ALREADY BEEN DONE TO THEM.
YOU'RE LUCKY I'D BEEN TRACKING THEM.
SIGH... STILL WITH US.
HOW'S IT DUCT TAPE'S GOT THIS ONE LOCKED DOWN?

Y'GOT ME. TOLD YOU THERE ARE DIFFERENT KINDS--
AND YOU SEE THEM ALL. COLE CASH A.K.A. GRIFTER SEES ALL, KNOWS ALL--
--BEATS SMART-ASSES TO WITHIN AN INCH OF THEIR LIVES.

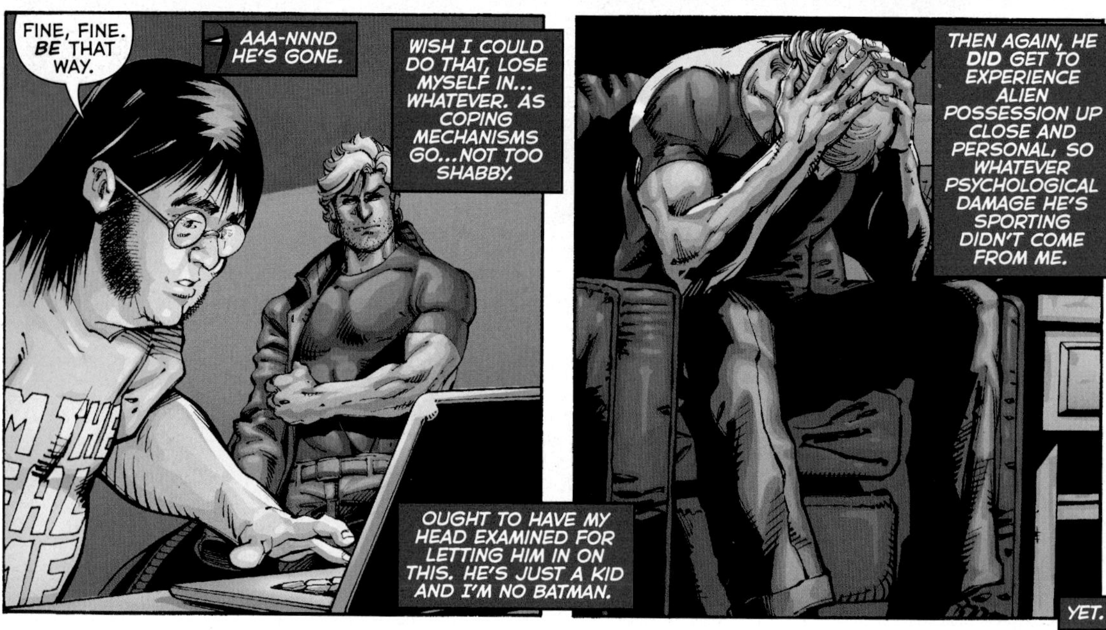
FINE, FINE. BE THAT WAY.
AAA-NNND HE'S GONE.
WISH I COULD DO THAT, LOSE MYSELF IN... WHATEVER. AS COPING MECHANISMS GO...NOT TOO SHABBY.
OUGHT TO HAVE MY HEAD EXAMINED FOR LETTING HIM IN ON THIS. HE'S JUST A KID AND I'M NO BATMAN.
THEN AGAIN, HE DID GET TO EXPERIENCE ALIEN POSSESSION UP CLOSE AND PERSONAL, SO WHATEVER PSYCHOLOGICAL DAMAGE HE'S SPORTING DIDN'T COME FROM ME.
YET.

THEN THERE'S THE FACT THAT HE IS USEFUL.
CATALOGUING KNOWN ALIEN TYPES, REVERSE-ENGINEERING THEIR TECHNOLOGY, KEEPING TABS ON THOSE WE KNOW ABOUT...IF HE COULD MAKE A DECENT OMELET, I'D HAVE TO MARRY HIM.
LET'S SEE WHAT JUSTIN'S GOT FOR ME TODAY...

Walter Pearson
(Daemonite)
921-C Bleecker St.
NYC, NY
PEARSON
Pretty much the same established patterns, although he did switch gyms. You want me to dig into this FITNESS 4 FUN franchise? Find out if it might be fronting a nest?

Amanda Greer
(Unknown)
131 Maplewood Dr.
Chatham, NJ
GREER
So, they really are after our women? The bastards! This one's playing it so low-key, I'm beginning to doubt you saw it right. Even her weekly recovery meeting reeks of "some-one just shoot me." Easy on the eyes, though.

Elizabeth Hargrove
(Unknown)
547 Hickory Terrace
Barnegat, NJ
HARGROVE
I know you already took her down, but she's back. I don't know how, and I'm betting you don't either. I'd prioritize this one. If they're coming back from the dead, we're all screwed. Pencil in your own zombie gag.

Timothy Sutton
(Durlan)
1908 Spruce St.
Derby, CT
SUTTON
The kid stuff always freaks me out. I mean, how do his parents not know? Unless they're aliens as well, which, according to you, they're not. He's just playing out typical kid stuff. Not too disturbing.

Roger DeMarco
(Martian)
2242 E. 46th St.
NYC, NY
DEMARCO
Still a no-show. No local credit card tags. My guess is he's walked away from this version of his cover. But then, what do I know about what motivates a (and I can't believe I'm writing this) Martian?

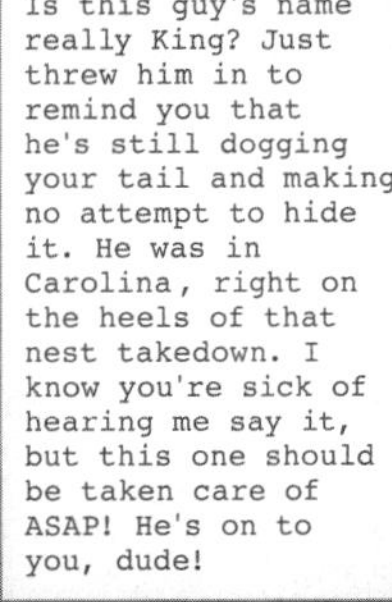
King Faraday
27 Driftwood Circle
Cape May, NJ
FARADAY
Is this guy's name really King? Just threw him in to remind you that he's still dogging your tail and making no attempt to hide it. He was in Carolina, right on the heels of that nest takedown. I know you're sick of hearing me say it, but this one should be taken care of ASAP! He's on to you, dude!

SO MUCH TO DO AND SO LITTLE TIME...

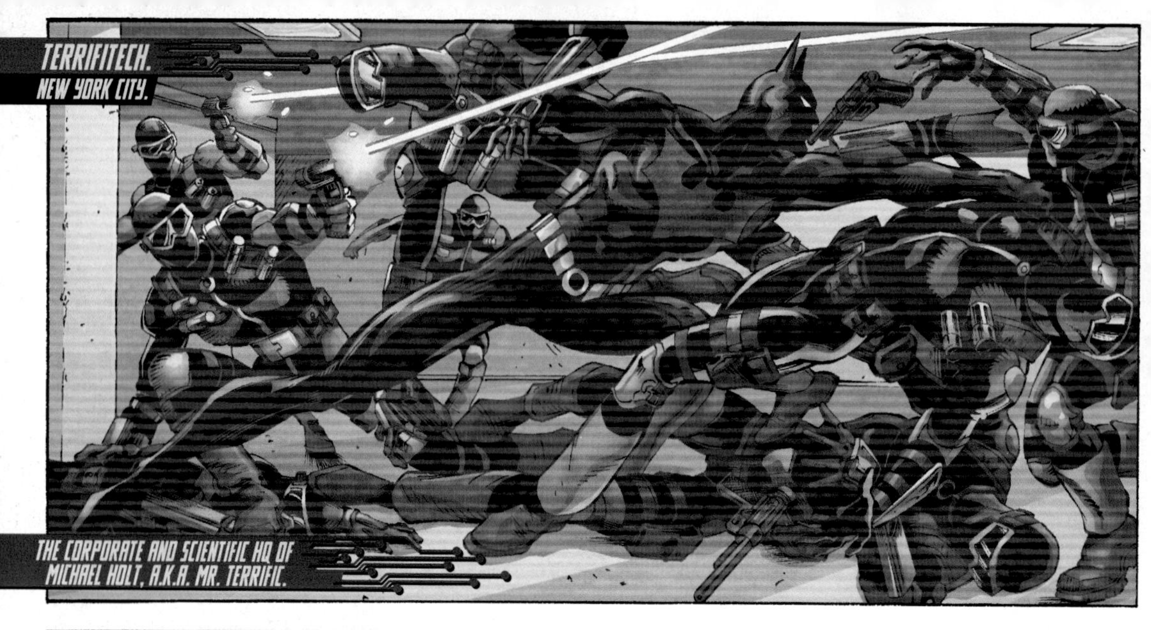

SO WHO ARE WE LOOKING AT, *NATHAN?*

SOMEONE WHO *BELIEVED* WE COULDN'T SEE HIM, T.

WHAT HE DID TO THE CAMERAS WAS PRETTY DOPE. ELECTRONICALLY LOOPED THE TAPE, JUST BEFORE HE BROKE INTO THE TOWER.

THREE SECONDS OF THE SAME FOOTAGE, BUT WITH AN ACTUAL TIME CODE.

GOOD THING WE HAVE OUR OWN COVERT SECURITY SYSTEM INSTALLED.
GOOD THING.
"SO...BATMAN HAVE A BEEF WITH YOU?"
"NO MORE THAN HE DOES WITH EVERYONE ELSE, NATHAN. COMES WITH 'PARANOID' AS YOUR DEFAULT SETTING."

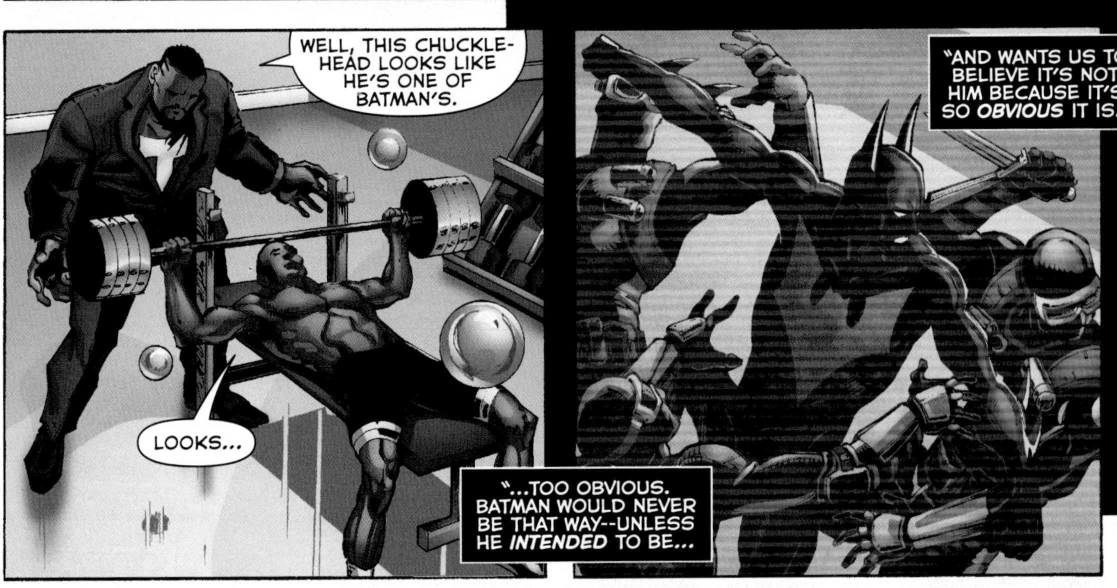
WELL, THIS CHUCKLE-HEAD LOOKS LIKE HE'S ONE OF BATMAN'S.
"AND WANTS US TO BELIEVE IT'S NOT HIM BECAUSE IT'S SO OBVIOUS IT IS."
LOOKS...
"...TOO OBVIOUS. BATMAN WOULD NEVER BE THAT WAY--UNLESS HE INTENDED TO BE...

NOW WHO'S BEING PARANOID...
HE GET ANYWHERE NEAR THE uSPHERE PROJECT, MR. COOLIDGE?

NO, SIR, MR. HOLT. NOT WITHIN TWELVE FLOORS OF IT.
SEE...WHAT'S HAPPENING...

"WE'RE *SUPPOSED* TO THINK IT'S BATMAN..."

WHO, BY THE WAY, HAS THE TECH CAPABILITIES TO LOOP OUR CAMERAS.

YOU SURE THE PROJECT WASN'T COMPROMISED?

HELL, YEAH. THERE'S AN ARMY GUARDING IT. ON TOP OF THE ARMY THAT SCARED HIM OFF.

"THE BUILDING LOCKED DOWN AFTER SECURITY ENCOUNTERED HIM. EVERY DOOR, EVERY COMPUTER.

"THERE WAS *NOWHERE* FOR THE INTRUDER TO GO..."

...AND I'M NOT ABOUT TO LOSE IT.
TERRIFITECH IS A GLOBAL BRAND I BUILT--

--AND TOGETHER WE ARE POISED TO CHANGE THE FUTURE OF SAID GLOBE.

I'LL LOAD OUR FAUX BATMAN'S IMAGE ONTO THE SERVERS. SEE IF WE CAN'T GET A VISUAL MATCH.

WE'LL KEEP IT IN HOUSE FOR NOW, BUT I CAN'T AFFORD TO IF WE COME UP BLANK.

NO, NOT WITH WHAT'S AT STAKE.
I NEED TO FIND OUT WHO HE IS...

AND WHAT THE HELL HE'S UP TO.

NEW YORK CITY.

Wounded Duck

...AND AN EMERALD MARTINI, PLEASE.

COMIN' RIGHT UP, LADIES. BUT I'M AFRAID I NEED TO SEE SOME I.D.

CAN I HAVE YOUR EARTH CARDS, PLEASE?

Willa Tomlinson
Age/DNA protocol verified

Kaylee Barnes
Age/DNA protocol verified

OKAY, YOU CHECK OUT AS *ONES.*

WELCOME TO THE WOUNDED DUCK.

OUT.
UGH!

BOTH OF YOU.
KRAKKT

NOW.

SET FOOT IN HERE AGAIN AND YOU'LL END UP IN THE INTENSIVE CARE UNIT!

SORRY ABOUT THOSE JERKS.
THE NEXT ROUND IS ON ME.
WELL, WELL, WELL.

THE MYSTERIOUS BOX'S FIRST CLUE--THE MATCHBOOK--SEEMS TO HAVE PAID OFF.
SEEING YOU IN PERSON, COMBINED WITH ALL THE BACKGROUND WORK I'VE DONE, LEADS ME TO ONE CONCLUSION.

RED ROBIN LIVES.
The FAST
RED ROB
DEAD
Last Titan falls during the Battle of Paris
By Lois Lane
PARIS—The losses for Earth's defenders continued to mount as they battled in defense of Western Europe today.
Red Robin, current Teen Titan and former associate of the Batman, was found dead in a severely bombed section of Paris that saw some of the war's heaviest fighting to date.
Scroll down for more

SOOK

WRITERS
•Brian Azzarello
•Jeff Lemire
•Dan Jurgens
•Keith Giffen
PENCILLER
•Aaron Lopresti
INKER
•Art Thibert
ART CONSULTANT
•Keith Giffen
COLORS
•Hi-Fi
LETTERS
•Taylor Esposito
COVER
•Ryan Sook

FIVE YEARS FROM NOW.

S.H.A.D.E.NET NOW ONLINE--PLEASE ENTER PASSWORD--
PASSWORD ACCEPTED. WELCOME TO S.H.A.D.E.NET, THE SUPERHUMAN ADVANCED DEFENSE EXECUTIVE'S PRIVATE INTERNET DATABASE.
QUERY--WHAT IS THE ANT FARM?
DATA INCOMING...97% DOWNLOADED...
THE ANT FARM: A MOBILE, 3-INCH INDESTRUCTIBLE METAL GLOBE THAT HOUSES S.H.A.D.E. CITY... S.H.A.D.E.'S MICRO-SCOPIC HEADQUARTERS.
CURRENT LOCATION OF THE ANT FARM, 700 KM ABOVE TOKYO.

ONLY S.H.A.D.E. OPERATIVES CAN ACCESS THE ANT FARM VIA A HYBRID OF TELEPORTATION AND MINIATURIZATION TECHNOLOGY.

TELEPORTATION AND BIO-REDUCTION IN PROGRESS. SUPER AGENT FRANKENSTEIN NOW ONBOARD--
HRRN...I ALREADY KNOW ALL TOO WELL WHAT THE ANT FARM IS, S.H.A.D.E.NET...

WHAT I WANT TO KNOW IS WHY THE HELL S.H.A.D.E. ATTACKED ME, AND IF YOU THINK I SHOULD BOTHER LEAVING ANY OF THESE PUNY LITTLE MAGGOTS ALIVE LONG ENOUGH TO EXPLAIN.
QUERY NOT UNDERSTOOD, AGENT FRANKENSTEIN. PLEASE REPHRASE YOUR QUERY--
HRRN...

GENTLEMEN, LOWER YOUR WEAPONS-- THIS IS NO INTRUDER! HAVEN'T YOU STUDIED YOUR S.H.A.D.E. ARCHIVES? THIS IS ONE OF OUR--WELL, LET'S NOT MINCE WORDS--HE *IS* OUR GREATEST AGENT...FRANKENSTEIN HIMSELF!
WAS, DR. BELROY. I RETIRED FROM S.H.A.D.E. LONG AGO AND MADE IT *VERY CLEAR* I NEVER WANTED YOU TO LOOK FOR ME. FOR YEARS I'VE FOUND PEACE AND SOLITUDE IN THE NORTH... YET YOU DARE ATTACK ME IN MY NEW HOME?!

IT TOOK ME NEARLY A WEEK TO FIND THE ANT FARM...TO TRACK DOWN S.H.A.D.E. BUT YOU *MUST* HAVE KNOWN YOU COULD *NEVER* HIDE FROM ME. IN FACT, I WOULD WAGER YOU DID NOT WANT TO HIDE. YOU WANTED ME TO FIND YOU...YOU WANTED TO DRAW ME OUT. WHY?
GULP!

WHY? SIMPLE, FRANK. WE NEED YOU BACK IN THE FOLD. THE UNIVERSE NEEDS YOU.
FATHER TIME!!
HOW DARE YOU TRY TO MANIPULATE ME INTO COMING BACK HERE!
BY THE LOOKS OF IT, I DIDN'T JUST TRY. AS USUAL, I SUCCEEDED COMPLETELY, FRANK.
HRRN...

I QUIT S.H.A.D.E. BECAUSE I COULD NO LONGER TRUST YOUR DUPLICITOUS NATURE, YOU LITTLE FIEND!
AND WHILE YOU MAY CURRENTLY RESIDE IN THE BODY OF AN INNOCENT LITTLE GIRL, I KNOW YOU FOR THE TREACHEROUS IMMORTAL SCUM YOU ARE!

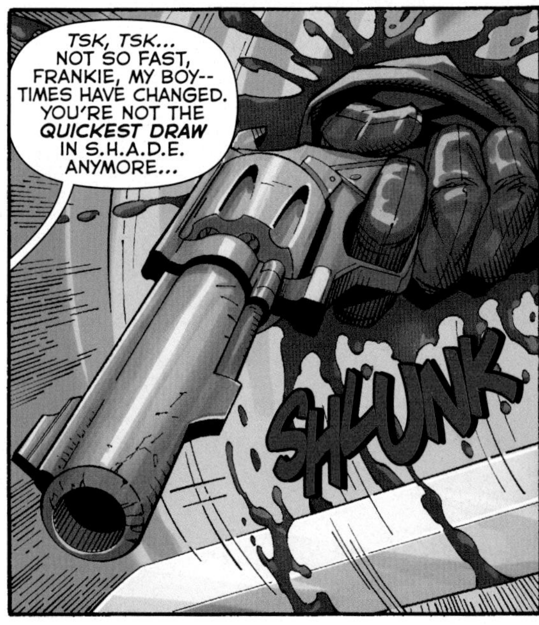
TSK, TSK... NOT SO FAST, FRANKIE, MY BOY-- TIMES HAVE CHANGED. YOU'RE NOT THE *QUICKEST DRAW* IN S.H.A.D.E. ANYMORE...
SHUNK

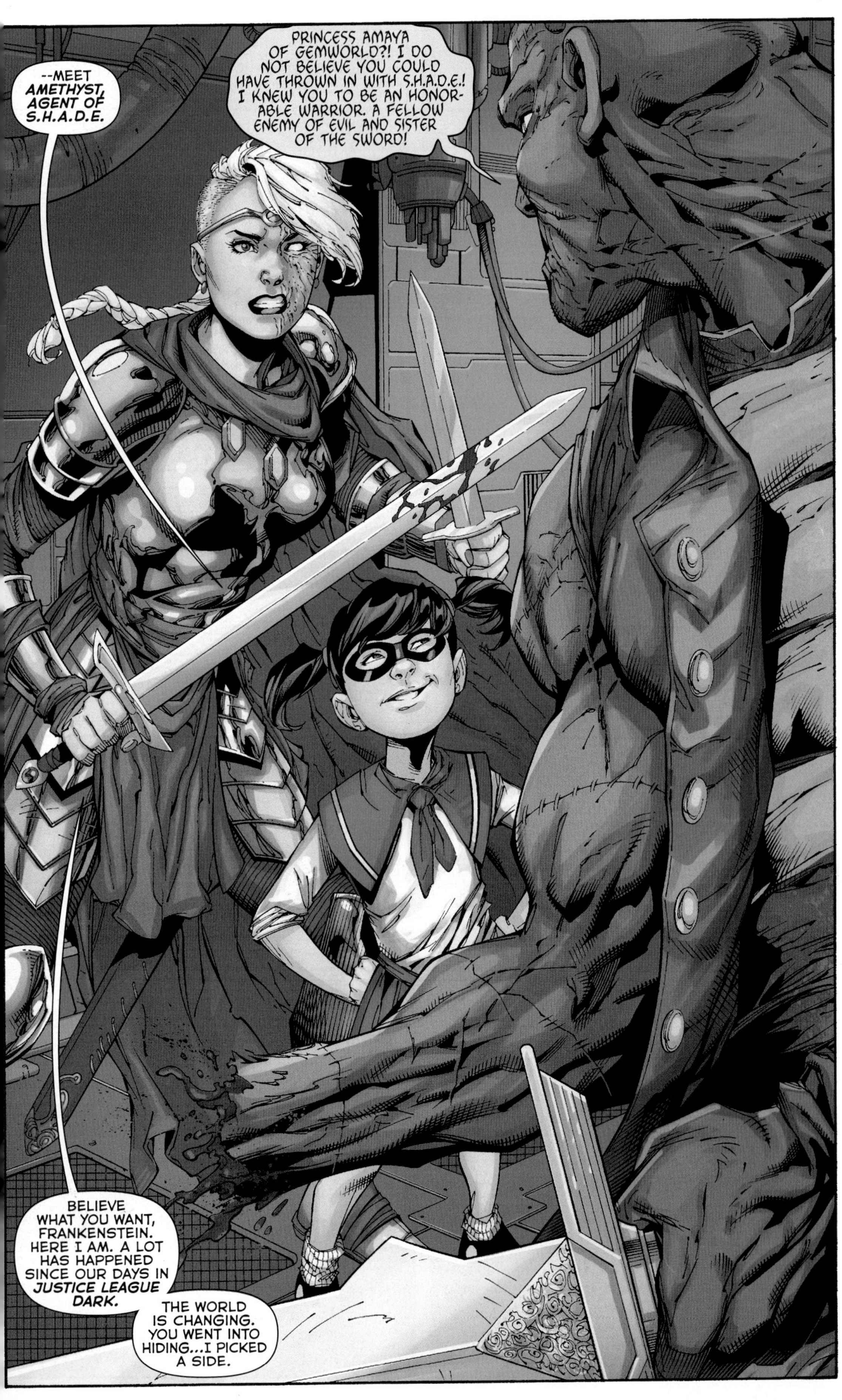
--MEET AMETHYST, AGENT OF S.H.A.D.E.
PRINCESS AMAYA OF GEMWORLD?! I DO NOT BELIEVE YOU COULD HAVE THROWN IN WITH S.H.A.D.E.! I KNEW YOU TO BE AN HONOR-ABLE WARRIOR. A FELLOW ENEMY OF EVIL AND SISTER OF THE SWORD!
BELIEVE WHAT YOU WANT, FRANKENSTEIN. HERE I AM. A LOT HAS HAPPENED SINCE OUR DAYS IN JUSTICE LEAGUE DARK.
THE WORLD IS CHANGING. YOU WENT INTO HIDING...I PICKED A SIDE.

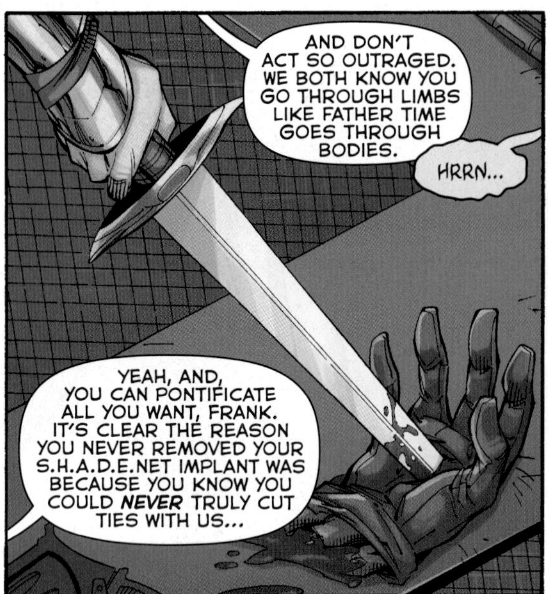
AND DON'T ACT SO OUTRAGED. WE BOTH KNOW YOU GO THROUGH LIMBS LIKE FATHER TIME GOES THROUGH BODIES.
HRRN...
YEAH, AND, YOU CAN PONTIFICATE ALL YOU WANT, FRANK. IT'S CLEAR THE REASON YOU NEVER REMOVED YOUR S.H.A.D.E.NET IMPLANT WAS BECAUSE YOU KNOW YOU COULD NEVER TRULY CUT TIES WITH US...

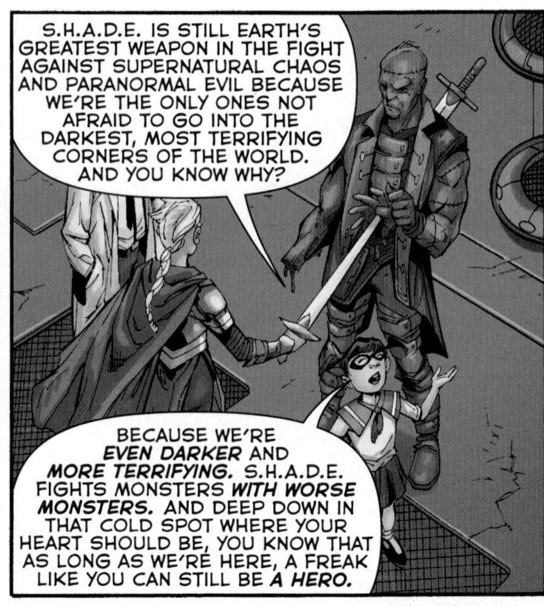
S.H.A.D.E. IS STILL EARTH'S GREATEST WEAPON IN THE FIGHT AGAINST SUPERNATURAL CHAOS AND PARANORMAL EVIL BECAUSE WE'RE THE ONLY ONES NOT AFRAID TO GO INTO THE DARKEST, MOST TERRIFYING CORNERS OF THE WORLD. AND YOU KNOW WHY?
BECAUSE WE'RE EVEN DARKER AND MORE TERRIFYING. S.H.A.D.E. FIGHTS MONSTERS WITH WORSE MONSTERS. AND DEEP DOWN IN THAT COLD SPOT WHERE YOUR HEART SHOULD BE, YOU KNOW THAT AS LONG AS WE'RE HERE, A FREAK LIKE YOU CAN STILL BE A HERO.

NOW...IF YOU'RE DONE PISSING AND MOANING, LET'S GET BACK TO WORK. LIKE I SAID, THE UNIVERSE IS IN BIG TROUBLE, FRANK. AND IF WE'RE GONNA GET THROUGH THIS ONE, I NEED MY BEST MONSTERS ON THE CASE.

S.H.A.D.E.NET, OPEN A NEW MIND PORTAL AND LINK AGENT FRANKENSTEIN, AGENT AMETHYST AND MYSELF.
AFFIRMATIVE, FATHER TIME. PREPARING FOR PRIVATE BROWSING NOW...
LINK ACHIEVED. REPLAYING SUBFILE SW 110-FG.

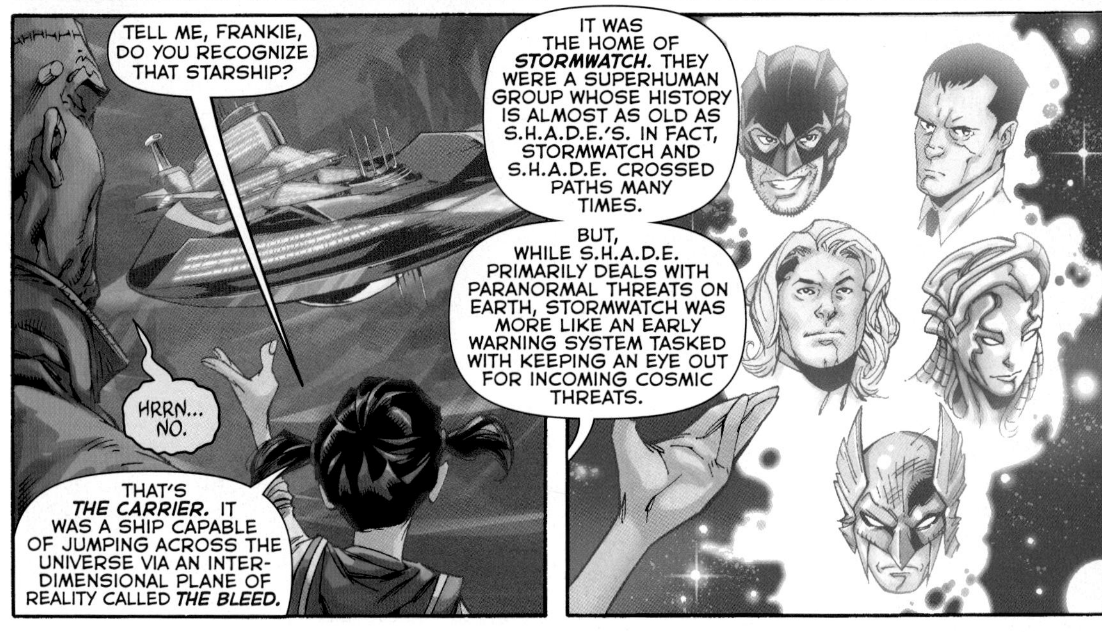
TELL ME, FRANKIE, DO YOU RECOGNIZE THAT STARSHIP?
HRRN... NO.
THAT'S THE CARRIER. IT WAS A SHIP CAPABLE OF JUMPING ACROSS THE UNIVERSE VIA AN INTER-DIMENSIONAL PLANE OF REALITY CALLED THE BLEED.
IT WAS THE HOME OF STORMWATCH. THEY WERE A SUPERHUMAN GROUP WHOSE HISTORY IS ALMOST AS OLD AS S.H.A.D.E.'S. IN FACT, STORMWATCH AND S.H.A.D.E. CROSSED PATHS MANY TIMES.
BUT, WHILE S.H.A.D.E. PRIMARILY DEALS WITH PARANORMAL THREATS ON EARTH, STORMWATCH WAS MORE LIKE AN EARLY WARNING SYSTEM TASKED WITH KEEPING AN EYE OUT FOR INCOMING COSMIC THREATS.

HAWKMAN? I FOUGHT BESIDE HIM IN THE JUSTICE LEAGUE.
YEAH. OL' HAWKY-PUCK ONLY JOINED STORMWATCH WHILE YOU WERE M.I.A. BAD CAREER MOVE, I'D SAY...

...BECAUSE THREE WEEKS AGO, THE CARRIER WAS PULLED OUT OF THE BLEED BY AN UNKNOWN FORCE AND INTO A SOLAR SYSTEM ABOUT SEVEN MILLION LIGHT-YEARS FROM EARTH.
AND, DESPITE HAVING A NUMBER OF VERY FORMIDABLE **SUPERHUMANS** ABOARD, INCLUDING THE SUPERMAN-LEVEL APOLLO, THEY WERE DESTROYED IN **LESS THAN FOUR MINUTES.**
THOOM
DESTROYED?! BY **WHAT,** FATHER?!

WE DON'T KNOW. BUT I THINK THIS IS IT... THE BIG ONE. I THINK THIS IS **THE STORM** THEY WERE CREATED TO WARN US ABOUT.

THAT'S WHY I WANT TO SEND YOU AND AMETHYST OUT THERE TO DEEP SPACE, FRANK. WE NEED TO KNOW WHAT THE HELL COULD DO THIS TO STORMWATCH AND IF IT HAS ANY INTENTION OF COMING HERE.

HRRN...SPACE TRAVEL DOES NOT AGREE WITH ME, FATHER. BESIDES...YOU SAID IT YOURSELF, I AM **NOT** YOUR TOP AGENT ANYMORE. I AM NO LONGER YOUR PET MONSTER. YOU HAVE AMETHYST FOR THAT NOW.
HEY!

YOU DON'T GET IT, FRANK. I DIDN'T CALL YOU BACK JUST BECAUSE **I** NEED **YOU.** I DID IT AS **A FAVOR.**
A FAVOR?! ARE YOU MAD?!

PROBABLY, BUT THAT'S NOT THE ISSUE HERE. YOU SEE, STORMWATCH HAD A NEW RECRUIT OF ITS OWN WHO DIED IN THAT EXPLOSION, FRANK...
YOUR OLD S.H.A.D.E. TEAMMATE... AND YOUR EX-LOVER... NINA MAZURSKY A.K.A. THE MERMAID... WAS ABOARD THAT SHIP.
...NINA!?
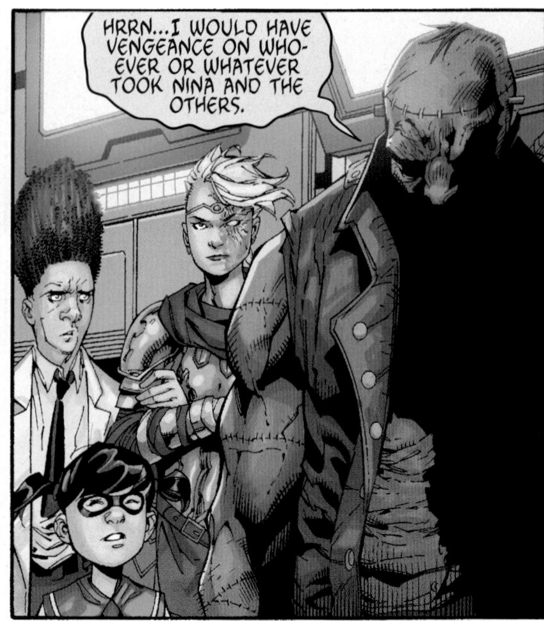
HRRN...I WOULD HAVE VENGEANCE ON WHO-EVER OR WHATEVER TOOK NINA AND THE OTHERS.

BUT, FATHER, YOU SAID THE DESTRUCTION OF STORMWATCH WAS THREE WEEKS AGO IN A STAR SYSTEM FAR ACROSS THE GALAXY. HOW CAN WE HOPE TO GET THERE IN TIME TO DO ANYTHING ABOUT IT?

WELL, YOU WON'T EXACTLY BE TRAVELING IN THE CONVENTIONAL WAY, FRANK.
HEY, DOC, YOU STILL THERE?

FRANK, I PRESUME YOU REMEMBER S.H.A.D.E.'S OLD SCIENCE LIAISON, DR. RAY PALMER?
DR. PALMER?!
HE OF COURSE DEVELOPED OUR MINIATURIZATION TECH AS WELL AS A NUMBER OF OTHER S.H.A.D.E. GOODIES.
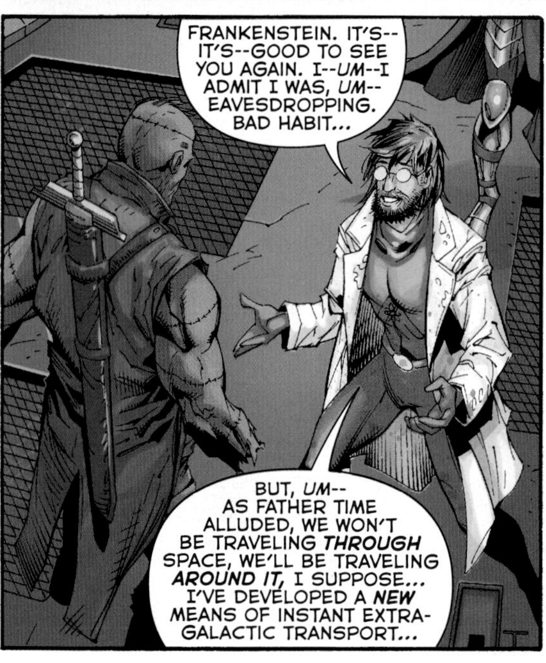
FRANKENSTEIN. IT'S--IT'S--GOOD TO SEE YOU AGAIN. I--UM--I ADMIT I WAS, UM--EAVESDROPPING. BAD HABIT...
BUT, UM--AS FATHER TIME ALLUDED, WE WON'T BE TRAVELING THROUGH SPACE, WE'LL BE TRAVELING AROUND IT, I SUPPOSE... I'VE DEVELOPED A NEW MEANS OF INSTANT EXTRA-GALACTIC TRANSPORT...

YOU SEE, FRANKENSTEIN, WE'LL BE TAKING A SHORTCUT...THROUGH THE PHANTOM ZONE.

NEW YORK CITY.
CENTRAL PARK.
NICE THAT YOU COULD GET OUT FOR THE DAY, CAL.
WHEN I DECIDED TO MANAGE BARS FOR A LIVING, I DIDN'T REALIZE HOW MESSED UP MY SCHEDULE WOULD BE.
BUT ON A DAY THIS NICE, YOU CAN'T LET YOURSELF BE TRAPPED INSIDE.

HOW'S THE KNEE?
FINE, MADISON. DISTANCES AREN'T A PROBLEM.
TORQUE AND CHANGE OF DIRECTION ARE ANOTHER STORY.

YOU SAID IT WAS A DRUNK DRIVER?
YEAH. BACK WHEN I LIVED IN GOTHAM.
I THOUGHT ABOUT GOING TO COLLEGE THERE, BUT MY DAD WAS LIKE, "NO WAY. IT'S FULL OF MURDERERS, RAPISTS AND TOTAL NUT CASES."
CAN'T ARGUE WITH THAT.

DO YOU EVER GO BACK?
NEVER.
YOU SAY YOUR IMMEDIATE FAMILY IS LONG DEAD, BUT WHAT ABOUT FRIENDS?
NONE.
NO REASON TO VISIT.

SOME WOMEN ARE ATTRACTED TO GUYS WITH AN AIR OF MYSTERY, BUT YOU BEAT THEM ALL, MR. CORCORAN.
I LIKE TO KEEP YOU ON YOUR TOES, MS. PAYNE.

SO WHAT IS IT, THEN?

WHAT IS WHAT?

THE REASON YOU WON'T TELL ME ANYTHING ABOUT YOURSELF!

LOOK, I'VE *TOLD* YOU THAT--

--THAT OUR LIVES TOGETHER BEGAN THE DAY WE MET, THAT ANYTHING BEFORE THEN DOESN'T MATTER, *BLAH, BLAH, BLAH.*

A NICE SENTIMENT, BUT I CAN'T HELP BUT WONDER.

I APPRECIATE THE PERSON YOU ARE NOW--

--BUT I'D LIKE TO KNOW WHAT ACTUALLY *FORMED* THAT PERSON.

IT DOESN'T *MATTER.*

THE PERSON I WAS IS *GONE.* HE DOESN'T *EXIST.*

YOU CAN UNDERSTAND WHY I FIND THAT KIND OF SCARY?
DON'T LET IT GET TO YOU, MAD.
THE WAR CHANGED US ALL.
LOTS OF PEOPLE LOOK BACK ON IT AS A FRESH START.

LET'S TAKE YOU AND YOUR FAMILY, FOR EXAMPLE.
OH, GREAT.
YOU KNOW I DON'T WANT TO TALK ABOUT THE FACT THAT MY FATHER--
IS IN PRISON FOR BETRAYING OUR WORLD AND BEING A WAR PROFITEER?

THAT DOESN'T MATTER TO ME.
MY POINT IS THAT I ONLY CARE ABOUT THE HERE AND NOW--
--AND YOU.
THE WAY YOU ARE TODAY.

I HATE IT WHEN YOU TRY TO MAKE ME CRY.
WAIT UP!

I'VE NEVER KNOWN ANYONE QUITE LIKE YOU, CAL.
IS THAT GOOD OR BAD?
WAY GOOD.

WHAT--
--THE HELL?

WHO--?
YOU HAVEN'T SEEN THAT YET? SOME NEW GUY IN A BATMAN SUIT.
NO ONE REALLY KNOWS MUCH ABOUT HIM.

ANOTHER ONE.
ANOTHER CHUNK OF BEEF TO BE RAMMED THROUGH BRUCE'S MEAT GRINDER.
WHAT DID YOU SAY?

NOTHING.
LET'S HEAD HOME.
GOOD IDEA. MY STUDY GROUP IS GETTING TOGETHER THIS AFTERNOON, ANYWAY.
IF JASON RUSCH EVER DECIDES TO SHOW UP AGAIN, THAT IS.

NOW THAT I'VE ANSWERED THE *WHO*--

--I NEED TO KNOW THE *WHY.*
TIME FOR US TO TALK...

"...RED ROBIN."
BOOM

KNOCK IT OFF, PLASTIQUE. WE DON'T NEED THE ATTENTION.

BOOM

DID YOU HEAR WHAT I--WHAT'S WRONG WITH YOU?
ME?

NOTHING, KEY.
THERE HE IS NOW...

COIL! WE'RE OVER HERE!

I'M ON PAROLE. I'D PREFER IT IF YOU CALLED ME *EDDIE.*

SORRY, *EDDIE.*
DO YOU HAVE THE MONEY?

OKAY. YOU HAVE *TWO MINUTES.*
TWO MINUTES FOR *THAT* KIND OF COIN?

GOOD-BYE.

NO NO NO--SIT.
WE GOT A *JOB.*

UNLESS IT COMES WITH A TIME CARD AND WITH-HOLDING TAX, NOT INTERESTED.
LEGIT, *HUH?* HEARD YOU WAS GUN-SHY...

HAVE A REASON TO BE.
NO.
THE FLASH?

HELL, NO.
HE PUT YOU AWAY, RIGHT?

HE CAUGHT ME. I DID WRONG.
ROLLIN' OVER ON A PARTNER LIKE THAT, YEAH, *YOU DID.*

YOU HAVE *ONE MORE MINUTE...*
TICK TOCK...

...FRESH OUT THE CELL BLOCK.
YOU'RE MISSIN' SOMETHIN', BROTHER--AN' IT'S YOUR--

WHAT THE HELL DO YOU WANT?!

YOU.
YOU AND YOUR SKILLS. YOU WERE ACTIVE FOR HOW MANY YEARS BEFORE YOU GOT CAUGHT? BEFORE ANYONE EVEN KNEW YOU WERE THE BEST--

--I'M RETIRED.
--NO, YOU ARE NOT...

IT'S A LAST JOB.

?
YEAH. ONE OF THOSE.
A GRAIL. MONEY BEING OFFERED, IT'S A "BUY YOUR OWN ISLAND" PAYDAY.

YOU GOT KIDS?
THAT'S NONE OF--

THEIR FUTURE? BE SET. THEIR KIDS, TOO.
IT'S THE *LAST* JOB.
IF WE PULL IT OFF.

THIS GRAIL... WHERE IS IT?

THAT'S THE THING, WHERE IT IS...

...IS IN *TERRIFITECH.*

BOOM

CHATHAM, N.J.
MAYBE JUSTIN'S NOT CUT OUT FOR THIS. KID DOES A HELL OF A JOB KEEPING ME BUSY AS GRIFTER, BUT HE SPOOKS TOO EASY. GOING ON AND ON ABOUT SOMEONE NAMED "FARADAY."
IF THIS FARADAY GUY REALLY HAS IT OUT FOR ME, I'LL TAKE CARE OF IT. I ALWAYS DO.
GIFFEN COMMUNITY CENTER

JUSTIN SHOULD KNOW THAT BY NOW. HE'S SENT ME OUT ON A MILLION OF THESE MISSIONS AND I ALWAYS COME THROUGH. AND BELIEVE ME--THAT AIN'T EASY. EXTRATERRESTRIALS ARE SURPRISINGLY GOOD AT HIDING IN PLAIN SIGHT.
CONFERENCE ROOMS

NO BETTER WAY TO WALK AMONG HUMANS THAN TO CHOOSE SOMETHING WE'D ALL RATHER IGNORE IN THE FIRST PLACE.

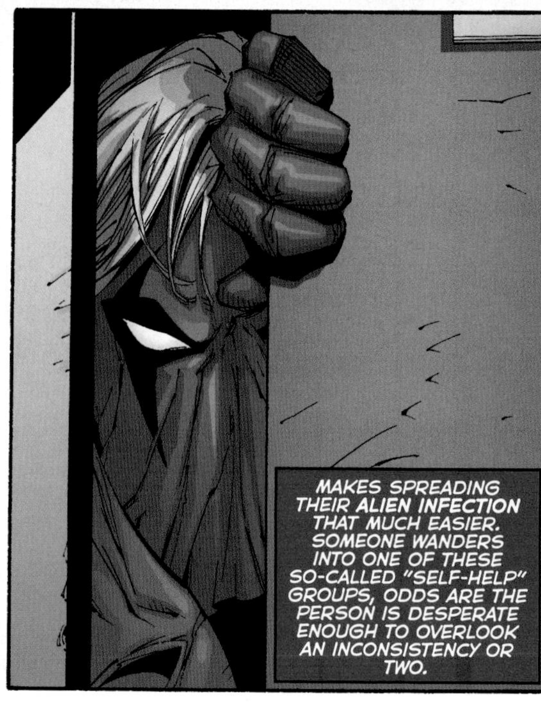
MAKES SPREADING THEIR ALIEN INFECTION THAT MUCH EASIER. SOMEONE WANDERS INTO ONE OF THESE SO-CALLED "SELF-HELP" GROUPS, ODDS ARE THE PERSON IS DESPERATE ENOUGH TO OVERLOOK AN INCONSISTENCY OR TWO.

ENTER AN ADDICT, EXIT A DAEMONITE OR A DURLAN OR...WHATEVER.
UNLESS I HAPPEN ALONG. IN WHICH CASE IT'S EXIT IN A BODY BAG.

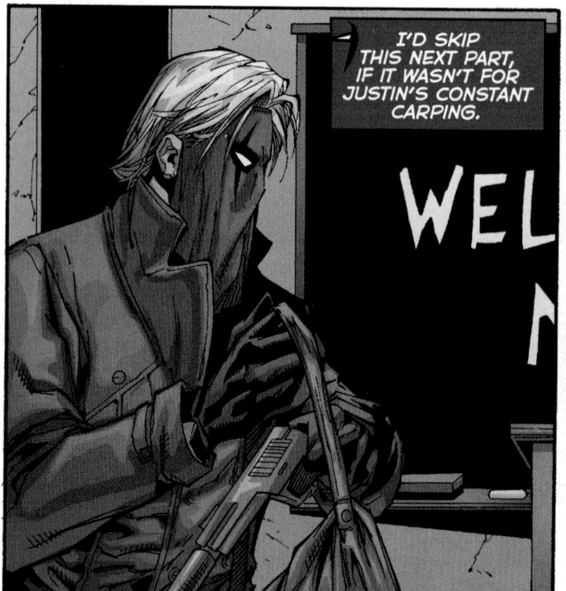
I'D SKIP THIS NEXT PART, IF IT WASN'T FOR JUSTIN'S CONSTANT CARPING.
WEL

"JUST BECAUSE IT LOOKS LIKE A CELL PHONE, DOESN'T MEAN IT IS."
"YOU'RE NOT TAKING ADVANTAGE OF OPPORTUNITY WHEN IT PRESENTS ITSELF."

AND JUST LIKE THAT, I'M BACK IN SCHOOLBOY MODE, DOING **ANYTHING** TO AVOID THE LECTURE.

'COURSE, IT DOESN'T HELP MATTERS THAT HE'S RIGHT. TURNS OUT ALIENS ARE AS GOOD AT CONCEALING THEIR TECH AS THEY ARE AT CONCEALING THEMSELVES.

WOULD HELP IF I COULD SEE THEIR TECH SAME'S I SEE THROUGH THEIR DISGUISES.
TERRIFITECH
AHH, GEEZ...

I **HATE** BEING AROUND WHEN THEY COOK OFF. THE STINK STAYS WITH YOU WORSE THAN SKUNK SPRAY.

I'D FEEL BAD FOR THE COPS WHO HAVE TO TRY TO MAKE SENSE OUT OF WHAT'S LEFT BEHIND IF IT WEREN'T FOR THE FACT THAT I'M DOING THEIR JOB.

I KNOW THAT WASN'T FAIR, THAT THEY CAN'T SEE WHAT I SEE, BUT STILL--
DAMMIT! WHAT NOW?
BREEE
BREEE
BREEE

YES, JUSTIN, I REMEMBERED TO GATHER ALL OF THE--
COLE CASH... A.K.A. GRIFTER. YOU DO KNOW WHAT YOU DO WHEN YOU ASSUME, DO YOU NOT? YOU MAKE AN ASS OUT OF U AND ME.

IT'D MAKE YOUR LIFE ONE HELLUVA LOT LESS COMPLICATED IF THIS TURNS OUT TO BE A WRONG NUMBER.
I SUPPOSE. UNFORTUNATELY, THAT IS NOT THE CASE.

YOUR VOICE DOESN'T SOUND MUFFLED. THAT MEANS YOU'VE REMOVED THAT DREADFUL BANDANNA.
MISSION ACCOMPLISHED, THEN?

WE SHOULD MEET.
IN YOUR DREAMS.
REALLY? NO CURIOSITY AT ALL? AND AFTER ALL OF THE TROUBLE I'VE BEEN THROUGH.

YOU'RE THAT FARADAY, AIN'TCHA? ONE'S BEEN TAILING ME.
GUILTY AS CHARGED.
WHY'RE YOU PLAYING IT CUTE? YOU KNOW WHO I AM, WHAT I DO, SO WHY NOT JUST RAT ME OUT TO YOUR E.T. BUDDIES?

"E.T. BUDDIES." YOU **ARE** FIXATED IF YOU CAN'T SEE PAST THAT. TRUTH IS THAT I'VE NEED OF A MAN WITH YOUR... TALENTS.
PASS.
OF **COURSE** YOU WOULD. LET'S SEE HOW YOU FEEL ONCE YOU'VE NO CHOICE IN THE MATTER.

H-HNK!
P-KOW

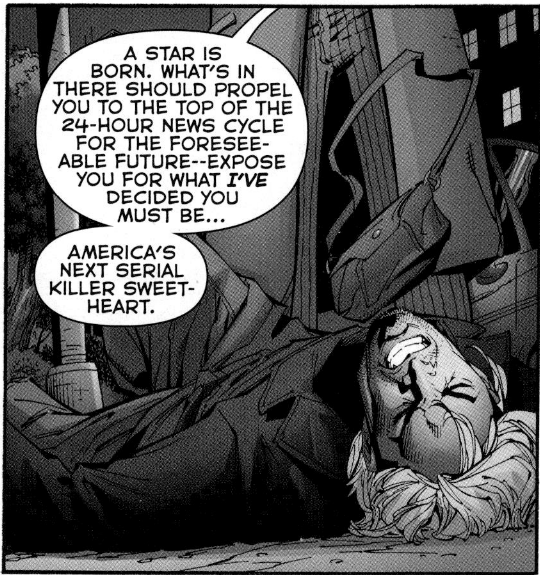
A STAR IS BORN. WHAT'S IN THERE SHOULD PROPEL YOU TO THE TOP OF THE 24-HOUR NEWS CYCLE FOR THE FORESEE-ABLE FUTURE--EXPOSE YOU FOR WHAT ***I'VE*** DECIDED YOU MUST BE...
AMERICA'S NEXT SERIAL KILLER SWEET-HEART.

OH, DON'T WORRY ABOUT YOUR ALIEN FRIENDS, I WON'T LET ANY HARM COME TO YOU...WELL, SHORT OF THE SPINAL CORD TRAUMA THAT SHOULD LEAVE YOU QUITE PARALYZED...QUITE VULNERABLE.
QUITE REVERSIBLE, ACTUALLY. SHOULD YOU DECIDE TO SEE THINGS MY WAY. ISN'T SUPER-SCIENCE WONDERFUL?
TILL THEN, MISTER CASH.

W...W... WONDERFUL...
AWWW BRAWWWW

WRITERS
• Brian Azzarello
• Jeff Lemire
• Dan Jurgens
• Keith Giffen
PENCILLER
• Jesús Merino
INKER
• Dan Green
COLORS
• Hi-Fi
LETTERS
• Carlos M. Mangual
COVER
• Ryan Sook

IVE YEARS FROM NOW.
EW YORK.
2:56
--WOULDN'T BE THE THIRD WEDNESDAY OF JUNE-- THE DAY GEEKS HAVE DUBBED TECHMAS-- WITHOUT TERRIFITECH ANNOUNCING THEIR NEXT-GENERATION DEVICE TO A RABID PUBLIC, JOAN.
THE FUTURE IS NOW
THE FUTURE IS U
TERRIFITECH
TERRIFITECH
TERRIFITECH
TERRIFITECH
THEY SHOULD BE FOAMING AT THE MOUTH, GORDON-- IF ANY OF THE PAST WEEK'S LEAKS HOLD WATER!
BABA BOOEY!
READY, T.?
LET'S DO THIS.
WE GO LIVE IN FOUR, THREE, TWO...
ONE.
CHUNK
WORLD.

YOU.
PEOPLE.
TOGETHER.
WHERE CAN THAT HAPPEN?
I SAY THE FUTURE.
I KNOW WHAT YOU'RE THINKING. BUT THE WAR IS IN THE PAST, AND THAT'S WHERE IT NEEDS TO STAY.
SEE, WE DON'T HAVE TIME FOR THE PAST ANYMORE BECAUSE WE ARE ABOUT TO BE SPENDING ALL OUR TIME BECOMING OURSELVES...
WHEN I REALIZED THAT WHAT UNIFIED US AS PEOPLE WAS FEAR, I KNEW I HAD TO TAKE A STEP FORWARD...
TO YOU.
WITH YOU. BECAUSE WHAT MATTERS...
...IS YOU.
PRESENTING THE uSPHERE.
IT'S MORE THAN YOUR PHONE, OR YOUR COMPUTER.
YOUR G.P.S.
YOUR TABLET.
IT'S YOU. YOUR LIFE AND THE LIVES OF THOSE IN IT.

IT'S YOUR BRAIN'S BACKUP. IT'S WHAT'S IN HERE...
TAP
AND ALL AROUND YOU.
BEING LABELED THE WORLD'S SMARTEST MAN--WHILE AN HONOR--IS NOT SOMETHING I BELIEVE I AM.
THERE ARE OTHERS OF YOU--WHO ARE JUST AS INTELLIGENT AS I AM.
YOU JUST NEED A CHANCE TO PROVE IT.
THIS IS YOUR CHANCE. THE FIRST STEP.
A STEP FORWARD, WHERE ONE WORLD HAS INFINITE POSSIBILITIES THAT ONLY YOU CAN DREAM OF.
AND WHEN DREAMS BECOME REALITY--THAT'S WHAT THE FUTURE IS.
ALL THAT'S MISSING...
THE FUTURE. I CAN'T WAIT TO GET THERE.

...IS YOU.
CUT!
AND THAT, MY FRIENDS...
...IS HOW TO BE A SUPER-HERO.

UTTERS COVE, MARYLAND.
COMFORTABLE?
ASIDE FROM BEING PARALYZED FROM THE NECK DOWN BECAUSE YOU SHOT ME, YOU MEAN?
LOOK... "GRIFTER" OR MR. CASH...I'M JUST BEING POLITE. I REALLY DON'T CARE, SO LET'S NOT MAKE THIS ANY MORE DIFFICULT THAN IT HAS TO BE.
YOU SHOULD BE GRATEFUL THAT I KNEW EXACTLY WHERE TO SHOOT TO GET THE DESIRED RESULT.
YEAH... ABOUT THAT.
MEDICAL TRAINING. FORENSICS ACTUALLY.
NOT WHERE I WAS GOING.
YES, I KNOW. BUT IT IS A PHYSICAL IMPOSSIBILITY...NOT TO MENTION THE RESPONSE OF CHOICE FOR THOSE WITH NO OTHER RECOURSE.
I JUST WASN'T IN THE MOOD TO HEAR IT AGAIN.
"AMERICA'S NEXT SERIAL KILLER SWEETHEART." THAT IS HOW YOU PUT IT, MR. FARADAY?
YOU'RE WELCOME. ALTHOUGH, IN ALL FAIRNESS, I DIDN'T HAVE TO WORK TOO HARD AT IT. IF IT'S A MASS MURDER, THE MEDIA'S ALL OVER IT.
QUITE PREDICTABLE, AND THANK GOD FOR THAT.

HOW DID YOU WIND UP WITH ME? LAST TIME I CHECKED, THE AUTHORITIES AREN'T BIG ON SHARING THEIR SERIAL KILLERS.
THAT WOULD FALL UNDER "NEED TO KNOW." YOU DON'T.
IF IT MEANS ANYTHING TO YOU, I'M SURE THEY'RE APPROPRIATELY PERPLEXED.
SO, UP FOR A JOB OFFER? I'VE NEED OF A MAN OF YOUR... TALENTS.
SAY *WHAT?*
YOU HEARD ME. ALTHOUGH "OFFER" MIGHT BE A BIT MISLEADING. A JOB *ULTIMATUM*, THEN.
ANY CHANCE'A ME TALKING WITH SOMEONE WHO KNOWS WHAT THEY'RE TALKING ABOUT?
OUCH. CONSIDER MY FEELINGS HURT.
DON'T SUPPOSE THERE'S MUCH I CAN DO TO STOP YOU.
RELUCTANT COOPERATION. ALL THINGS CONSIDERED, I'LL TAKE IT.
THEN GET ON WITH IT ALREADY.
DON'T MIND IF I DO.
LISTEN CLOSELY NOW. I'M ONLY GOING TO GO OVER THIS ONCE, THEN OFF TO THE ISLAND YOU GO.

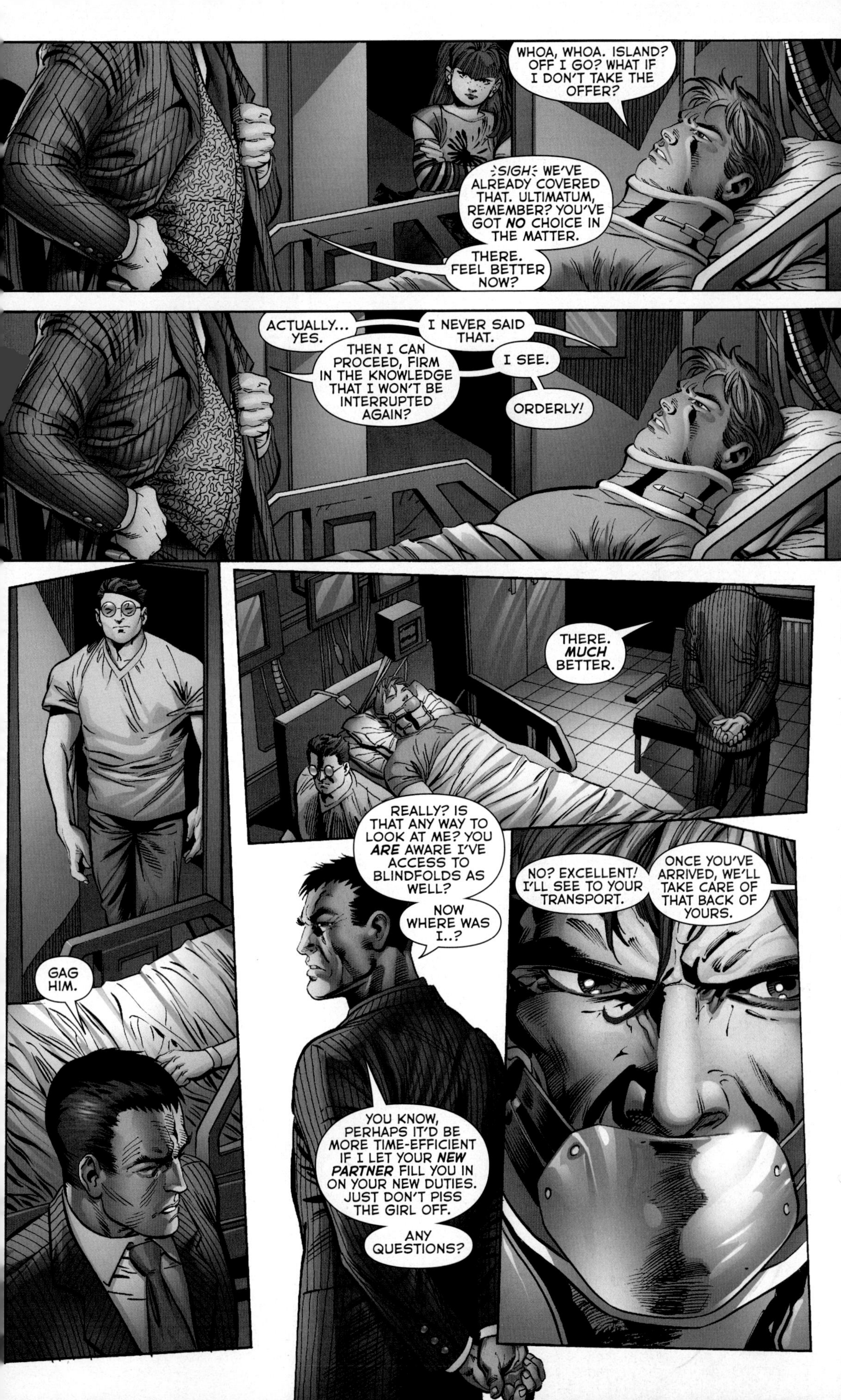
WHOA, WHOA. ISLAND? OFF I GO? WHAT IF I DON'T TAKE THE OFFER?
⁑SIGH⁑ WE'VE ALREADY COVERED THAT. ULTIMATUM, REMEMBER? YOU'VE GOT NO CHOICE IN THE MATTER.
THERE. FEEL BETTER NOW?
ACTUALLY... YES.
I NEVER SAID THAT.
THEN I CAN PROCEED, FIRM IN THE KNOWLEDGE THAT I WON'T BE INTERRUPTED AGAIN?
I SEE.
ORDERLY!
GAG HIM.
THERE. MUCH BETTER.
REALLY? IS THAT ANY WAY TO LOOK AT ME? YOU ARE AWARE I'VE ACCESS TO BLINDFOLDS AS WELL?
NOW WHERE WAS I..?
YOU KNOW, PERHAPS IT'D BE MORE TIME-EFFICIENT IF I LET YOUR NEW PARTNER FILL YOU IN ON YOUR NEW DUTIES. JUST DON'T PISS THE GIRL OFF.
ANY QUESTIONS?
NO? EXCELLENT! I'LL SEE TO YOUR TRANSPORT.
ONCE YOU'VE ARRIVED, WE'LL TAKE CARE OF THAT BACK OF YOURS.

"SEE THAT? SEE HOW EASILY THINGS FALL INTO PLACE ONCE YOU'RE FORCED TO COOPERATE?"
CADMUS ISLAND.
REPEAT. PERIMETER VIOLATION. BREACH AT SECTOR 07. IN PURSUIT.
I.D. INCONSISTENT WITH FACIAL MAPPING. ACCESSING VISUAL RECORDS... SCANNING...
FACIAL MAPPING MATCH ACQUIRED. VIOLATOR CONFIRMED AS CODE NAME FURY--
SQUAR-RRK
CHUK
THROKTCH
PATHETIC TECHNORGANIC FREAK!

OMAC DOWN. LETHAL FORCE APPROVED. ENGAGING.
BRING IT!
CHUDDA CHUDDA CHUDDA
SHLOR-RRKTCH
I HAVE FOUGHT... PARADEMONS. YOU...ARE POOR SUBSTITUTES...
I'M TRYING TO SULK HERE!
!

THIS IS WHERE I COME TO SULK IN PEACE. IN ***PEACE.***

ARE YOU...GOING TO STOP ME?

NOT SURE.

KNEW YOU WERE FAKING IT. APOKOLIPTIAN HALF-BREEDS LIKE YOU DON'T GET SICK. YOU ***MAKE*** PEOPLE SICK.

MEDI-UNIT'S GOT SECURITY ISSUES. EVEN ***I*** CAN SEE THAT.

DID YOU KILL HER? MOLLY HUTCHINS? IS THAT HER BLOOD?

TOO BAD FOR YOU THAT I CAN READ THE BAR CODE BADGE.

I LIKED MOLLY, SO... YEAH. I GUESS I ***AM*** GOING TO STOP YOU.

CHILD, I...

SHAK-KKT

DO NOT CALL ME "CHILD."

NEW YORK.

SO THAT'S WHAT A PARTY AT THE PLAYBOY MANSION IS LIKE.

TALK ABOUT A WILD NIGHT!

JASON, EVEN YOU HAFTA ADMIT THAT WAS ***FUN.***

JASON?

OH, C'MON.

YOU AREN'T GOING ALL SILENT ON ME ***AGAIN***, ARE YOU?

I KNOW YOU'RE IN THERE SOMEWHERE, MR. LESSER HALF.

NOTHING? NO COMMENT?

OKAY, SO YOU'RE SORE. I GET IT.

BUT YOU CAN'T CARRY A GRUDGE FOREVER...

"...CAN YOU?"

I CAN'T RESPOND.

I'M...I DON'T KNOW WHAT I AM.

NORMALLY, FROM INSIDE THE MATRIX, I SEE WHAT FIRESTORM SEES.
EXPERIENCE WHAT HE EXPERIENCES.
NOW, I'M... NUMB.
BEYOND NUMB.
THERE IS NO SENSE OF TACTILE SENSATION HERE.
IT'S LIKE...I'M FOLDING IN ON MYSELF.
FADING AWAY.
AS THOUGH I'LL CEASE TO EXIST.
IT'S BEEN SO LONG SINCE MY FEET WERE ON THE GROUND.
SINCE I ACTUALLY SPOKE WITH SOMEONE.
OR FELT THE TOUCH OF AN ACTUAL HUMAN BEING.
I HAVE ONLY EXPERIENCED MY JAILER.
MY TORMENTOR.
TIME TO WAKE UP, JASON.
WE'RE HOME.
...?

YOU OKAY?
YOU'RE... ASKING ME THAT NOW? AFTER HOLDING ME IN A SENSORY DEPRIVATION TANK?
YOU KEPT ME IN THERE FOR WEEKS!
I MISSED FINALS BECAUSE OF YOU!
I MIGHT'VE LOST MY INTERNSHIP BECAUSE OF YOU!
MAYBE EVEN MY SCHOLAR-SHIP!
I BEGGED YOU TO LET ME OUT!
BUT YOU WOULDN'T LISTEN!
YOU DIDN'T CARE!
YOU STOLE FROM ME!
MY LIFE, MY TIME, MY INTERESTS, MY GOALS...
EVERY-THING!
YOU BETRAYED ME!
BEFORE WE GO OUR SEPARATE WAYS, WE GOTTA TALK.
UH!
THAT'S BECAUSE YOU--
--WERE GOING TO BETRAY ME.

YOU WERE GOING TO TELL THE LEAGUE THAT OLLIE DIED BECAUSE--
YOU BETRAYED HIM, TOO! ALL YOU CARE ABOUT IS YOURSELF!
THAT'S ALL YOU'VE EVER CARED ABOUT!

THAT'S NOT TRUE AND YOU KNOW IT.
YOU KNOW WHAT I'VE LOST.
YOU KNOW THE PRICE I PAID FOR BEING FIRESTORM.

IT WAS THE WAR, RONNIE.
WE COULDN'T SAVE EVERY-ONE.

SOMEONE WITH THE POWER OF FIRESTORM--
--SHOULD'VE BEEN AROUND TO SAVE HIS OWN MOTHER.

I'M DONE.
I'VE HAD IT.

SAME HERE.

I WON'T LET YOU PUT ME IN THE MATRIX AGAIN.
EVER.
I CAN'T TRUST YOU ANYMORE, RONNIE.

FINE.
I HAVEN'T WANTED TO BE FIRESTORM FOR A LONG TIME NOW.
IT'S OVER.
FOREVER.

973 TEXTS?
62 VOICE-MAILS?
IS THERE ANYONE WHO WASN'T LOOKING FOR ME?
JASON! IS THAT YOU?

DR. YAMAZAKE! YOU'RE IN EARLY.
I'VE ACTUALLY BEEN HERE ALL NIGHT WORKING ON MY EXPERIMENTAL TRANSPORTER, JASON.
WHERE HAVE YOU BEEN ALL THIS TIME?
WE'VE BEEN LOOKING EVERYWHERE FOR YOU!
IT WAS A...FAMILY MEDICAL EMERGENCY, SIR.
AND THEN I LOST MY PHONE.

WELL, I GUESS THAT EXPLAINS IT.
COME! LET ME SHOW YOU WHAT YOU MISSED!

AUTHORIZED PERSONNEL ONLY
IDENTITIES CONFIRMED. ADMISSION GRANTED.
YOU FINISHED...?
NO, BUT I'M PROCEEDING NICELY. I CERTAINLY COULD HAVE USED YOUR ASSISTANCE, JASON.
SORRY. I KNOW HOW IMPORTANT THIS IS TO YOU.

INDEED.
FROM THE DAY THE WAR TOOK MY WIFE ALONG WITH SO MANY OTHERS WHO WERE TRAPPED IN THAT HIGH-RISE OFFICE FIRE, I REALIZED A TRANSPORTER SYSTEM WOULD HAVE SAVED THEM.
I CONSIDER IT CRIMINAL THAT THE HEROES OF THE WORLD--THE SO-CALLED JUSTICE LEAGUE--
--WITH-HOLD THAT TECHNOLOGY.
BUT THAT'S WHAT THEY DO.
USE THEIR TECH FOR THEM-SELVES.
LIKE A RING THAT CAN GENERATE ANYTHING WITH A THOUGHT. OR EXOSKELETONS THAT COULD HELP THE PARALYZED WALK.
THEY PURPORT TO HELP US ALL, YET PRIVATIZE SCIENTIFIC KNOWLEDGE.
MAYBE THEY'RE AFRAID OF WHAT WOULD HAPPEN IF IT FELL INTO THE WRONG HANDS.
THROUGH-OUT THE COURSE OF HISTORY, EVERY SOLDIER WITH SUPERIOR FIREPOWER HAS SAID THE SAME THING, JASON.
WHOA!
I MADE A LOT OF PROGRESS IN YOUR ABSENCE--
--BUT AM NOW ON THE PRECIPICE OF AN INCREDIBLE DISCOVERY.
THAT WHICH THE GODS WOULD KEEP SECRET IS ABOUT TO BE THE PROVINCE OF MAN.
TERRIFIC'S NEWLY ANNOUNCED μSPHERES WILL BE NOTHING COMPARED TO THIS.

BLAAARRGH!
WHERE'D YOU FIND HIM, TOMMY?
RIGHT WHERE YOU SAID HE'D BE.
...
SORRY.

HE OKAY?
UM... HE'S SEEN BETTER DAYS.
FFFFWWHHHHHAAA

I'M FINE.
WHERE AM I?
KANSAS.

VERY FUNNY, TOTO.
NO, SERIOUSLY. YOU'RE IN KANSAS...

...CONSTANTINE.
'AVE A LIGHT?

I QUIT.
THOSE TWO WORDS... DEFEAT ME LIKE NO OTHERS.

WHY?
I WANTED TO LIVE LONGER.
YOU... DON'T REMEMBER ME?

...

MIDGE.

SO TELL ME, WHAT AM I DOING IN KANSAS, MIDGE?
THERE'S SOME UNEXPLAINED PHENOMENA, JOHN...

EVERY-THING'S UN-EXPLAINED.

JUS' 'CAUSE I KNOW IT, WHY MUST I TAKE THE TIME TO PROVE IT...

STREWTH.
THIS HAPPENED HERE?

'COURSE IT DID.
THIS GROUND...IT'S DEAD. PRIMORDIALLY SO. CAN YOU FEEL IT SUCKING THE LIFE OUT THROUGH YOUR SOLES?
IT'S A KILLING FIELD, AND 'AS BEEN FROM BEFORE WE WAS LIVIN' IN CAVES.
THOSE ANCIENT ONES... BEAT WHAT WE CALL "EVIL" TO THE PUNCH.
PUNCH, TIMMY?
TOMMY.
MAKE THE NOTION OF OL' SATAN QUAINT BY COMPARISON.
THESE THREE... BLOBS...
NINE SKELETONS EACH, RIGHT? THEY LOOK BURNT.
AUTOPSY SAYS THEY'RE NOT.
AN' THERE'S NO BLOOD IN THEM EITHER, YEAH?
FORENSICS FOUND TRACES ON THE PERIMETER. IN THE CORN.
WHAT'S IT MEAN?
MEAN?...

MEANS YOU MIGHT AS WELL START SMOKING AGAIN.

former associate of the Batman, was found
dead in a severely bombed section of Paris that saw
of the Teen Titans
of the war to date.
ROBIN
by Lois Lane
enders continued to
as they battled in
ense of Western
ope today.
by Lois Lane
SOOK

WRITERS
• Brian Azzarello
• Jeff Lemire
• Dan Jurgens
• Keith Giffen
ARTIST
• Patrick Zircher
COLORS
• Hi-Fi
LETTERS
• Carlos M. Mangual
COVER
• Ryan Sook

IVE YEARS FROM NOW.
EW YORK.
TERRIFITECH
BREAK IN TO TERRIFITECH AND STEAL THE uSPHERE BEFORE IT GOES INTO PRODUCTION? THAT'S ALL?
THAT'S RIGHT.
THEY'RE NOT PAYING ENOUGH, KEY.
WHA? COIL, I TOLD YOU IT--
--AIN'T ENOUGH TO GO BACK TO PRISON.
THAT BUILDING MAY NOT LOOK LIKE MUCH, BUT IT'S A FORTRESS.
IT DOESN'T LOOK INPENEDABLE.
WHAT?
INPENEDABLE. LIKE A FORTRESS.
PLASTIQUE... YOU MEAN LIKE WE CAN'T GET IN.
YEAH. THAT'S WHAT I SAID.
IF THAT'S WHAT YOU MEANT, YOU SHOULD HAVE SAID "IMPENETRABLE."
AS LONG AS YOU UNDERSTOOD WHAT I WAS SAYIN', WHO CARES WHAT I SAID?
HEH.

LOOK, COIL, I CAN GET US IN THERE...
AND YOU CAN KEEP US IN.
YEAH? THERE ARE LITERALLY HUNDREDS OF ELECTROMAGNETIC FIELDS BEING GENERATED IN THERE.
HOW DO YOU KNOW?
I CAN FEEL THEM.
IT'LL BE LIKE WALKING INTO A MAZE THAT'S CONSTANTLY RECONFIGURING ITSELF BEHIND US.
I SHOULD BE ABLE TO DISRUPT THINGS ENOUGH ONCE WE'RE INSIDE...
IT'S GETTING OUT GONNA BE THE PROBLEM.
LEAVE THAT TO ME.
...
YEAH, I KNOW.

UM... A.L.F.R.E.D.?
I'VE NOTICED HER AS WELL, MASTER TERRY. RUNNING A PHYSIO-DIAGNOSTIC AGAINST THE CYBORG'S REMAINING TISSUE...
YES. THEY ARE ONE AND THE SAME.
THAT'S EITHER REALLY GOOD FOR US, OR REALLY BAD.
OR A COINCIDENCE.
I SUPPOSE THAT DEPENDS ON WHAT SHE'S DOING HERE.
I'LL ISOLATE AND AMPLIFY...
"WOULD HELP IF WE HAD SCHEMATICS OF THE INTERIOR."
IT SOUNDS LIKE SHE AND HER COMPANIONS ARE HERE FOR THE SAME REASON WE ARE.
THEY'RE PLANNING TO BREAK IN TO TERRIFITECH?
SO IS THAT GOOD, BAD...

"...OR A COINCIDENCE?"
OTHER THAN OUR OWN FOOTAGE, MR. HOLT? WE GOT ONE VISUAL HIT FOR OUR NEW BATMAN...
FROM THE 'NET. SNAPPED TWO DAYS BEFORE HE BROKE IN.
AND NOTHING ELSE--NO MATCHES PRIOR TO THAT.
NOT REALLY MUCH HELP.
NO, IT ISN'T. SO I DECIDED TO OPEN THINGS UP. WE RAN SCANS ON OUR PERIMETER SECURITY CAMERAS AND...
THAT HOMELESS MAN SHOWED UP IN THE PARK ACROSS THE STREET THE DAY AFTER THE PHOTO WAS TAKEN. HE'S BEEN THERE OFF AND MOSTLY ON EVER SINCE.
I RAN SOME COMPARATIVE ANALYSIS...
186 cm
WT: 75 to 85 kg
Body type: Mesomorph
HT: 176
WT: 75 to 85 kg
Body type: Mesomorph
COULD BE OUR MAN, MR. HOLT.
NICELY DONE, MR. COOLIDGE.
YOU WANT ME TO BRING HIM IN?
NO...
...LEAVE HIM TO ME.

THE ANT FARM: Mobile microscopic adquarters of S.H.A.D.E.
CURRENT CATION: 100 iles above Manhattan.
"HRRN...I AM NOT WEARING THIS."
OH, DON'T BE SUCH A BABY, FRANK. PUT THE DAMN THING ON, ALREADY. DR. PALMER IS WAITING.
PLEASE PUT THE JUMPSUIT ON, AGENT FRANKENSTEIN. IT'S NOT LIKE I LIKE WEARING THIS THING, EITHER.
I WANT TO GET MOVING WITH OUR INVESTIGATION OF STORMWATCH'S MURDER.
FRANK, THAT SUIT IS MADE OF A SPECIAL EXTRAMOLECULAR WEAVE THAT WILL PROTECT YOU FROM ANY RADIATION YOU MAY PASS THROUGH ONCE YOU THREE HIT THE PHANTOM ZONE.
MY INSIDES, LIKE THE REST OF ME, ARE ALREADY LONG DEAD, FATHER. I HAVE NO USE FOR THEM. SO LET'S QUIT ARGUING AND GET ON WITH THIS, SHALL WE?
AH! YOU'RE HERE! I'M, UH, GLAD TO SEE YOU'RE IN ONE PIECE, AGENT FRANKENSTEIN.
DR. PALMER, IS YOUR SHIP READY FOR LAUNCH INTO THE PHANTOM ZONE?
YES, YES-- JUST MAKING A FEW LAST-MINUTE TWEAKS TO THE NAN-KNIGHT'S NAVIGATIONAL SYSTEM. WANT TO MAKE SURE WE CAN CONTROL THIS THING ONCE WE GET IN THERE.
THE NAN-KNIGHT? YOU NAMED YOUR SHIP THE NAN-KNIGHT?
UH...YEAH.
I THOUGHT IT SOUNDED COOL.

HRRN...
YES, WELL, FRANKENSTEIN, AT ANY RATE, I MUST SAY I FEEL MUCH BETTER ABOUT THIS MISSION, KNOWING YOU'LL BE ALONG FOR THE RIDE!
NO OFFENSE, PRINCESS AMAYA.
NONE TAKEN, RAY. AND I'VE TOLD YOU BEFORE, I HAVEN'T BEEN A PRINCESS SINCE GEMWORLD FELL. PLEASE, JUST AGENT AMETHYST NOW.
AH, YES-- OLD HABITS, I SUPPOSE...
FATHER TIME, WHAT EXACTLY IS THIS PHANTOM ZONE? SOME SORT OF HAUNTED DIMENSION?
WHAT MANNER OF UNDEAD ENEMIES CAN I EXPECT TO FACE ENROUTE TO DEEP SPACE?
NOT THOSE KIND OF PHANTOMS, FRANK.
YOU SEE, FRANKENSTEIN, THE PHANTOM ZONE WAS FIRST DISCOVERED BY SUPERMAN. IT WAS A DIMENSION THAT EXISTED OUTSIDE ALL SPACE-TIME, BUT LAYERED RIGHT UNDER OUR OWN.
HIS PEOPLE, THE KRYPTONIANS, USED THIS "GHOST DIMENSION" AS A PRISON OF SORTS FOR THEIR WORST CRIMINALS AND OUTCASTS FOR EONS.
GET ON WITH IT, DR. PALMER...
AH, YES, WELL, ANYWAY. AFTER THAT, THE PHANTOM ZONE WAS DEEMED TOO DANGEROUS. MICHAEL HOLT, OLIVER QUEEN AND I MANAGED TO CONTAIN THE PHANTOM ZONE AND EVERYTHING IN IT INTO A MUCH MORE MANAGEABLE "POCKET UNIVERSE."
I IMMEDIATELY SAW THE POTENTIAL IN USING THE PHANTOM ZONE AS A SHORTCUT OF SORTS ACROSS THE EXPANSES OF SPACE.
LAUNCHING FROM THE ANT FARM AND ONLY OPENING A MICROSCOPIC PORTAL INTO THE ZONE ALLOWS US TO ENTER WITHOUT ANY OF ITS DANGEROUS CONVICTS ESCAPING.
AT OUR CURRENT MICROSCOPIC SIZE, WE WILL BE UNDETECTABLE INSIDE THE ZONE. AND WHEN WE NAVIGATE TO STORMWATCH'S POSITION AND EXIT, I'LL ENLARGE US BACK TO NORMAL SIZE.

OKAY, GANG...WE ARE ONLY GOING TO GET ONE SHOT AT THIS...SOMETHING OUT THERE IN DEEP SPACE BLEW STORMWATCH, EARTH'S SUPER-HUMAN EARLY WARNING DEFENSE TEAM, TO HOLY HELL, AND YOU NEED TO FIND OUT WHAT IT WAS.
WE WILL BE ABLE TO STAY IN CONTACT HOLOGRAPHICALLY ONCE YOU GET OUT OF THE PHANTOM ZONE, BUT UNTIL THEN, YOU WILL BE IN THE DARK. SO BE GOOD, AND DON'T RUN OUT OF GAS OR PICK UP ANY HITCHHIKERS.
WE'LL DO OUR BEST, FATHER.
YOU ALWAYS DO, AGENT AMETHYST. HOW ABOUT YOU, FRANK? READY TO GET BACK INTO THE FIELD?
I AM. NINA MAZURSKY WAS MORE THAN JUST A MEMBER OF STORM-WATCH. SHE WAS A GOOD WOMAN. SHE WAS MY--MY FRIEND.
I WOULD HAVE VENGEANCE ON WHATEVER KILLED HER.
VENGEANCE, HUH, FRANK? YOU'RE A MAN OF SIMPLE TASTES... I LIKE THAT.
POWERING UP EXTRA-DIMENSIONAL GATEWAY. ARE YOU READY, DOCTOR PALMER?
ALL SYSTEMS ARE LIVE. WE ARE READY TO LAUNCH.
PHANTOM ZONE OPENING IN FIVE... FOUR...THREE... TWO...ONE...
"--NAN-KNIGHT ENGAGE!"

W-WE DID IT! WE ACTUALLY DID IT!
UM... WHY DO YOU SOUND SO SURPRISED, DOC?
HONESTLY? I HAD NO IDEA IF THAT WAS REALLY GOING TO WORK OR NOT.
HRRN...

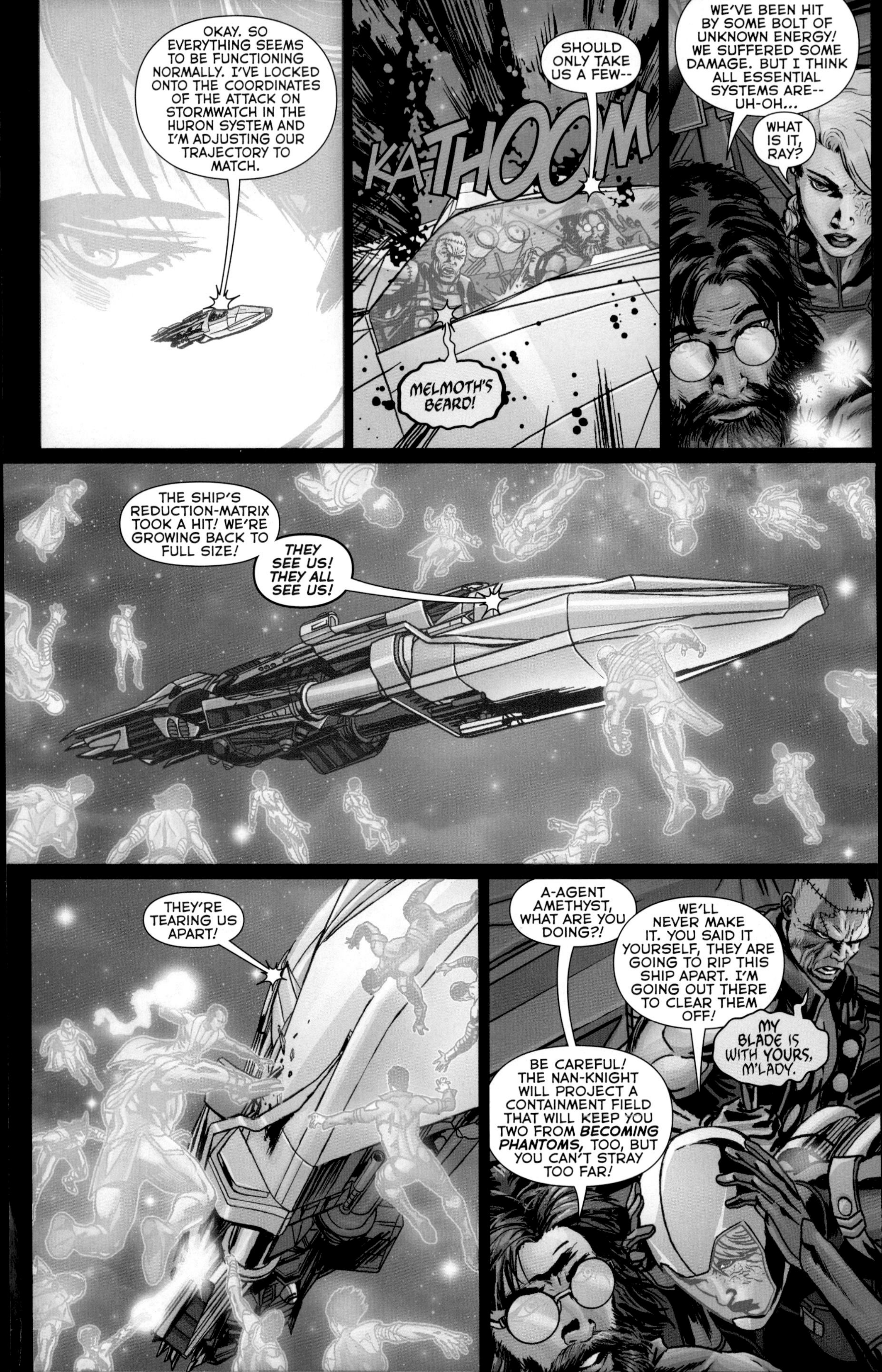

OKAY. SO EVERYTHING SEEMS TO BE FUNCTIONING NORMALLY. I'VE LOCKED ONTO THE COORDINATES OF THE ATTACK ON STORMWATCH IN THE HURON SYSTEM AND I'M ADJUSTING OUR TRAJECTORY TO MATCH.

SHOULD ONLY TAKE US A FEW--

KATHOOM

MELMOTH'S BEARD!

WE'VE BEEN HIT BY SOME BOLT OF UNKNOWN ENERGY! WE SUFFERED SOME DAMAGE. BUT I THINK ALL ESSENTIAL SYSTEMS ARE-- UH-OH...

WHAT IS IT, RAY?

THE SHIP'S REDUCTION-MATRIX TOOK A HIT! WE'RE GROWING BACK TO FULL SIZE!

THEY SEE US! THEY ALL SEE US!

THEY'RE TEARING US APART!

A-AGENT AMETHYST, WHAT ARE YOU DOING?!

WE'LL NEVER MAKE IT. YOU SAID IT YOURSELF, THEY ARE GOING TO RIP THIS SHIP APART. I'M GOING OUT THERE TO CLEAR THEM OFF!

MY BLADE IS WITH YOURS, M'LADY.

BE CAREFUL! THE NAN-KNIGHT WILL PROJECT A CONTAINMENT FIELD THAT WILL KEEP YOU TWO FROM ***BECOMING PHANTOMS,*** TOO, BUT YOU CAN'T STRAY TOO FAR!

KEEP YOUR WITS ABOUT YOU, LADY AMETHYST! THESE FIENDS ARE LEGION!
FOOM
FOOM
I CAN HANDLE MYSELF, OLD MAN.
HRRN... INDEED.
A PARADEMON?!
HAIL DARKSEID!
YOU'RE A LITTLE LATE FOR THAT!
I THINK YOU GUYS SCARED THEM OFF. THEY'RE RETREATING!
YES...RUNNING LIKE THE SPINELESS COWARDS THEY ARE.
I-I DON'T THINK IT'S US THEY'RE SCARED OF, FRANKENSTEIN.
--UNGH!!
LOOK OUT!
THOOM

IF YOU CAME FOR A FIGHT, MONSTER... YOU'VE FOUND ONE.
BLACK ADAM?!

MORNINGSIDE HEIGHTS.
NEW YORK CITY.
WOUNDED DUCK
THE FUTURE IS
THE FUTURE
CLOSING TIME, FOLKS. TIME TO CALL IT A DAY.
SEE YOU TOMORROW NIGHT, CORCORAN.
THAT MEANS YOU, TOO, BUD. IT'S BEEN A LONG DAY.
C'MON. ONE MO... MORE.
SORRY. LAST CALL WAS HALF AN HOUR AGO.
THA'S A CRIME AGAINST NATURE, BUT Y'CAN MAKE IT UP TO ME.
WANNA TAKE ME HO...HOME AND *TUCK ME IN?*
WHOA!
NAME'S RON.
IF Y'GO TO ANY OF THE CO...COLUMBIA GAMES, THA'S ME AT QB.
AN' LADIES *LOVE* TO LOVE THE QB.
NOT THIS ONE.
LEAVE, *RAYMOND.*
OH, SO YOU *DO* KNOW ME!
PLAYIN' HARD TO GET.
I LIKE THAT.

I'VE GOT THIS, MADISON.
I CAN TAKE CARE OF MYSELF, CAL.
THIS THE HERO RIDIN' TO THE RESCUE?
WE'RE CLOSED.
START WALKING.
NOT UNTIL THE HOTTIE JOINS ME.
SHE CAN TELL ME A BEDTIME STORY.
LAST CHANCE.
DUDE, YOU HAVE NO IDEA WHO YOU'RE MESSIN' WITH.
I CAN BURN THIS PLACE DOWN.
OR TURN YOU INTO A PILE OF MARSHMALL--
PAK
TODAY'S LESSON:
THUMP
WHEN YOU'RE TOLD TO LEAVE--
--LEAVE!

MUCH AS I APPRECIATE THE GALLANTRY...
...I WOULDN'T WORK IN A BAR IF I COULDN'T HANDLE A DRUNK.
MAYBE.
MY WAY WAS MORE... DIRECT.
WHAT IF HE STORMS BACK IN?
REPEAT PERFORMANCE.
I DON'T DOUBT THAT.
WHO--?
SORRY, MISS, BUT WE'RE TRYING TO CLOSE FOR THE NIGHT.
YOU'LL HAVE TO LEAVE.
MY NAME IS LOIS LANE.
IF YOU COULD SPARE A FEW MOMENTS, I'D LIKE TO ASK A COUPLE OF QUESTIONS.
YOU.
SHE'S A REPORTER. RUNS THE FAST LANE SITE.
OH, I KNOW. WE'VE MET.
SORRY, MS. LANE, BUT IT'S LATE. ANOTHER TIME.

CARE TO RECONSIDER?
... NO.
CAL? WHAT IS THIS ABOUT?
WHY WOULD SHE BE SHOWING YOU AN OLD HEAD-LINE...
...OF A DEAD TITAN?
RED ROBIN DEAD!
Last Titan Falls During The Battle of Paris.
's Lane
RIS—The losses for
's defenders continued to
t as they battled in
e of Western Europe
Red Robin, current Teen Titan and former associate of the Batman, was found dead in a severely bombed section of Paris that saw some of the war's heaviest fighting to date.
Scroll down for more
NO IDEA, MADISON.
PLEASE, MR. CORCORAN. I HAVE A BOX OF CLUES AND BACKGROUND WORK THAT SAYS OTHER-WISE.
YOU'RE DENYING THAT YOU WERE ONCE KNOWN AS RED ROBIN?
TEEN TITAN AND PARTNER TO BATMAN?

I WAS NEVER A "PARTNER" TO ANYONE.
YOU HAVE TO GO.
AND DON'T COME BACK.
EVER.
WE'LL TALK, "MR. CORCORAN."
COUNT ON IT.
IS IT TRUE?
WERE YOU...A TITAN?
HOW? I MEAN-- THEY ALL DIED IN THE WAR!
MADISON...
WERE YOU RED ROBIN?
SHE'S A REPORTER CHASING GHOSTS AND BOGUS HEADLINES.
I DO HAVE A HISTORY OF MY OWN WITH HER...
WHICH IS WHY YOU CAN IGNORE LOIS LANE--
--AND ALL HER CRAZY ACCUSATIONS.

I DOUBT IT.
BECAUSE SHE'S VERY, VERY GOOD AT WHAT SHE DOES, AND THAT MEANS SHE KEEPS HER WITS ABOUT HER.
ALTHOUGH A *LITTLE* TIPSY WOULD SIMPLIFY MATTERS CON-SIDERABLY.
IF I KNEW THAT, I'D BE MOVING ON THE PERSON WHO GAVE IT TO HER. ONE DOESN'T TAKE ON A REPORTER OF MS. LANE'S EXPERIENCE UNLESS ONE ABSOLUTELY HAS TO.
NOW THAT... *THAT* IS A NIGHTCLUB WALK.
WELL, IF I HAVE TO EXPLAIN IT, THEN ODDS ARE YOU WOULDN'T...
NEVER MIND. I'M MOVING IN.
WRONG.

NO, THAT WASN'T ME.
LET ME GET BACK TO YOU ON THAT.
IS THERE A PROBLEM?
NOT A WISE MOVE.
AND WHICH MOVE WOULD THAT BE?
MS. LANE IS OFF-LIMITS.
SAYS YOU?

SAYS YOU. RIGHT. OFF-LIMITS.

YOU'VE BEEN WARNED.

YES, I HAVE, HAVEN'T I? BUT BY WHOM? LOTS OF RUMORS ABOUT WHY YOU WEAR THAT MASK, SUPERMAN.
ONE OF THESE DAYS, I'LL FIND OUT FOR MYSELF.

IT'S ONLY PROVOCATION IF HE HEARS ME.
I SUPPOSE WE'LL JUST HAVE TO LET MS. LANE FIND HER WAY TO US. AND SHE WILL. COUNT ON IT.
A PITY, THAT.
SIGH
NO GOOD DEED GOES UNPUNISHED.

whos
Afraid

WRITERS
•Brian Azzarello
•Jeff Lemire
•Dan Jurgens
•Keith Giffen
PENCILLER
•Aaron Lopresti
INKER
•Art Thibert
COLORS
•Hi-Fi
LETTERS
•Dave Sharpe
COVER
•Ryan Sook

E YEARS FROM NOW.
PHANTOM ZONE.
I *WILL* EXACT REVENGE FROM SUPERMAN FOR PUTTING ME HERE!
YOU'RE TAKING ME OUT OF HERE, MONSTER, OR *I'M GOING TO RIP YOU APART!*
HRRN... DR. PALMER... DO YOU HEAR ME?

I'M HERE, FRANK!
ARE YOU STILL ABLE TO PILOT YOUR SHIP OUT OF HERE?
BLACK ADAM DAMAGED A LOT OF THE *NAN-KNIGHT'S* SYSTEMS, BUT I THINK I CAN STILL MAKE IT TO OUR EXIT POINT AND GET US BACK INTO REAL-SPACE.

GOOD... THEN, GET MOVING. I WILL HOLD THIS FIEND OFF LONG ENOUGH FOR THE *LADY AMETHYST* AND YOURSELF TO ESCAPE.
I DON'T THINK SO, *AGENT FRANKENSTEIN...*

NO WAY I'M LETTING YOU HAVE ALL THE FUN!
SZZZRRK
AH... I SENSE MAGIC ON YOU! EVEN HERE IN THIS PLACE BETWEEN PLACES, IT FLOWS. IT LED ME TO YOUR TINY SHIP... EXPOSED YOU. YOU DOOMED YOUR CREWMATES, WITCH.

I'VE BEEN IN THIS PLACE SO LONG...FEELS LIKE EONS. IT WILL TAKE MORE THAN SOME ENCHANTRESS AND HER PET ZOMBIE TO KEEP ME ANY LONGER!
--UNGH!
M'LADY!

FOOM
I AM NO ZOMBIE, BLACK ADAM. I SHOULD KNOW, I'VE FACED A FEW IN MY LONG WALK THROUGH HISTORY.

--AK!
I AM NO MINDLESS GHOUL... I AM A POET AND A WARRIOR. I AM GOD'S HOLY VENGEANCE MADE UNFLESH!
I... AM...
--FRANKENSTEIN!!
KA-THOOM

LADY AMETHYST, YOUR SPIRIT AND COURAGE ARE NOBLE, BUT IF WE BOTH STAY AND ENGAGE THIS FIEND, WE RISK BEING TRAPPED HERE FOREVER. TAKE DR. PALMER AND GET OUT OF HERE!

BUT AGENT FRANKENSTEIN--

GO!

SHAZAM!
SHRACK
HUURRGH!

LIGHTNING?

I WAS BORN FROM LIGHTNING, EVIL ONE.

--AK!
YOU'VE ONLY MADE ME MORE ALIVE.

DR. PALMER, AMETHYST--
BLACK ADAM IS INCAPACITATED. I AM GOING TO TRY AND CATCH UP TO YOU.

WE ARE GOING THROUGH THE PORTAL NOW, FRANK...ONCE WE'RE THROUGH, IT WILL ONLY STAY OPEN FOR A FEW SECONDS.
HURRY, FRANKENSTEIN!

HRRN?
I AM ON MY WAY!

YOU THINK A SWORD CAN STOP ME, MONSTER? DON'T YOU KNOW WHERE YOU ARE?!

UNHAND ME, MADMAN!
THIS PLACE IS HELL...

ARRRGGH!
...AND I AM THE DEVIL!

WHAP
AND I MAY HAVE BEEN BORN A MONSTER...BUT I HAVE BECOME SOMETHING MORE THAN MY FLESH, BEAST. I AM FRANKENSTEIN...
UNGH!

--AND I SHALL ENDURE.
FRANK! YOU MADE IT!

N--NOT ALL OF ME, I'M AFRAID, M'LADY...BUT I WILL LIVE... SO TO SPEAK.
WELL, THAT'S GOOD...

...BUT IT LOOKS LIKE STORMWATCH WASN'T AS LUCKY!

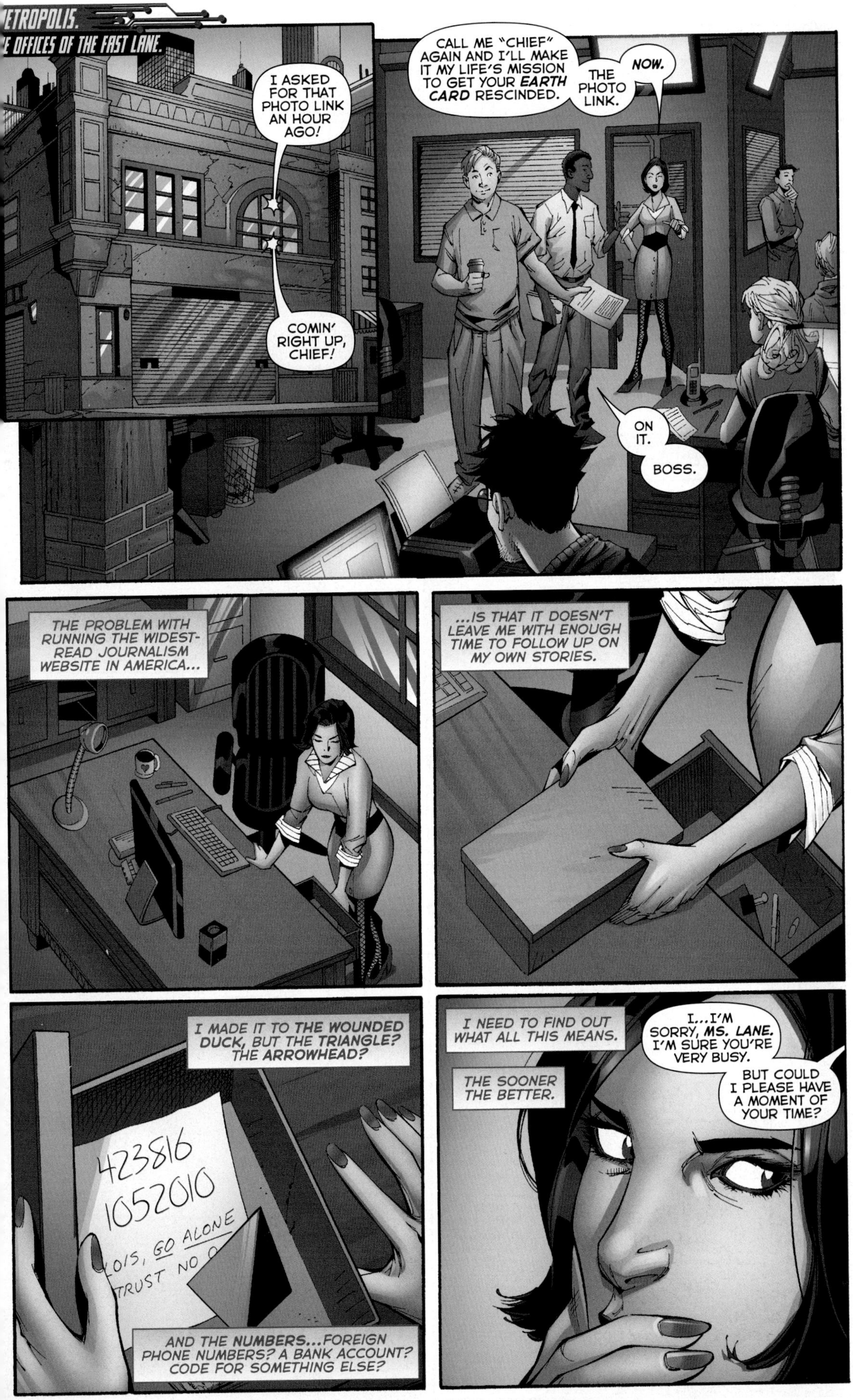

ETROPOLIS.
E OFFICES OF THE FAST LANE.

I ASKED FOR THAT PHOTO LINK AN HOUR AGO!
COMIN' RIGHT UP, CHIEF!
CALL ME "CHIEF" AGAIN AND I'LL MAKE IT MY LIFE'S MISSION TO GET YOUR **EARTH CARD** RESCINDED.
THE PHOTO LINK.
NOW.
ON IT.
BOSS.

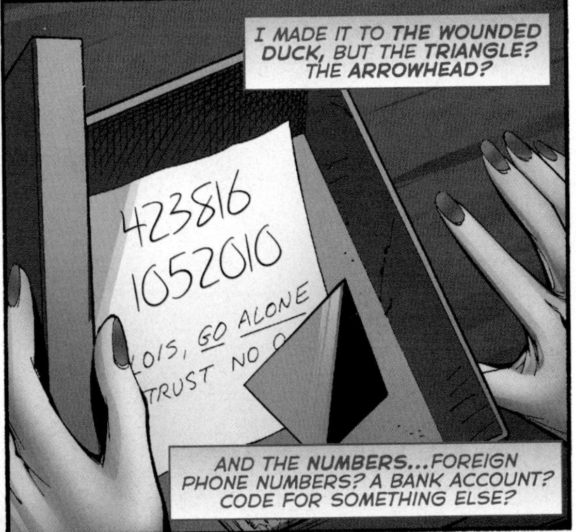

MY NAME IS *MADISON PAYNE.* WE MET--
AT THE *WOUNDED DUCK* A FEW NIGHTS AGO. I REMEMBER.
WHAT CAN I DO FOR YOU, MADISON?
I WANT TO ASK...*NEED* TO ASK YOU ABOUT MY BOYFRIEND, *CAL CORCORAN.*

YOU SAID THAT HE USED TO BE RED ROBIN OF THE *TEEN TITANS.*
WHY DO YOU *THINK* THAT? RED ROBIN AND THE TITANS ARE *DEAD!*
I'M SURE YOU ASKED HIM ABOUT IT. WHAT DID HE SAY?

CLASSIC REPORTER STRATEGY. FORGET HUMAN DIGNITY AND CONVERSATION AND BORE RIGHT IN FOR THE STORY.
YOU CAME TO *ME,* MADISON. I'M SURE YOU ASKED HIM ABOUT IT.

HE SAID THERE'S NOTHING TO IT, THAT EVERYONE KNOWS THE TITANS DIED IN *THE WAR* AND THAT I SHOULD NEVER MENTION THOSE NAMES AGAIN.
IF ANY OF THAT WERE TRUE, HE WOULD HAVE *TOLD* ME.

ARE YOU SURE?
HOW MUCH DO YOU REALLY KNOW ABOUT HIM?

HE DOESN'T LIKE TO TALK ABOUT HIS LIFE BEFORE WE MET.
IT WAS A MISTAKE FOR ME TO COME HERE.
JUST... LEAVE HIM ALONE, OKAY?
I ALSO KNOW WHO *YOU* ARE, MADISON. I RECOGNIZE YOU FROM THE *TRIAL.*

I REMEMBER YOU, TOO, MS. LANE.
AND EVERY LAST MEAN, TERRIBLE WORD YOU WROTE ABOUT MY FATHER.
BEING *MAXWELL PAYNE'S DAUGHTER* MUST'VE BEEN HARD.

THAT'S WHAT *I* DON'T WANT TO TALK ABOUT.
WHEN I WRITE ABOUT A MAN'S CRIMES, I WORRY ABOUT HOW MY STORY IMPACTS HIS FAMILY.
IF MY STORIES HURT YOU...I APOLOGIZE.

BUT HE SOLD ARMS AND INFORMATION TO THE *ENEMY* DURING *WARTIME.*
SOME PEOPLE WOULD SAY HE BETRAYED THIS WORLD.
FOR *MONEY.*
I CAN'T IMAGINE WHAT YOU WENT THROUGH.

YOU WANNA KNOW?
DO YOU REALLY WANT TO KNOW WHAT IT'S LIKE FOR A 17-YEAR-OLD GIRL TO LOSE *EVERYTHING?*
HER HOME? EVERY LAST POSSESSION AND DOLLAR? TO WATCH HER MOTHER FALL INTO CHEMICAL DEPENDENCY OUT OF SHAME WHILE HER FATHER *ROTS* IN *PRISON?*

YOU'RE LIKE ALL THE OTHER REPORTERS!
YOU'RE *JACKALS,* FEEDING ON THE CARCASSES OF WHATEVER STORY PUTS MONEY IN YOUR POCKETS.
LEAVE US *ALONE* AND LEAVE THE PAST WHERE IT BELONGS!

SEEMS AS THOUGH YOU AND YOUR BOYFRIEND HAVE MORE IN COMMON THAN I THOUGHT.

NEW YORK CITY.
COLUMBIA UNIVERSITY.
YOU MADE INCREDIBLE PROGRESS WHILE I WAS AWAY, DR. YAMAZAKE. I'M IMPRESSED.
THE WORLD NEEDS THIS, JASON. TRANSPORTERS WILL SAVE LIVES.
YEAH, BUT WE'RE FAR FROM THAT POINT.
CAUTION
CAUTION
NO. WE HAVE TO PUSH OURSELVES.
NOW THAT THE ELECTRICAL TEAM DID ITS WORK BY DIVERTING EXTRA POWER TO THE LAB--
--I DARE SAY WE MIGHT RUN OUR INITIAL TEST AS EARLY AS NEXT WEEK.
WAIT.
REALLY?
WHAT ABOUT THE MAGNETIC FIELD STABILITY EQUATIONS?
SOLVED WHILE YOU WERE AWAY, JASON.
I HAVE ONE GOAL, AND THAT'S TO BRING REVOLUTIONARY, SUPERIOR TECHNOLOGY TO THE MASSES.
WE DESERVE EQUALITY WITH THOSE WHO DEEM THEMSELVES SUPERIOR.
SUPPOSE EVERY COMMUNITY--MAYBE EVERY HOUSE--HAD A TRANSPORTER DURING THE WAR!
CAN YOU IMAGINE HOW MANY LIVES WOULD HAVE BEEN SPARED?!
NOW, WE HAVE A LOT OF HEAVY EQUIPMENT TO MOVE.
WE COULD USE SOME HELP. MAYBE THAT FRIEND OF YOURS? THE QUARTERBACK FELLOW?
YOU MEAN RONNIE RAYMOND.
TURNS OUT WE REALLY WEREN'T FRIENDS, AFTER ALL.
FRANKLY, I DON'T HAVE ANY IDEA WHERE HE IS...

Leigh Ragland
Thomas Raleigh
Millicent Raven
Greta Rawlins
Jonathan Rawson
Joanne Raymond
William Reicher
Juan Reynaldo

Joanne Raymond

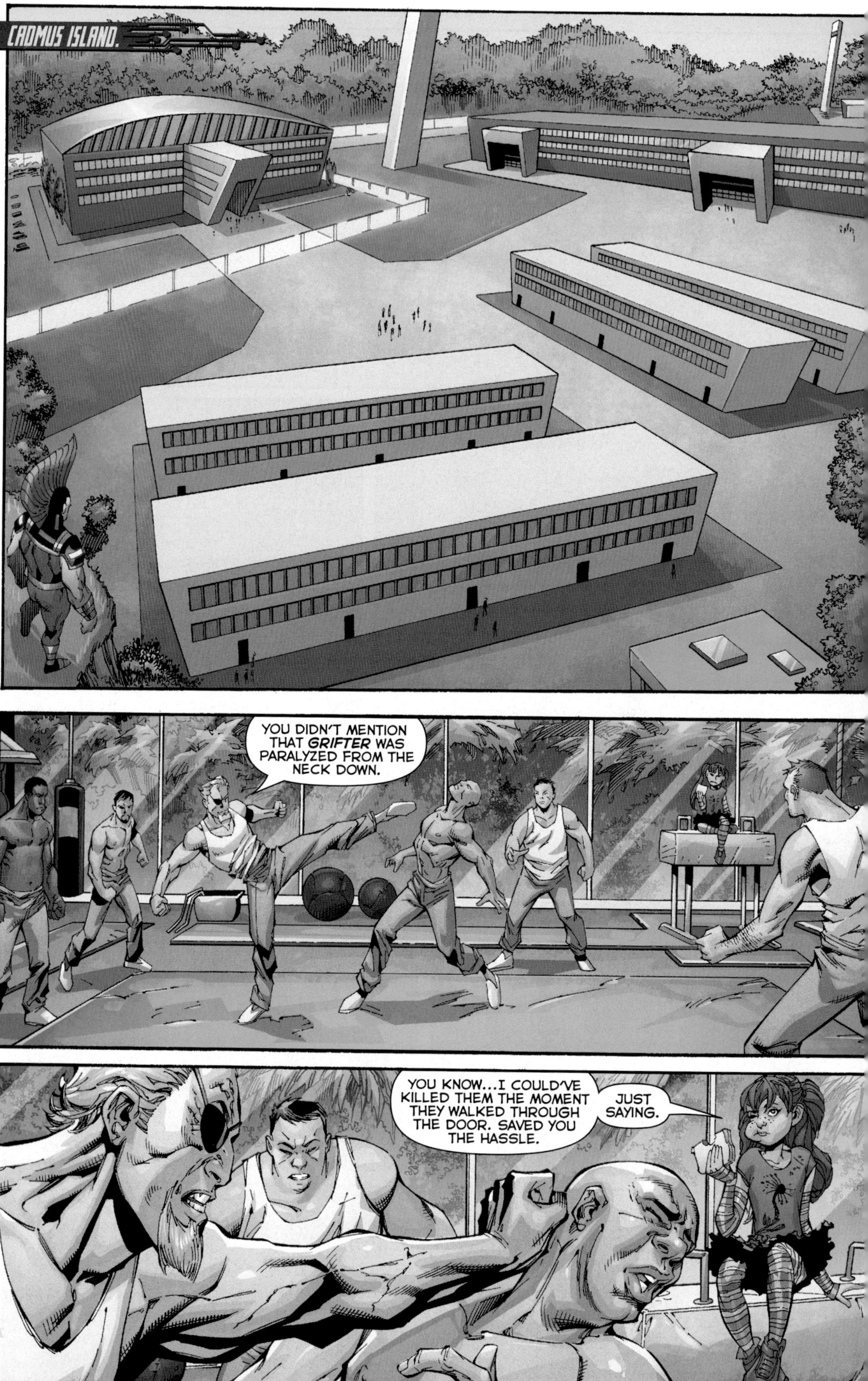

CADMUS ISLAND.

I'M *TRAINING!* NOT TRYING TO KILL THEM!

HE'S ONLY GOT *ONE* EYE! BLIND SIDE! HEL-*LO!*

I'M SURE THEY APPRECIATE THE TIP.

PARALYZED? NECK DOWN?

NOT AN ISSUE, MR. WILSON, *SIR.* THEY'LL FIX HIM UP NOW THAT THEY'VE GOT HIM HERE.

SO WHAT'S THE STORY? I THOUGHT YOU AND ME WERE A TEAM.

WE ARE.

THAT DIDN'T SOUND VERY HAPPY.

I DON'T DO "HAPPY."

I DON'T DO "REJECTION."

NAME LIKE DEATHSTROKE, I FIGURED ***YOU'D*** PAY ***FARADAY.***

I DON'T KILL FOR FUN.

LET ME GUESS. YOU DON'T DO "FUN"?

DON'T MESS WITH HIM TOO BADLY. FARADAY MAY BE RIGHT.

WHAT MAKES YOU THINK I'M GOING TO MESS WITH HIM AT ALL?

YOU'RE NOT?

MENS

LADIES

YOU THINK YOU KNOW SO MUCH.

I KNOW YOU.

YOU DON'T KNOW DI--

LANGUAGE!

CADMUS ISLAND MEDICAL FACILITY.

AH, MISTER CASH, UP AND ABOUT ALREADY. VERY GOOD. ALTHOUGH THERE'S NO REASON YOU SHOULDN'T BE.
MAKES IT THAT MUCH EASIER TO BEAT SOME ANSWERS OUT OF YOU.

THERE'S THAT SENSE OF HUMOR THAT I'M SURE WE'LL ALL COME TO KNOW AND LOVE. HOW MUCH DO YOU KNOW?
I KNOW FARADAY SHOT ME IN THE BACK, STASHED ME AWAY AND, SOMEHOW, MANAGED TO LAND ME HERE--WHEREVER HERE IS--WITHOUT MY HAVING ANY SAY IN THE MATTER.
QUITE SO.

I ALSO KNOW THAT YOU'RE A SORRY REPLACEMENT FOR THE NURSE WHO--
YES... SHE'S NOT CLEARED FOR THIS.

SHORT FORM, MISTER CASH, YOU HAVE BEEN BROUGHT HERE BECAUSE WE HAVE NEED OF SOMEONE WITH YOUR GIFT.

MY "GIFT" USUALLY LEADS TO BLOODSHED. FOR THOSE THAT GOT BLOOD, THAT IS.

I THINK MR. SLADE WILL FIND THAT TO HIS LIKING.
SLADE? SLADE WILSON?! *DEATHSTROKE?*
YOU'VE HEARD OF HIM?
ENOUGH TO KNOW BETTER THAN TO CROSS PATHS WITH HIM.

MR. FARADAY BELIEVES THAT YOUR "GRIFTER" SKILL SET WILL COMPLEMENT MR. WILSON'S--
SKILL SET! SLADE'S A PROFESSIONAL KILLER WHO'S NOT SO DISCRIMINATING ABOUT WHO HE'S AFTER--I JUST HANDLE ALIENS!

YES, YOU CAN DETECT ALIENS. *AND* DOPPELGANGERS *AND,* JUST RECENTLY, YOU'VE BEGUN SEEING ENHANCED LIFE FORMS-- SUPERBEINGS, IF YOU WILL.
HOW DO YOU--?

WE HAVE OUR WAYS.
MR. WILSON WILL SEND FOR YOU SHORTLY. UNTIL THEN, YOU'VE THE RUN OF THE COMPOUND, EXCEPTING RESTRICTED AREAS. DO *NOT* GET THE GIRL WORKED UP. IT NEVER ENDS WELL.
OH, AND *PLEASE* DON'T FEED THE OMACS.

WHAT? GIRL? *OMACs?* WHAT THE HELL IS AN OMAC? HEY! *HEY!*
HAY IS FOR HORSES.

FIFTY SUE. THAT'S MY NAME. LAUGH AND DIE. "PLEASED" TO MEET YOU.
YOU'D BETTER NOT BE A DORK.
...WONDERFUL.

NEW YORK CITY.
MADISON SQUARE PARK.
HERE'S HOW IT IS: THE ELECTRONIC SECURITY IN *TERRIFITECH* IS SELF-HEALING, AND LEARNS FROM ITS MISTAKES.

FROM WHAT I'M SENSING MAGNETICALLY, IT'S JUST AS DIFFICULT TO BREAK *OUT* OF TERRIFITECH AS IT IS TO BREAK *IN.*
SO IT'S LIKE A PRISON...

"EXACTLY. WHICH I'M NOT INTERESTED IN RETURNING TO."
"WELL, THEN, **COIL**, MAKE SURE YOU GET US OUT OF THERE."

KEY, DO YOU ONLY LISTEN WHEN IT'S SOMETHING YOU WANT TO HEAR?
YES.
WHAT?

"I'M NOT SURE I **CAN** GET US OUT OF THERE!"

HMM.

I'VE ALWAYS KNOWN BUMS HAVE A NOSE FOR MONEY.

BUT YOU'RE NOT A BUM...

...*ARE YOU?*

WHAKKK
MASTER TERRY, DIRECT CONTACT AT THIS POINT WITH MR. TERRIFIC--

SOKKK

--IS MOOT?

ISN'T THAT--?
TERRIFIC.

"LET'S GET OUT OF HERE."
SLAAMMM
EVASIVE ACTION RECOMMENDED. IMMEDIATELY.
NO, A.L.F.R.E.D. I CAN'T LET HOLT GET HIS HANDS ON THE CYBORG.
TERRIFITECH SECURITY HAS US SURROUNDED.
OUR BEST COURSE OF ACTION...
...IS TO TAKE THE HIGH ROAD.
?

WHAT IS *THAT?*
SIR, ARE YOU...?

I'M...
...FINE?

LET'S GO...
PLASTIQUE, MOVE!
WAIT! LOOK AT--
IT'S--

MY, MY, WHAT DO WE HAVE HERE?

WRITERS
•Brian Azzarello
•Jeff Lemire
•Dan Jurgens
•Keith Giffen
PENCILLER
•Scot Eaton
INKER
•Drew Geraci
COLORS
•Hi-Fi
LETTERS
•Carlos M. Mangual
•Dezi Sienty
COVER
•Ryan Sook

VE YEARS FROM NOW.
OMUS ISLAND.

GRIFTER'S NO FOOL. FIRST THING HE DID, ONCE WE'D ASSIGNED HIM QUARTERS, WAS WALK THE ISLAND PERIMETER. GUESS HE HAD TO SEE FOR HIMSELF THAT HE REALLY *IS* ON AN ISLAND.

I'M SURE THE OMACs WERE THRILLED.

FIFTY SUE DOESN'T CARE FOR HIM.

AND THIS SURPRISES YOU?

I DON'T SEE WHY YOU DIDN'T DESTROY HER WHEN YOU HAD THE CHANCE.

ONE OF THESE DAYS SHE'S GOING TO OVERHEAR YOU SAYING THAT.

AND?

"MY PLEASURE..."
SO...THIS IS GOING TO BE A DAILY AFFAIR, YOU FOLLOWING ME AROUND?
SUE ME FOR CARING.
WHY WOULD YOU CARE ABOUT ME?
WHO SAID ANYTHING ABOUT CARING ABOUT YOU?
I WAS ON THE OMAC'S SIDE WHEN YOU BREACHED THE PERIMETER.

YOU SAW THAT?
I SEE ALL, KNOW ALL.
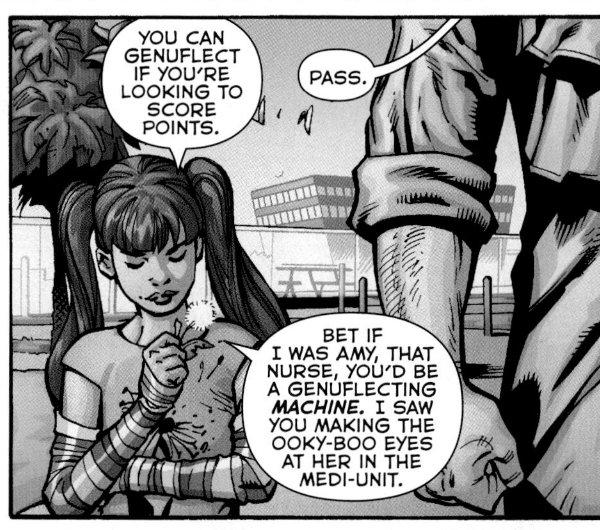
YOU CAN GENUFLECT IF YOU'RE LOOKING TO SCORE POINTS.
PASS.
BET IF I WAS AMY, THAT NURSE, YOU'D BE A GENUFLECTING MACHINE. I SAW YOU MAKING THE OOKY-BOO EYES AT HER IN THE MEDI-UNIT.

THANKS, FIFTY SUE.
THANKS?
FOR REMINDING ME WHY I DON'T HAVE KIDS.
OUCH. THIS IS GONNA HURT.

AAAAAAAAAAAGH

AAAAAAGGHHH!

SPLUNCH

MEDICAL CENTER
ARRIVALS / HELIPORT
STAFF QUARTERS
SPECIAL NEEDS
SOLITARY
VILLAGE SQUARE
DOCKS
DON'T BE SUCH A SOURPUSS. IF I'D ***REALLY*** WANTED TO HURT YOU, I'D HAVE PEELED YOUR SKIN OFF BEFORE YOU HIT THE WATER. SALT 'N' LIKE THAT, Y'KNOW?
YOU CAN DO THINGS LIKE THAT...LIKE TOSSING ME INTO THE OCEAN ON A WHIM--

THAT WAS NOTHING.
--AND YOU'RE ALLOWED TO WANDER FREE?

THIS IS ME DOING WHAT I WANT, WHEN I WANT, AND THERE'S NOT A DAMN THING ***ANYONE*** ON THIS CHUNK OF GEOGRAPHY CAN DO TO STOP ME.
LIFE IS GOOD.
IS THERE A REASON YOU'VE ZEROED IN ON ME?

METROPOLIS.
THE FAST LANE OFFICES.
OUR INTELLIGENCE SPECIALIST LOOKED AT THOSE NUMBERS EVERY POSSIBLE WAY, LOIS.
HER EXPERT OPINION IS THAT THEY'RE MAP COORDINATES.
PLACING US WHERE, EXACTLY?

MIDDLE OF THE INDIAN OCEAN, WEST OF AUSTRALIA.
NOTHING BUT WATER AND SHARKS.
THERE MUST BE SOMETHING MORE.
423816
1052010
GO ALONE
ONE

SOMEONE SENT ME THAT BOX OF MYSTERY ITEMS FOR A REASON.
THE WOUNDED DUCK MATCHBOOK LED ME TO A MAJOR FIND, SO I'M WILLING TO BET THOSE COORDINATES--IF THAT'S WHAT THEY ARE--WILL AS WELL.
THE RED ROBIN THING. SO WHEN ARE YOU GOING TO PRINT THE STORY?
WHEN I KNOW HOW ALL OF THIS CONNECTS.

COULD BE A SMALL ISLAND, BOAT OR PLATFORM OF SOME KIND.
CHARTER A PLANE, TY. I WANT TO SEE FOR MYSELF.
WE HAVE THE BUDGET FOR THAT?

OF COURSE NOT.
PUT IT ON MY PERSONAL CARD.
THIS STORY IS BIGGER THAN MONEY.
REALLY?

THIS OPERATION IS A HAND-TO-MOUTH EXISTENCE, LOIS. IF ANYTHING HAPPENS-- IF YOU GO ALL AMELIA EARHART ON US-- WE'RE DONE!
WHICH IS WHY WE NEED THIS STORY.
BOOK
THE
PLANE.

NEW YORK CITY.
COLUMBIA UNIVERSITY.
THE LIBR OF COLU UNIVERSITY
POWER INPUT LEVELS HAVE REACHED 88 PERCENT, DR. YAMAZAKE.
STAND BY TO ENGAGE.

THANK YOU, JASON.
GIVEN THE CIRCUMSTANCES--
--I CANNOT THINK OF A MORE APPROPRIATE OBJECT FOR OUR FIRST TEST.

THAT'S YOUR WIFE?
YES. FOR US, IT'S CUSTOMARY TO HAVE A COMMEMORATIVE PLATE OF ONE'S WEDDNG DAY.
KAI WAS THE MOST BEAUTIFUL BRIDE I'D EVER SEEN.
I FEEL THE PAIN OF HER DEATH TO THIS DAY.

I CAN'T BEGIN TO IMAGINE.
POWER LEVELS AT 97 PERCENT.
98... 99...
IN MEMORY OF KAI AND THE OTHERS WHO DIED BECAUSE THEY WERE UNABLE TO ESCAPE THE BURNING TOWERS...

...EVEN AS OPERATIONAL TRANSPORTER TECHNOLOGY WAS WITHHELD BY OUR "PROTECTORS"...
...LET US *DO THIS.*
100 PERCENT!
FULL POWER!

HISTORY SHALL REMEMBER THIS MOMENT.
NOW.

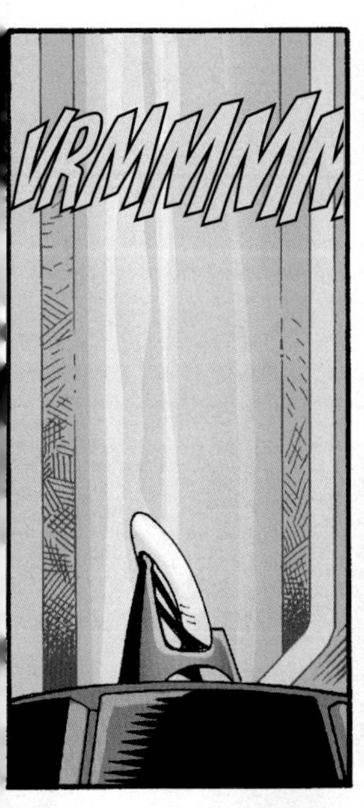
VRMMMMM

COME ON...
...COME ON...

MMMMMM

ORIGINATING TUBE EMPTY.
THE PLATE'S MATRIX IS NOW IN THE MAGNETIC STREAM.

POWER LEVELS HOLDING, BUT WE'RE DRAWING MORE THAN WE ANTICIPATED.

MMMMM
RECEIVING TUBE HAS A LOCK ON THE PLATE. MATERIALIZATION UNDER WAY.

DR. YAMAZAKE! STOP THE PROCESS! POWER LEVELS HAVE SURGED INTO THE DANGER AREA!

NO! ADD POWER!
WE MUST NOT--

MMMBWHOOMBROOWWWW

I'M CUTTING THE POWER BEFORE THE WHOLE LAB BLOWS!

THIS...
...CAN'T BE.
KAI.

I...DON'T UNDERSTAND.
THE COMPUTER SIMULATIONS SAID IT WOULD WORK!
IT *SHOULD* HAVE *WORKED!*
I'M REALLY SORRY, DR. YAMAZAKE.

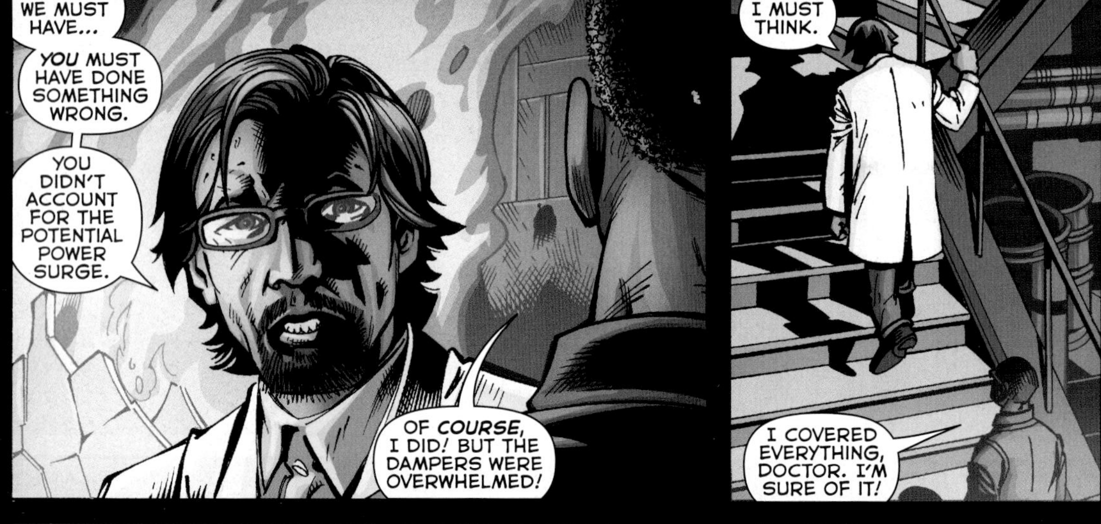

SKASSH
SUPERMAN?
WHAT ARE YOU DOING HERE?
I COULD ASK THE SAME OF YOU.

FIRESTORM HAS MISSED THE LEAGUE'S LAST TWO MEETINGS.
THERE IS NO FIRESTORM.
NOT ANYMORE.

EXPLAIN.
TWO PEOPLE SHARING ONE BODY? IT SHOULDN'T HAVE WORKED AS LONG AS IT DID.
IT'S OVER.
I'VE MOVED ON.

TO BUILD A TRANSPORTER.
LOOKS A LOT LIKE OURS.
USING JLA TECH?

WHAT--?
NO!
I WOULD NEVER--!
YOU SHOULD KNOW THAT!

OF COURSE.
IT FAILED, ANYWAY. NOT SURE WHY...
SOME KIND OF POWER SURGE, I GUESS.

TOO BAD.
HAVE YOU EVER ASKED YOURSELF IF THIS IS A GOOD THING?
THE DOWNSIDE MIGHT DWARF THE UPSIDE.

WAIT! YOU DIDN'T DO ANYTHING TO--!
FIX YOUR PROBLEM WITH RAYMOND.

FIRESTORM IS NEEDED.
NO!

NEVER...
...AGAIN.

HIS IS S.H.A.D.E. SPECIAL SCIENCE LIAISON OCTOR RAY PALMER, BROADCASTING OUT ON ALL KNOWN S.H.A.D.E. TELEPATHIC NETWORKS.
IT HAS BEEN THREE DAYS SINCE AGENT RANKENSTEIN, AGENT AMETHYST AND I ARRIVED IN THE HURON SYSTEM, APPROXIMATELY ONE MILLION LIGHT-YEARS FROM EARTH, TO INVESTIGATE THE MURDER OF STORMWATCH.
IN THAT TIME, I HAVE BEEN UNABLE TO MAKE ANY CONTACT WITH S.H.A.D.E. OR S.H.A.D.E.'S HEAD, FATHER TIME. I CAN ONLY HOPE THAT THESE DAILY THOUGHT JOURNALS ARE MAKING THEIR WAY BACK TO HEADQUARTERS, BUT OF COURSE, I HAVE NO WAY OF KNOWING.
ESSENTIALLY, WE ARE ALL ALONE AND IN THE DARK OUT HERE IN DEEP SPACE.
UPON EXITING THE HANTOM ZONE WORM-OLE AND ARRIVING HERE, WE FOUND STORMWATCH'S HIP, THE CARRIER, EVERELY DAMAGED. THE VESSEL WAS SSENTIALLY SPLIT INTO TWO.
WE CHOSE TO BOARD THE RGER SECTION, AND I USED PORTABLE NANO-FIELD TO AL IT OFF AND PROTECT US OM THE VACUUM OF SPACE. ALSO THINK THIS SECTION THE CARRIER WILL PROVIDE WITH THE BEST CHANCE OF REBOOTING THE SHIP'S MPUTER AND GLEANING SOME CLUE AS TO WHO OR WHAT ATTACKED THEM.
ENT FRANKENSTEIN ONCE AIN PROVED HIMSELF TO BE QUITE DURABLE.
LOST HIS LEFT M IN THE BATTLE TH THE PHANTOM ZONE FUGITIVE BLACK ADAM.
BUT HE REMAINS IN OOD SPIRITS...OR AT AST, I THINK HE IS N GOOD SPIRITS. I MIT FRANKENSTEIN'S MOOD IS SOMEWHAT HARD TO READ.
I DO HAVE AN IDEA PERCOLATING AS TO HOW TO HELP REPAIR FRANKENSTEIN... BUT MORE ON THAT LATER...

AFTER SETTING UP BASE IN THE CARRIER, AGENTS AMETHYST AND FRANKENSTEIN VOLUNTEERED TO RETRIEVE THE BODIES OF THE FALLEN STORMWATCH MEMBERS.
CONSIDERING FRANKENSTEIN'S "HANDICAP," AMETHYST VOLUNTEERED TO GO ALONE.

BUT FRANKENSTEIN INSISTED ON JOINING HER.
RECOVERING THE BODIES HAS ADDED A ***SECOND MYSTERY*** TO THIS MISSION, ONE THAT IS PERHAPS JUST AS DISTURBING TO ME AS THE MYSTERY OF WHAT WAS POWERFUL ENOUGH TO DESTROY THE TEAM.
HAWKMAN, THE MIDNIGHTER, JACK HAWKSMOOR AND ***THE MERMAID*** HAVE BEEN SALVAGED.
BUT THE BODIES OF ***APOLLO*** AND ***THE ENGINEER*** ARE ***NOWHERE TO BE FOUND.***
BUT LIKE ANY MAN OF SCIENCE, I MUST DO THE BEST I CAN WITH THE CLUES AND EVIDENCE THAT ARE PRESENT. SO...IT IS WITH A HEAVY HEART THAT I NOW BEGIN ***THE AUTOPSY OF STORMWATCH...***

...BUT FIRST, BACK TO A MORE IMMEDIATE CONCERN...

DOCTOR PALMER, HAVE YOU HAD ANY SUCCESS IN CONTACTING FATHER TIME OR S.H.A.D.E.?

HMM? OH, NO. NOT YET, FRANKENSTEIN.

AGENT AMETHYST, MAY I BORROW YOUR SWORD FOR A MOMENT?

WHAT? WHY?

...JUST CURIOUS ABOUT SOMETHING.

UH... OKAY. HERE.

THANK YOU.

I ALWAYS WANTED A SWORD.

DR. PALMER, PLEASE. THIS IS NO TIME FOR FLIGHTS OF THE IMAGINATION. WE NEED TO FIND A WAY TO RECONNECT WITH S.H.A.D.E.

I ASSURE YOU, FRANKENSTEIN, THE SWORD IS MORE THAN JUST A PROP FOR MY DAY-DREAMS.

SEE, THE SAWS I BROUGHT JUST WON'T CUT IT... ***LITERALLY.***

DR. PALMER?

MELMOTH'S BEARD!!!
SCHLUNK
DOCTOR PALMER?!!?
WHAT?
...IT LOOKED LIKE THE BEST FIT.

SOUTHEAST ASIA.
COME IN, HO, COME IN...

HE'S NOT RESPONDING.
NO DUH.

REMEMBER WHEN THIS WAS ALL FOREST?
SURE. DAMN WAR.
WRECKED EVERYTHING.

YEAH.
YOU THINK THEY SAID THAT ON EARTH 2?

I MEAN, WE WENT TO WAR WITH EARTH 2. AND WHILE WE NEVER CALLED OURSELVES EARTH 1...
IT'S KINDA OBVIOUS THAT'S WHERE WE RANKED OURSELVES, RIGHT?
FONG?

I'M HERE, HO.
...WE'VE MADE A TERRIBLE MISTAKE.

"WHAT DO YOU MEAN? THE GUIDE SAID THAT THE BOMBINGS FROM THE WAR EXPOSED A CAVE AND A TEMPLE WAS INSIDE!
"IF THAT'S NOT TRUE? GOOD GOD, WE'VE LOST NEARLY A HUNDRED THOU--"

"NO...IT'S TRUE.

"THERE'S A TEMPLE.

"AND A GOD."

GET OUT OF HERE...
WHAT SORT OF TREASURE DO YOU HAVE YOUR HANDS ON, HO?
HEH.
THE WAR... AS BAD AS IT WAS, I THINK IT'S OPENED THE WAY FOR SOMETHING *WORSE.*
TAKE THE BOAT AND LEAVE *NOW.*
WHA--? WHY? WHAT DID YOU FIND?
WHAT ARE YOU KEEPING FROM ME, HO?
NO, *BROTHER*... YOU DON'T UNDERSTAND...

I WANT TO KEEP YOU FROM IT.

OH MY...

...GOD?

CRUUUNCH

SNAP

NEW ORLEANS.
AAAH!
HUH
HUH
HUH.
HUH?
YOU WAS DREAMIN', MIDGE...
...IN CHINESE.
IT WAS LAOTIAN.
JOHN...
THE END...IT'S COMING.
I KNOW, LUV.
I KNOW.
I MIGHT NEED HELP THIS TIME STAVIN' IT OFF.

FINALLY, THE POWER
BEHIND...
SOOK

WRITERS
• Brian Azzarello
• Jeff Lemire
• Dan Jurgens
• Keith Giffen
ARTIST
• Patrick Zircher
COLORS
• Hi-Fi
LETTERS
• Taylor Esposito
COVER
• Ryan Sook

FIVE YEARS FROM NOW.
THE INDIAN OCEAN.
RUN THOSE COORDINATES BY ME AGAIN, MS. LANE?
42 DEGREES SOUTH, 38 MINUTES, 16 SECONDS BY 105 DEGREES EAST, 20 MINUTES, 10 SECONDS, BUCK. HOW MUCH LONGER?
WE'RE ON TOP OF THAT RIGHT NOW.
SO WHAT IS IT WE'RE LOOKING FOR?
ANYTHING THAT SEEMS OUT OF PLACE OR UNUSUAL.
UNLESS YOU CONSIDER WATER UNUSUAL, THERE'S NOTHING HERE.
SONAR IS QUIET. NOTHING UNDER THE SURFACE.
HOW CAN THAT BE?
NO ISLANDS... NO BOATS... THOSE NUMBERS HAD TO HAVE MEANING.
KEEP CIRCLING.
NEGATIVE ON THAT.
WE'LL BE SUCKING FUMES BY THE TIME WE GET BACK AS IT IS.
THIS DOESN'T MAKE SENSE.
WHY WOULD SOME-ONE GO TO SUCH LENGTHS TO GET ME HERE--
--WHEN THERE'S ABSOLUTELY NOTHING TO SEE?

CADMUS ISLAND.
...STOP GETTING HER ANGRY, YOU WON'T KEEP GETTING DUMPED IN THE OCEAN.
WORD.
IT MUST BE DRIVING THE OMACs CRAZY.
COMMISSARY
SO...WHEN DO I FIND OUT WHAT I'M EXPECTED TO DO NOW THAT I'M HERE?
KILL YOURSELF?
WHATEVER I TELL YOU TO DO, MR. CASH. UNLESS YOU'VE BEEN TOLD DIFFERENT?
I HAVEN'T BEEN TOLD ANYTHING EXCEPT "DON'T PISS OFF THE GIRL."
WHICH, TRUTH BE TOLD, ISN'T WORKING OUT ALL THAT GREAT.
I'D WORK ON THAT.

"GRIFTER," YOU'RE OF NO USE TO ME--
AT ALL.
--UNLESS YOU'RE WILLING TO EMBRACE THE WHOLE OF IT.
I'M SUPPOSED TO BE OF USE TO YOU?
HATE TO BREAK THIS TO YOU, BUT ONCE YOU GET PAST "HE SEES ALIENS," THERE'S NOT A LOT--
MISTER FARADAY PAYS ME WELL--VERY WELL--TO TAKE CARE OF CERTAIN... PROBLEMS.
SLADE AND I, WE KILL PEOPLE.
ADMINIS
MEDICA
STAFF C
SOLITA
YES...WE DO, DON'T WE?
WAIT A MINUTE, WAIT A MINUTE. "EMBRACE THE WHOLE" OF WHAT?
NOT TOO SLOW ON THE UPTAKE THERE, EINSTEIN.
YOUR... POWER, FOR LACK OF A BETTER WORD.
ABILITY, TALENT, ENHANCEMENT--
YOU SEEM TO BE UNDER THE IMPRESSION THAT YOU ONLY SEE ALIENS.
ADMINISTR
THAT'S BECAUSE I ONLY SEE ALIENS. AND DOPPELGANGERS. AND, JUST RECENTLY...
OKAY. POINT TAKEN.
FARADAY SEEMS CONVINCED THAT YOU SEE DECEPTION.
THAT GIVEN ENOUGH TIME, AND A BIT OF EFFORT ON YOUR PART, YOU COULD REFINE THAT POWER AND BE OF USE.
USE? WHAT KIND OF USE?
ELIMINATING THE GUESSWORK. I KNOW THAT WOULD MAKE MY LIFE EASIER.
GUESS-WORK?

CONTRARY TO CERTAIN PERCEPTIONS, I--
WE.
...WE DO MORE THAN KILL PEOPLE, ALTHOUGH THERE ARE TIMES WHEN THAT BECOMES UNAVOIDABLE. WE ALSO HUNT DOWN AND PROCURE FOR CADMUS.
SUPERHUMANS. CLOSETED FOR THE MOST PART. ACTIVE IF THE OPPORTUNITY PRESENTS ITSELF.
"CLOSETED." AS IN, THEY HAVE THE COMMON SENSE NOT TO BROADCAST THE FACT THAT THEY CAN...WHATEVER.
THERE ARE MORE OF THEM THAN YOU THINK.
CADMUS IS INTERESTED IN THEM ALL, FROM THE MOST INNOCUOUS TO THE POTENTIAL POWERHOUSES.
AND ALL POINTS BETWEEN.
THAT'S WHERE I COME IN, RIGHT? THEY CAN'T HIDE FROM ME. IF THIS FARADAY IS RIGHT.
I THINK HE IS. I WOULDN'T BE WASTING MY TIME WITH YOU OTHERWISE.
I'M NOT A KILLER...OF HUMANS.
THEN DON'T. YOU POINT, I--
WE.
--DO WHAT NEEDS DOING.

A BLOODHOUND.
CLOSE ENOUGH.
MORE A POODLE, YOU ASK ME.

YOU DO REALIZE YOU'VE NO CHOICE IN THE MATTER, RIGHT?
KINDA FIGURED THAT.
I'M GOING TO ASSUME WHAT'S IN HERE WILL DRIVE HOME THAT POINT?
IN A MANNER OF SPEAKING.

I PREFER TO THINK OF IT AS THE POINT OF NO RETURN.
ONCE YOU'VE SEEN THIS, YOU BELONG TO CADMUS.
OR WE WHACK YOU. IT'S WHAT WE DO.
THOSE ARE...CADMUS HAS SUPER-HUMANS?!

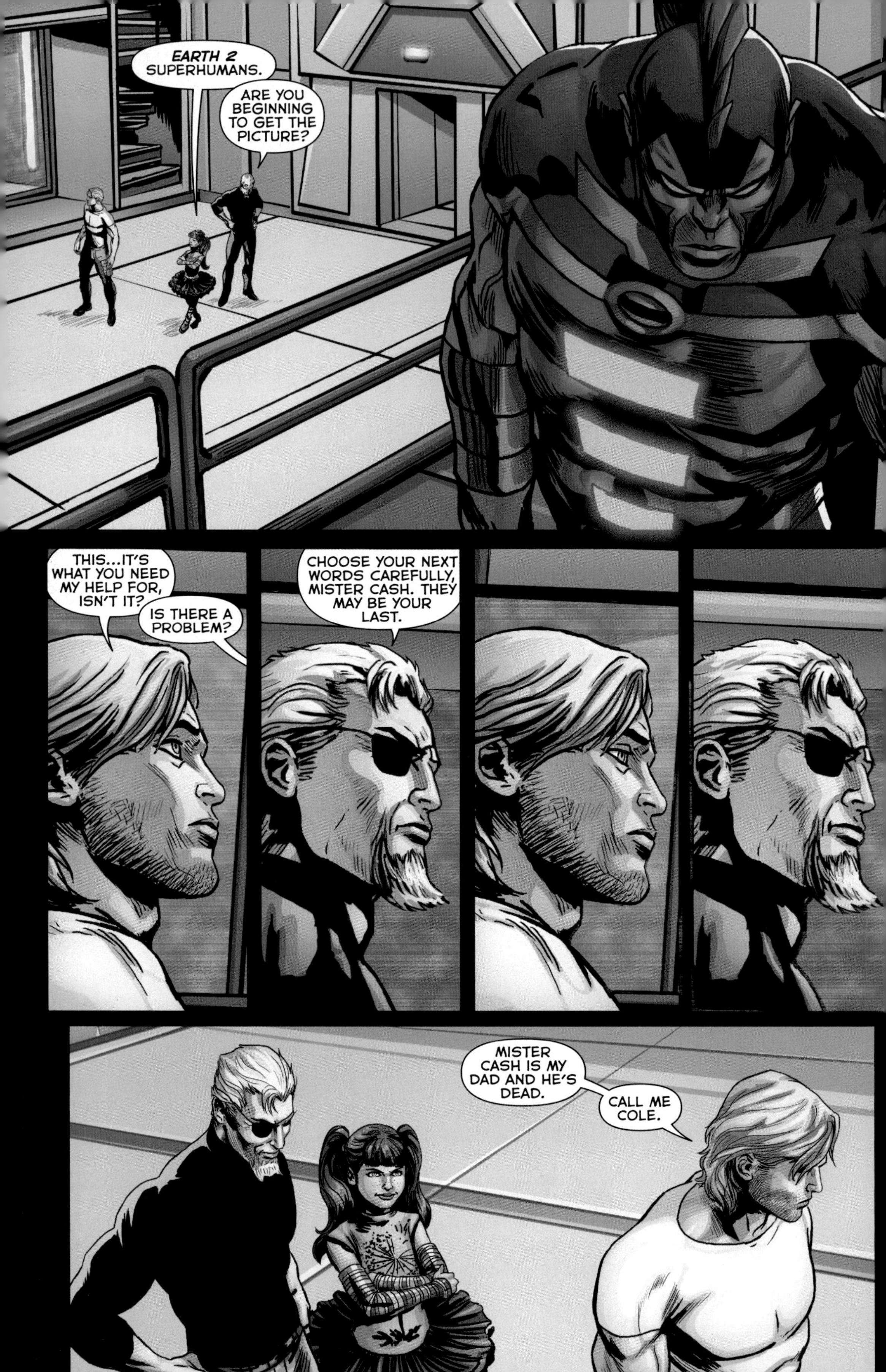
EARTH 2 SUPERHUMANS.
ARE YOU BEGINNING TO GET THE PICTURE?
THIS...IT'S WHAT YOU NEED MY HELP FOR, ISN'T IT?
IS THERE A PROBLEM?
CHOOSE YOUR NEXT WORDS CAREFULLY, MISTER CASH. THEY MAY BE YOUR LAST.
MISTER CASH IS MY DAD AND HE'S DEAD.
CALL ME COLE.

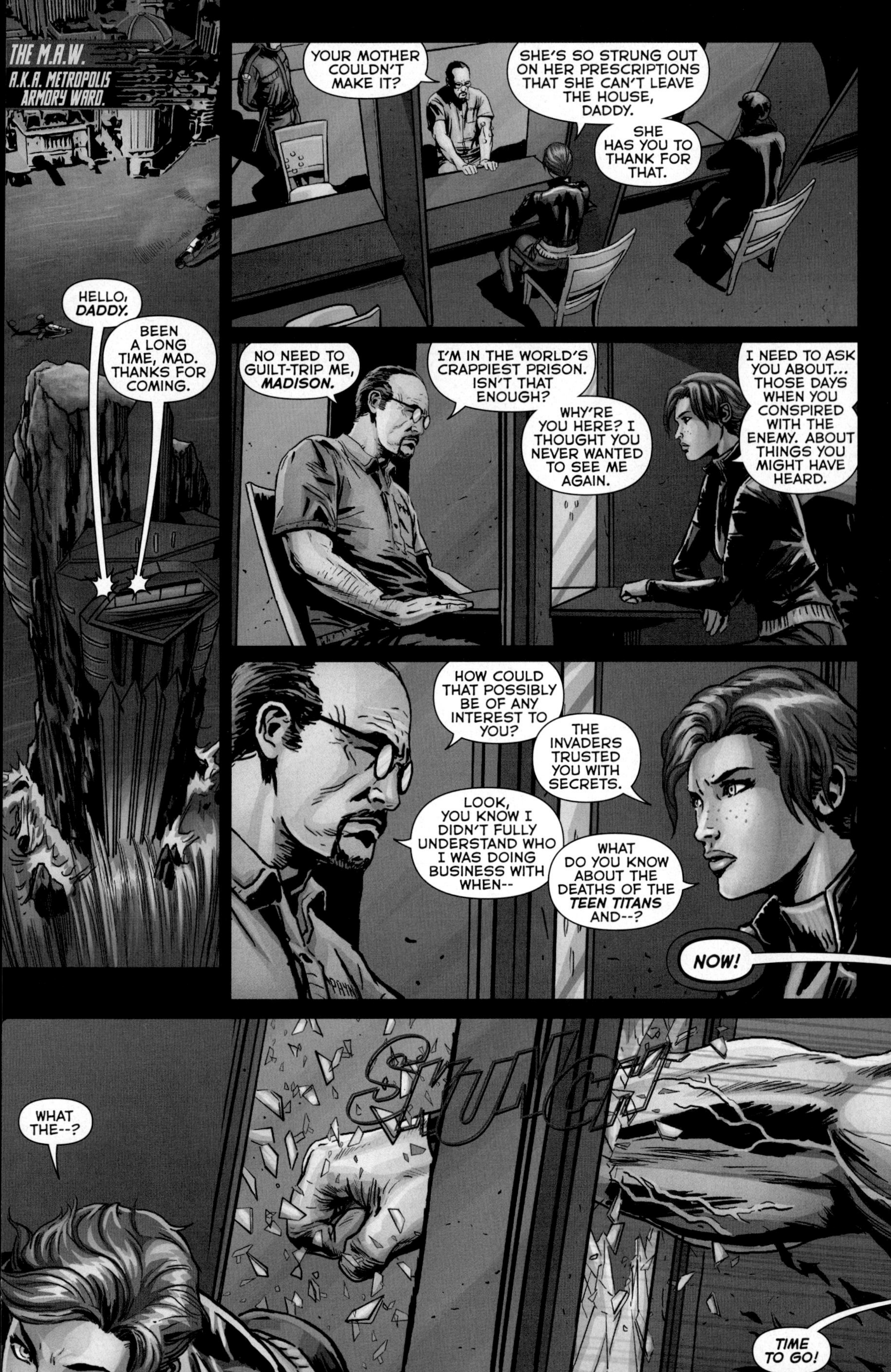
THE M.A.W.
A.K.A. METROPOLIS ARMORY WARD.
YOUR MOTHER COULDN'T MAKE IT?
SHE'S SO STRUNG OUT ON HER PRESCRIPTIONS THAT SHE CAN'T LEAVE THE HOUSE, DADDY.
SHE HAS YOU TO THANK FOR THAT.
HELLO, DADDY.
BEEN A LONG TIME, MAD. THANKS FOR COMING.
NO NEED TO GUILT-TRIP ME, MADISON.
I'M IN THE WORLD'S CRAPPIEST PRISON. ISN'T THAT ENOUGH?
WHY'RE YOU HERE? I THOUGHT YOU NEVER WANTED TO SEE ME AGAIN.
I NEED TO ASK YOU ABOUT... THOSE DAYS WHEN YOU CONSPIRED WITH THE ENEMY. ABOUT THINGS YOU MIGHT HAVE HEARD.
HOW COULD THAT POSSIBLY BE OF ANY INTEREST TO YOU?
THE INVADERS TRUSTED YOU WITH SECRETS.
LOOK, YOU KNOW I DIDN'T FULLY UNDERSTAND WHO I WAS DOING BUSINESS WITH WHEN--
WHAT DO YOU KNOW ABOUT THE DEATHS OF THE TEEN TITANS AND--?
NOW!
WHAT THE--?
TIME TO GO!

YOU'RE COMING WITH ME, *ETHAN.*
WHO-- ARE *YOU?*

FRIEND.
ONE I'VE NEVER MET.
IS SOMEONE PAYING YOU TO DO THIS?
NEED YOU.
WHOA.
TOTAL *RAMPAGE.*
I *LIKE* IT.
MOVE!
UH!
MADISON!
ENOUGH.
MEH.
THIS IS WHERE WE COWER IN FEAR?

SUPER--
ERGH!
GRRAHR!
MR.
BUZZKILL.
PAK
CHAK
POK
KRAK
THINK FOR A SECOND, HON.
YOU CAN'T WIN THIS WAY.

WUMP
DISTRACT HIM.
GIVE THE DO-GOODER SOMETHING MORE TO WORRY ABOUT.
HUH?
WHAT'RE YOU--
NOOOOOO!
THAT'S MORE LIKE IT.
HELP MEEEE!
OHMY GODOHMYGOD OHMYGODOH MYGODOHMY GODOHMY GOD--!
GOT YOU.
THANKYOU THANKYOUTHANK YOUTHANKYOUTHANK YOUTHANK--!
GONE.
WHY?
WHAT COULD SHE WANT WITH A SICKO LIKE ETHAN BOYER?

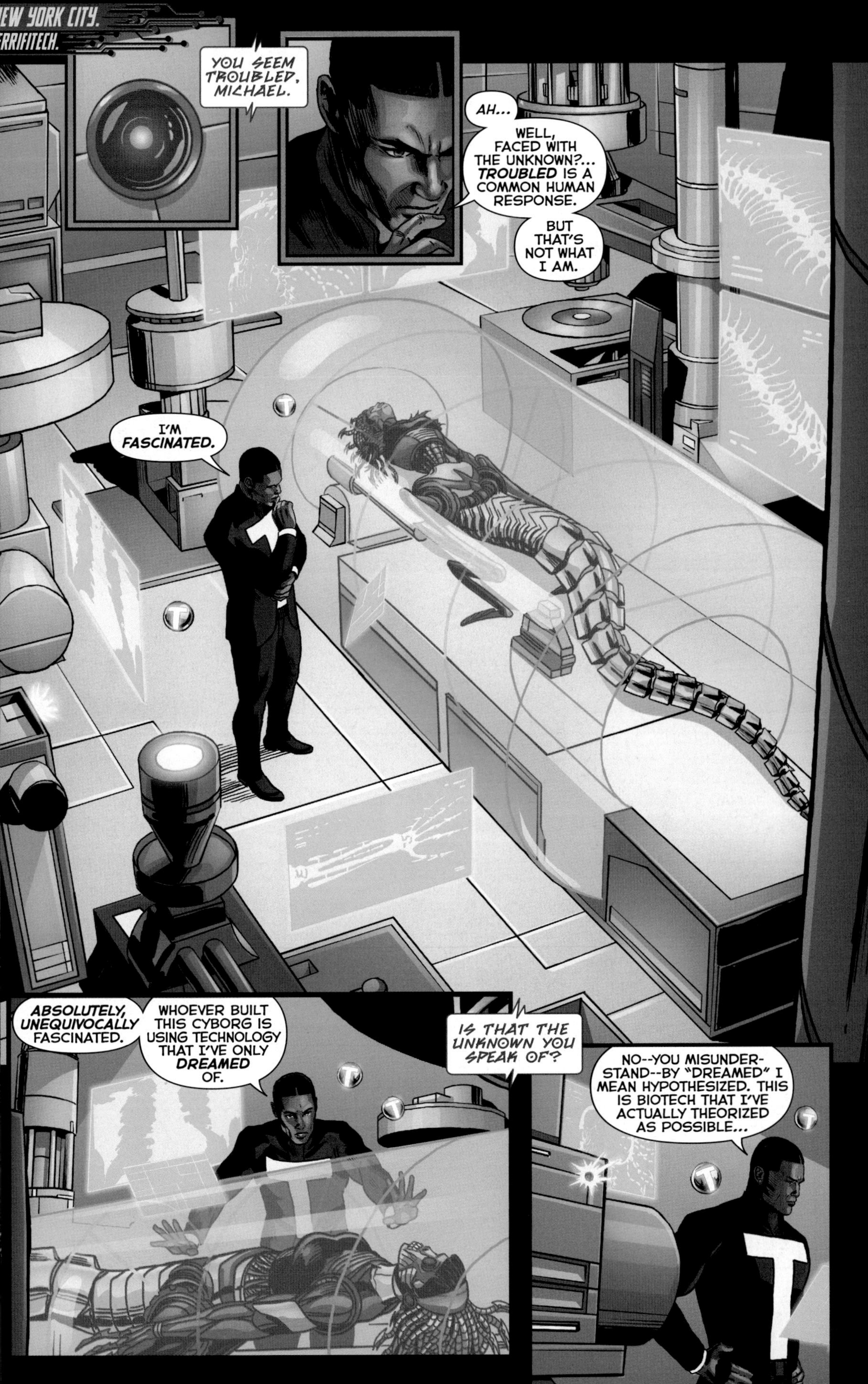

NEW YORK CITY.
TERRIFITECH.
YOU SEEM TROUBLED, MICHAEL.
AH...
WELL, FACED WITH THE UNKNOWN?... TROUBLED IS A COMMON HUMAN RESPONSE.
BUT THAT'S NOT WHAT I AM.
I'M FASCINATED.
ABSOLUTELY, UNEQUIVOCALLY FASCINATED.
WHOEVER BUILT THIS CYBORG IS USING TECHNOLOGY THAT I'VE ONLY DREAMED OF.
IS THAT THE UNKNOWN YOU SPEAK OF?
NO--YOU MISUNDERSTAND--BY "DREAMED" I MEAN HYPOTHESIZED. THIS IS BIOTECH THAT I'VE ACTUALLY THEORIZED AS POSSIBLE...

BUT NOT UNTIL TECHNOLOGY CATCHES UP WITH THE SCIENCE I PROPOSE. THIS IS TECH THAT CAN EAT CANCER, REPLACING IT WITH HEALTHY SYNTHETIC CELLS.
THIS IS NANOTECH EBOLA. DROPPED IN MY LAP OUT OF A BUM'S SHOPPING CART.
THE BUM? THAT'S OUR UNKNOWN.
CAN IT BE A REMNANT FROM THE DOPPELGANGER EARTH YOU'VE TOLD ME ABOUT?
UNLIKELY. SPENDING TIME THERE, I WOULD HAVE COME ACROSS THIS.
WHAT ABOUT...?
MICHAEL, I CAN'T HELP YOU. I'M IN CONTACT WITH YOU ONLY TO OBSERVE.
THAT CAN BE FRUSTRATING.
AND DRIVING.
I'M SURE YOU'LL FIGURE THIS CYBORG OUT. AFTER ALL, YOU, SIR, ARE THE SMARTEST MAN...

"...ON YOUR WORLD."

NOW WHAT?

FOR SOMEONE WHO TREATS ME WITH SUCH DISREGARD, YOU DO TURN TO ME FOR ADVICE VERY OFTEN, **MASTER TERRY.**

WELL, YOU TEND TO ALWAYS POINT ME IN THE WRONG DIRECTION, *A.L.F.R.E.D.* THAT HELPS.

EXCUSE--

--ASSESSMENT.

OUR GOAL IN RETURNING TO THE PAST WAS TO STOP **BROTHER EYE** FROM BEING CREATED, THEREBY DIVERTING THE FUTURE WE'VE TRAVELED FROM.

HOWEVER, WE'VE ARRIVED TOO LATE--

OR WOULD THAT BE NOT LATE ENOUGH?

"WHY DIDN'T WE KNOW THAT IN THE FUTURE?"
"THE EYE CONTROLLED MEDIA, INFORMATION, THEREFORE HISTORY..."

"AND OUR *BLINDNESS.*"

YOUR COURSE OF ACTION?
OUR FUTURE IS PROOF THE SATELLITE GETS REACTIVATED. WE NEED TO PREVENT THAT OCCURRENCE.

WOUNDED DUCK
RIGHT. MEANING WE BREAK INTO *TERRIFITECH.*
AGAIN? BUT IT WENT SO WELL LAST TIME.
"WELL, LAST TIME ALL I HAD WAS YOU..."

...ON MY TEAM.
I WAS AFRAID YOU WERE GOING TO SAY THAT...

HOLD STILL, FRANKENSTEIN!
HRRN...
WHAT IS THAT THING, DOCTOR PALMER?
KZZT
I'M ATTEMPTING NANOSURGERY TO ATTACH THIS CYBERNETIC COUPLING TO THE EXISTING NERVE ENDINGS IN FRANKENSTEIN'S SHOULDER, AGENT AMETHYST.
JUST BE QUICK ABOUT IT, PALMER. I FIND THIS WHOLE AFFAIR SOMEWHAT LURID.
OH, COME ON, FRANKENSTEIN. IT'S NOT LIKE HAWKMAN IS GOING TO NEED HIS ARM ANYMORE.

I'D LOVE TO STUDY YOUR PHYSIOLOGY FURTHER AT A LATER DATE.
WHATEVER THAT NECROTIC FLUID YOU CALL BLOOD IS, IT'S REALLY SOME-THING, FRANK. IT'S ALREADY ADAPTING TO THE EXISTING CIRCULATORY SYSTEM IN HAWKMAN'S ARM.
YOU KNOW, NOW THAT I'M GETTING A CLOSER LOOK, IT'S NOT JUST YOUR BLOOD THAT'S A BIT ODD--
--HHHHNNN...
UH... GUYS...
WHAT THE HELL DID YOU DO TO MY ARM!?!
AHHHH! HE'S A ZOMBIE!
MELMOTH'S BEARD!

STOP RIGHT THERE AND LET GO OF DOCTOR PALMER, HAWKMAN! I DO NOT WISH TO REMOVE YOUR HEAD AS WELL.
NOW...THIS IS ALL A TERRIBLE MISUNDER-STANDING.
MISUNDER-STANDING? YOU'RE DAMN RIGHT IT IS! THAT'S MY ARM!
I--I SWEAR I THOUGHT YOU WERE DEAD!
SPEAKING OF WHICH... WHY THE HELL AREN'T YOU DEAD?!
SIGH--I AM NOT A DAMNED ZOMBIE, PALMER!
I--THE NTH METAL. IT'S IN MY BLOOD. FUSED TO ME. IT DOES AMAZING THINGS. I DON'T EVEN KNOW IF I CAN DIE.
I TOLD YOU--SPACE ZOMBIE!

NTH METAL?
LONG STORY, PALMER. WHAT THE HELL ARE YOU THREE DOING HERE, ANYWAY?! THE LAST I REMEMBER I WAS--
--NO!
I--I'M SORRY, HAWKMAN. STORMWATCH IS DEAD. S.H.A.D.E. SENT US TO INVESTIGATE...TO TRY TO FIGURE OUT WHAT THE HELL DID THIS TO YOU ALL.
I--I DON'T KNOW. THE CARRIER WAS SOMEHOW PULLED OUT OF THE BLEED. THE COMPUTER SYSTEM WENT NUTS, TURNED THE SHIP'S DEFENSES AGAINST US.
APOLLO WENT OUT AFTER IT, AND IT--WHAT-EVER IT WAS--IT INCINERATED HIM.
BUT APOLLO IS AS POWERFUL AS SUPERMAN...WHAT THE HELL COULD HAVE DONE THAT TO HIM?
I WISH I KNEW. BUT WHAT WORRIES ME NOW IS THAT WHATEVER IT WAS...

"...IT'S STILL OUT THERE SOMEWHERE."
RTH.
S.H.A.D.E.'S MICROSCOPIC, MOBILE HEAD-QUARTERS. CURRENT LOCATION FIFTY-SIX MILES ABOVE THE GREAT PYRAMID OF GIZA, EGYPT.
ARE YOU SURE AGENT AMETHYST AND HER TEAM HAVE NO IDEA WE'RE MONITORING THEIR ACTIONS OUT THERE IN DEEP SPACE, FATHER TIME?
NONE. I TOOK PRECAUTIONS. AS FAR AS THEY KNOW, THEY ARE OUT OF RANGE OF ANY POSSIBLE CONTACT WITH S.H.A.D.E.
WE CAN SEE THEM, BUT THEY CAN'T SEE US, DR. BELROY. IT'S BETTER THAT WAY FOR NOW, ANYWAY.
HMM...THEY STILL SEEM TO HAVE NO IDEA WHAT THEY ARE REALLY UP AGAINST OUT THERE, DO THEY?
IF THEY HAD ANY CLUE...HELL, IF ANYONE ON EARTH HAD ANY CLUE WHAT WAS REALLY COMING...WELL, LET'S JUST PRAY FRANKENSTEIN AND HIS TEAM CAN NEUTRALIZE IT BEFORE THAT EVER HAPPENS.
AND IF THEY CAN'T?
IF THEY CAN'T...THEN IT WILL BE THE END OF EVERY-THING.

WRITERS
•Brian Azzarello
•Jeff Lemire
•Dan Jurgens
•Keith Giffen
PENCILLER
•Aaron Lopresti
INKER
•Art Thibert
COLORS
•Hi-Fi
LETTERS
•Taylor Esposito
COVER
•Ryan Sook

VE YEARS FROM NOW.
TROPOLIS.
ZAKT
ZAKT
SHOULD'VE EXPECTED THIS.
SKAZZ
ZAKT

BRIPPT
SHRIPP
GIVE IT UP, BOYER!
SKAZZ
I KNOW YOU'RE HERE!

IF YOU THINK THESE TOYS OF YOURS CAN STOP ME--
BRAK

BRUNK
--YOU FORGET WHO YOU'RE DEALING WITH.

MAKE ME COME FIND YOU AND I'LL RIP YOUR HEAD RIGHT OFF YOUR SHOULDERS.
TOO LATE.

HOPE YOUR FRIENDS KNOW WHAT TO DO WITH YOUR REMAINS.

SKAZZ

GET OUT HERE.

NOT HERE.
DAMN.
SUPERMAN?!
WHAT ON EARTH ARE YOU DOING HERE?

YOU HAVE THE ENTIRE CITY ON HIGH ALERT!
LOIS.
BOYER DISAPPEARED DAYS AGO.

FIGURED HE MIGHT BE HERE.
HERE? SUPERMAN, ARE YOU SERIOUS?

BOYER ABANDONED THIS GENETIC EXPERIMENTATION LAB LONG AGO.
YOU'RE THE ONE WHO TOLD ME, IN FACT.
IT WOULD'VE BEEN DEMOLISHED BY NOW, IF NOT FOR ALL THE TOXIC WASTE.

WHICH... IS WHY I THOUGHT HE MIGHT BE HERE.
LIKE HIDING IN PLAIN SIGHT.

HAVE TO KEEP LOOKING.
SEE YA.
OF COURSE.
WHATEVER THAT HAS COME TO MEAN.

NEW YORK CITY.
THE WOUNDED DUCK.
SO WE DOING THIS?

"WE"? WE AIN'T "WE" YET, KEY. LIKE I'VE SAID BEFORE, THE HARDEST PART ABOUT BREAKING INTO TERRIFITECH...

WHAT ARE YOU DOING?
FEELING MY SKULL. YOU THINK IT'S METAL?

AS I WAS SAYING, STAYIN' IN LONG ENOUGH TO GET WHAT WE'RE THERE FOR? THAT'S A PROBLEM.

YOU NEED AN INSIDE MAN?

I DON'T THINK I KNOW WHAT YOU'RE TALKING ABOUT, FRIEND.

I'M NOT YOUR *FRIEND,* AND I KNOW YOU'RE TALKING ABOUT BREAKING INTO TERRIFITECH.
I THINK YOU'RE MISTAKEN.

IT WOULDN'T BE THE FIRST TIME.
FLOP

YOU'RE THE *BAT GUY* WHO--

--DOESN'T NEED TO BE REMINDED WHO HE IS.
WHAT YOU NEED, THOUGH, IS *ME.*
WHY'S THAT?

BECAUSE I'VE BEEN *INSIDE* T-TECH.

THIS IS THE FLOOR PLAN.

HOW'D YOU--?
THAT *BATSUIT*-- APPEARED WHEN YOU MIXED IT UP WITH *TERRIFIC.*

RIGHT.
FIRST FLOOR...

SECOND FLOOR...

TENTH FLOOR...
GET IT?

WHAT WAS IN YOUR *SHOPPING CART?*

HIS GROCERIES-- WHAT THE HELL IS WRONG WITH YOU, *PLASTIQUE?*

WHAT THE HELL IS GOING ON *PERIOD?*
YOU BUYIN' THIS, *COIL?*

I'M LISTENIN'...

--TO A HEAP OF STEAMING BULL! AM I THE ONLY ONE THAT SMELLS IT?

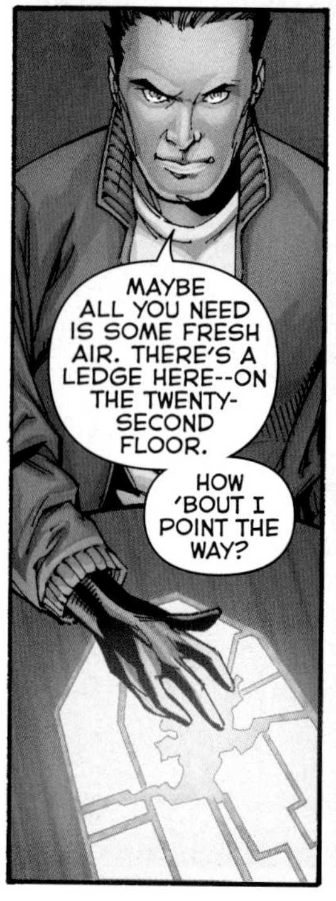
MAYBE ALL YOU NEED IS SOME FRESH AIR. THERE'S A LEDGE HERE--ON THE TWENTY-SECOND FLOOR.
HOW 'BOUT I POINT THE WAY?

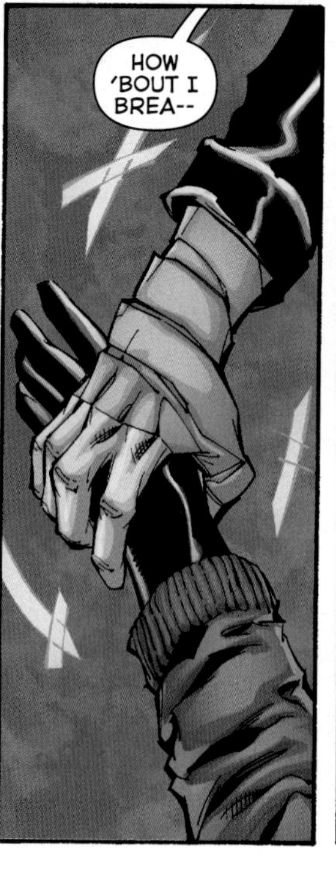
HOW 'BOUT I BREA--

--SERIOUSLY.
ALLOW ME.
THWIK

HUUUH...

I'LL GET A RAG.

WHAT YOU JUST DID?
SORRY.

THAT WAS A VARIATION ON THE *TONGA DEATH STRIKE.*

WHAT DO *YOU* KNOW ABOUT THE TONGA DEATH STRIKE?

I KNOW THE MAN WHO CAME UP WITH THE *DEATHLESS* VARIATION.

HAS HE MENTIONED ME?

I WOULDN'T KNOW.

CAN HE WALK?
I THINK SO.
GOOD.

I'D LIKE TO CONTINUE OUR CONVERSATION SOMEWHERE ELSE.

LATER...
MADISON! ARE YOU STILL OBSESSING OVER LANE'S ACCU-SATIONS?
UCK
WOUNDED DUCK

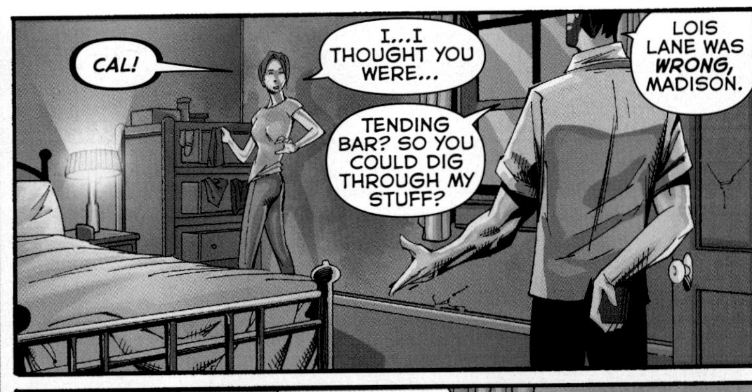
CAL!
I...I THOUGHT YOU WERE...
TENDING BAR? SO YOU COULD DIG THROUGH MY STUFF?
LOIS LANE WAS WRONG, MADISON.

IT'S A WELL-DOCUMENTED FACT THAT THE TEEN TITANS, RED ROBIN INCLUDED, WERE KILLED BY...WHAT WERE THEY CALLED?
PARADEMONS.
SHE'S CHASING RUMORS AND GHOSTS.
MAYBE SO, BUT--!

WE'RE ALL ABOUT THE HERE AND NOW, MAD.
I WAS SCARED TO DEATH WHEN YOU GOT CAUGHT UP IN BOYER'S JAILBREAK.
WHICH IS WHY I GOT YOU THIS.

CAL!
IT'S BEAUTIFUL!
I KNOW YOU LOST 'MOST EVERYTHING--JEWELRY INCLUDED, WHEN YOUR DAD WENT TO PRISON.

YOU ARE AWESOME.

MUCH AS I'D LIKE TO SEE WHERE THIS CONVERSATION GOES, I HAVE TO GET BACK TO THE BAR.
HIGH-STRUNG CROWD TONIGHT.
I'LL BE DOWN TO HELP IN A COUPLE MINUTES.
AFTER I PUT THIS ON, OF COURSE!

THE HURON SYSTEM.

YOU WERE RIGHT. IT HAPPENS QUICKLY.

WHA--?

YOUR ARM. THE HEALING IS INCREDIBLE.

...YES. THE NTH METAL *IS* INCREDIBLE IN THAT RESPECT. I JUST WISH--WELL, I WISH THE *REST OF STORMWATCH* WERE SO LUCKY.

IT DOES MAKES ME WONDER, THOUGH--WHAT IS THAT NTH METAL IN YOUR OLD ARM GOING TO DO TO *FRANKENSTEIN?*

ALL DUE RESPECT, FRANKENSTEIN IS THE LEAST OF MY CONCERNS. RIGHT NOW, ALL I CARE ABOUT IS HEALING QUICK ENOUGH AND GETTING BACK OUT THERE TO *HUNT DOWN* WHOEVER DID THIS TO STORMWATCH.

OH...I UNDERSTAND.
I UNDERSTAND THAT YOU'RE AS PIGHEADED AND FULL OF YOURSELF AS I'D ALWAYS HEARD.

I UNDERSTAND THAT THE ONLY REASON YOU ENDED UP OUT HERE IN DEEP SPACE WITH STORMWATCH IN THE FIRST PLACE IS THAT THE JUSTICE LEAGUE FINALLY GOT TIRED OF YOUR ACT.

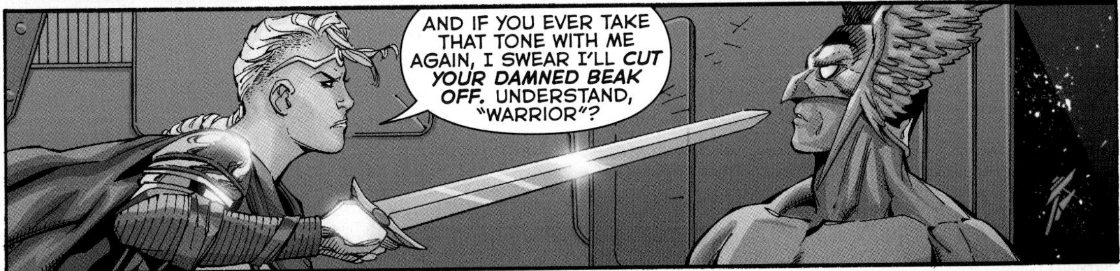
AND IF YOU EVER TAKE THAT TONE WITH ME AGAIN, I SWEAR I'LL CUT YOUR DAMNED BEAK OFF. UNDERSTAND, "WARRIOR"?

WHAT THE HELL ARE YOU SMILING AT?!
...I THINK I JUST FELL IN LOVE.

--EEP BEEP BEEP
WHAT IS THAT?
MY STORMWATCH EMERGENCY COMMUNICATOR--
WE KEPT THESE AS BACKUP IN CASE THE TELEPATHIC UPLINK WE ALL SHARED WENT DOWN.

WHY IS IT GOING OFF NOW? A LITTLE LATE FOR AN EMERGENCY BEACON, ISN'T IT?
YOU DON'T UNDERSTAND. IF THE BEACON HAS BEEN TRIPPED, IT MEANS I'M NOT ALONE...IT MEANS SOMEONE ELSE FROM STORMWATCH SURVIVED!

CADMUS ISLAND.
OKAY...OKAY...LINE IT UP AND SEE WHAT YOU'VE GOT HERE.
I'M AMBUSHED BY KING FARADAY, WHO PACKS ME OFF TO AN ISLAND SERVING AS A BLACK OPS GITMO FOR E2 SUPERHUMANS BY CADMUS WHICH, UP UNTIL RECENTLY, I THOUGHT WAS JUST ANOTHER BRANCH OF BIG PHARMA.

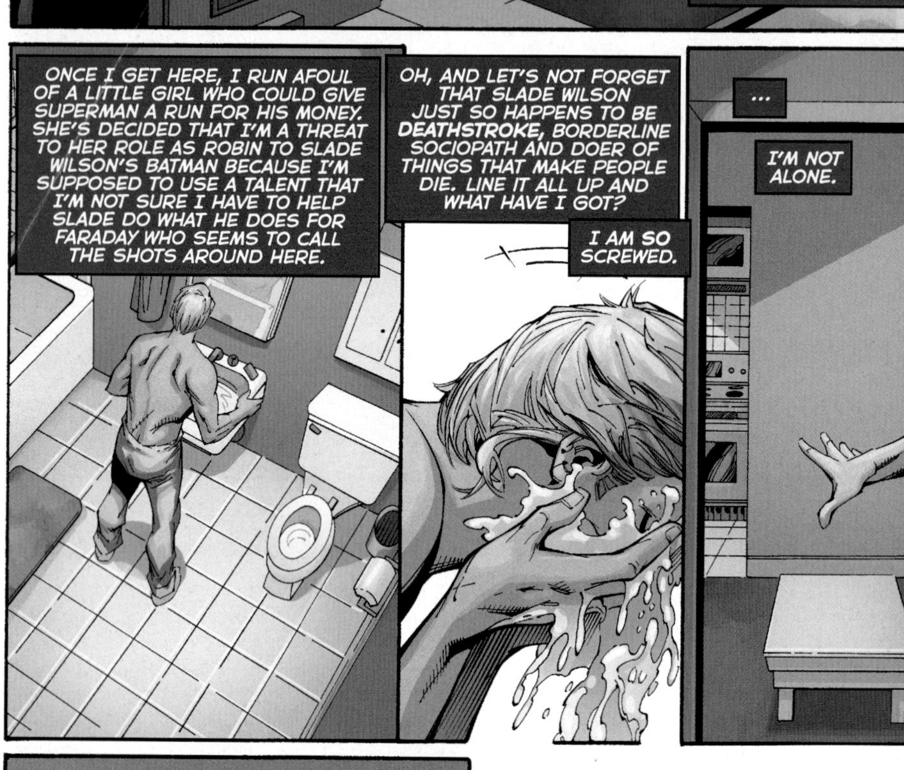
ONCE I GET HERE, I RUN AFOUL OF A LITTLE GIRL WHO COULD GIVE SUPERMAN A RUN FOR HIS MONEY. SHE'S DECIDED THAT I'M A THREAT TO HER ROLE AS ROBIN TO SLADE WILSON'S BATMAN BECAUSE I'M SUPPOSED TO USE A TALENT THAT I'M NOT SURE I HAVE TO HELP SLADE DO WHAT HE DOES FOR FARADAY WHO SEEMS TO CALL THE SHOTS AROUND HERE.
OH, AND LET'S NOT FORGET THAT SLADE WILSON JUST SO HAPPENS TO BE **DEATHSTROKE,** BORDERLINE SOCIOPATH AND DOER OF THINGS THAT MAKE PEOPLE DIE. LINE IT ALL UP AND WHAT HAVE I GOT?
I AM **SO** SCREWED.
...
I'M NOT ALONE.

SWEAR TO GOD, IF IT'S THAT FIFTY SUE PSYCHO PLAYING AROUND WITH M--

THWOK

INVISIBLE? OH, WONDERFUL! JUST WONDERF--

NO. NOT INVISIBLE. CLOAKED.

PLAYING SEMANTICS WHILE SOMEONE'S TRYING TO TAKE MY HEAD OFF! SMART, COLE! REAL SMART!

I'M NOT LOOKING FOR TROUBLE. YOU GOT AN ISSUE WITH ANYTHING I'VE DONE--
WHICH HAS BEEN DAMN ALL SO FAR!
--JUST SPELL IT OUT.
OH, YEAH, THAT OUGHTA WORK!

WHRACKT

C'MON... C'MON! AT LEAST TRY TO MAKE IT A FIGHT!

HNNGHH!
POK-KRUNCH
SLAM
WHUMP
CHAKK

WHU...NO!
NO, NO, NO, NO,
NO...SAY SOMETHIN'!
SAY ANYTHIN'! A' LEAS'
GIVE ME A HINT!
WHA'
JUS' HAPPEN?
WH-WHY..?

JUS'
TELL M'
WH...

SIGH...
ON THE PLUS SIDE, YOU GET TO HANG OUT WITH AMY, YOUR LITTLE NURSE FRIEND, AT THE MEDI-UNIT.

ON THE OTHER PLUS SIDE, SEEMS LIKE I'M NOT THE ONLY ONE WHO WOULDN'T MIND SEEING YOU DEAD. THAT WAS AN OMAC, IN CASE YOU WERE WONDERING, BUT NOT LIKE ANY KIND I'VE EVER SEEN.
O... OMAC?

HERE'S YOUR CHANCE TO IMPRESS ME.
HAH?
IT'LL BE JUST LIKE A SCOOBY-DOO CARTOON.

HAH!?
LET ME GET YOU SOME MEDICAL ATTENTION. THEN, WE CAN GET RIGHT DOWN TO IT.
DOWN TO...DOWN TO WHAT?
THE GAME'S AFOOT! CONGRATULATIONS, COLE, YOU JUST GOT INTERESTING.

VANCOUVER, CANADA.
ST. CHRISTOPHER'S HOUSE
HOMELESS SHELTER

GOD BLESS YOU, JANE.

NO PROBLEM, WILL. JUST STAY WARM TONIGHT, YEAH?

...YOU GONNA EAT THAT, SWEET-HEART?
HMM?
YER FOOD?

NO. YOU CAN HAVE IT. I'M NOT HUNGRY.

WHY ARE YOU FOLLOWING ME?!

HEY!

WHO THE HELL ARE YOU?!
MY NAME IS EMIKO...BUT I'VE BEEN CALLED MANY THINGS. NONE OF THEM IMPORTANT RIGHT NOW. WHAT'S IMPORTANT IS WHERE YOU REALLY COME FROM.

WHO ARE YOU? G.P.A.?
I'M NOT WITH THE GLOBAL PEACE AGENCY. I CAME BECAUSE I NEED YOUR HELP.

BUT I NEED THE REAL YOU. NOT "JANE KIRBY," THE WOMAN WHO'S BEEN WORKING IN DAMNED SOUP KITCHENS SINCE THE WAR, TRYING TO EASE HER GUILTY CONSCIENCE.
I NEED A HERO...
MARKET

...I NEED BARDA.

WRITERS
•Brian Azzarello
•Jeff Lemire
•Dan Jurgens
•Keith Giffen
PENCILLER
•Georges Jeanty
INKER
•Cam Smith
COLORS
•Hi-Fi
LETTERS
•Taylor Esposito
COVER
•Ryan Sook

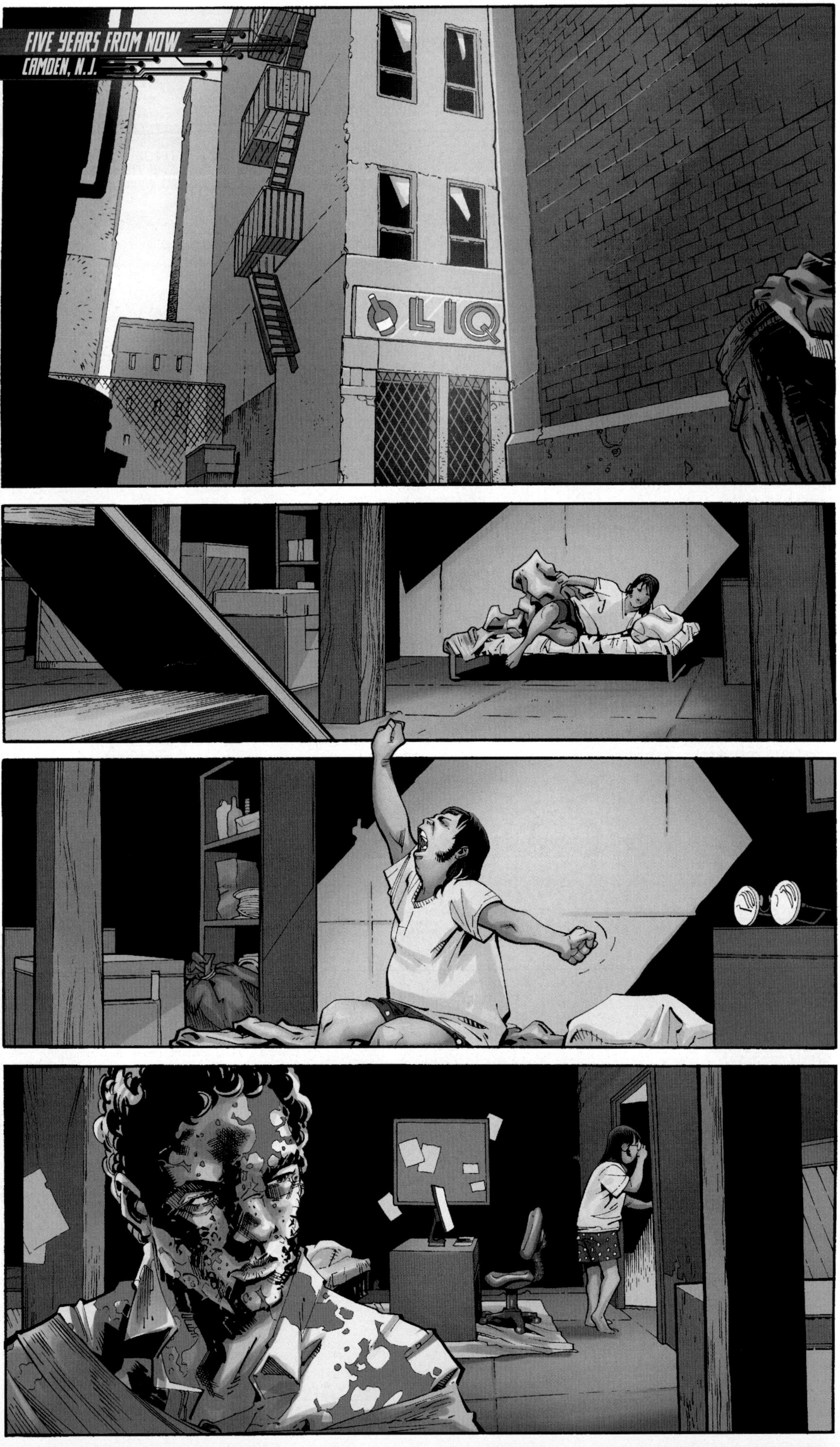

FIVE YEARS FROM NOW.
CAMDEN, N.J.

LIQ

SIGH...

DAMMITALL, COLE. BEEN A COUPLE A' WEEKS NOW.
MY NAME'S NOT COLE.

HOW MANY TIMES DO I GOTTA TELL YOU IT AIN'T TALKING TO YOURSELF IF SOME-ONE RESPONDS TO WHAT YOU'RE SAYING?

BLAM

IDJIT ALIEN.

AREN'T YOU SUPPOSED TO CUT AND RUN IF YOUR "GRIFTER" PARTNER DOESN'T CHECK IN AFTER FORTY-EIGHT HOURS?
CORRECT ME IF I'M WRONG, BUT YOU BLEW THAT DEADLINE.

HE'S NOT DEAD.
NO. JUST WISHING HE WERE IF ONE OF MINE CAUGHT HIM.

DUDE, I JUST SHOT YOU. SHOW A LITTLE RESPECT.
SHOT, ELECTROCUTED, POISONED, SLICED, DICED AND BURNT. HAVE I MISSED ANYTHING?
INFECTED.

NOT MY FAULT IF YOU'RE TOO STUPID TO DIE.

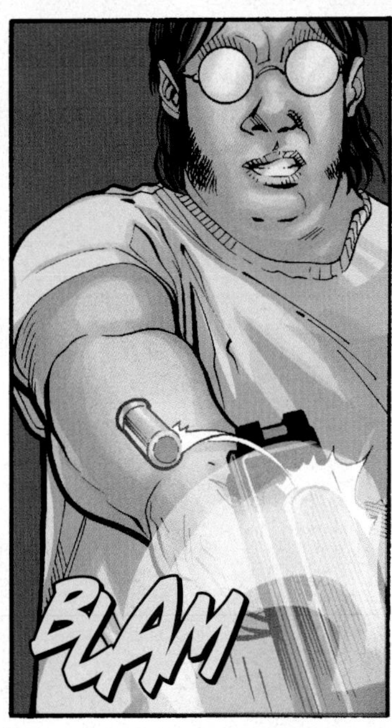
BLAM

FEELING SMARTER NOW?

DAMN E.T. HAD A POINT. I WAITED WAY TOO LONG. COLE'D BE FURIOUS.
"CUT BAIT AND RUN." THE GOSPEL ACCORDING TO COLE.

JUST... JUST LET HER BE SOBER.
JUST THIS ONCE. I'LL GIVE HER THE REST OF THE TIME, BUT JUST THIS ONCE...
1510

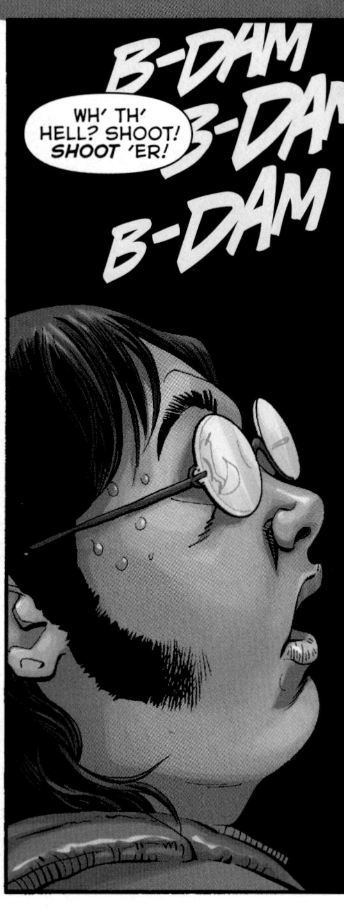
B-DAM
B-DAM
WH' TH' HELL? SHOOT! SHOOT 'ER!
B-DAM

HIT 'ER F'GODSAKE! HI--
NGYAHHH
SNAKT

NO! DEAR GOD N--

NO! NONONO... *PLEASE!*

KR-RUNCH

HEY, *VOODOO.* AM I INTERRUPTING SOMETHING?
JUSTIN.
YEAH...
LET ME GATHER UP A FEW THINGS. THIS PLACE ISN'T SAFE ANYMORE.

COLE DEAD OR MISSING?
YOU MEAN IT *WAS?*
DEFINITELY MISSING.

HE DIDN'T DO YOU A FAVOR... THIS ARRANGEMENT. STILL, I *DID* AGREE TO TAKE YOU IN "JUST IN CASE."
WELCOME TO MY HELL.

DEEP SPACE.
THE HURON SYSTEM.
"HOW ARE THE CONTROLS HANDLING, HAWKMAN?"

FINE, PALMER. THIS ISN'T MY FIRST TIME FLYING A SPACECRAFT.
--RIGHT, RIGHT. I FORGOT YOU'RE FROM ANOTHER PLANET. ZANIBAR, RIGHT?
SIGH THANAGAR... THANAGAR.
RIGHT, GOT IT.

NOW, THE DISTRESS BEACON YOU'RE RECEIVING ON YOUR STORMWATCH COMMUNICATOR IS DEFINITELY COMING FROM THAT SMALL, UNCHARTED PLANET.
BUT, YOU'RE SURE IT'S NOT SOME KIND OF TRICK? IT'S POSSIBLE THAT WHOEVER DESTROYED STORMWATCH IS TRYING TO DRAW YOU OUT, HAWKMAN. MAYBE YOU ALL SHOULD HAVE STAYED ON THE CARRIER WITH ME UNTIL WE HAD A CHANCE TO THINK THIS THROUGH A BIT MORE.

IF IT'S A TRAP, THEN THE BASTARDS WILL BE SORRY THEY DIDN'T KILL ME WHEN THEY HAD THE CHANCE, DR. PALMER.

YOU'VE BEEN STARING AT ME FOR THE LAST TEN MINUTES, AGENT FRANKENSTEIN. DO I HAVE SOMETHING ON MY FACE?

WHA--?! NO, M'LADY. I AM SORRY. I DID NOT MEAN TO--

RELAX, FRANK. I WAS JUST MESSING WITH YOU. YOU KNOW--SOMETHING ON MY FACE--THE SCAR. SORRY. MY SENSE OF HUMOR CAN BE A BIT BLACK.
AH, YES, WELL, PRINCESS AMETHYST, AT LEAST YOU HAVE A SENSE OF HUMOR. I'M AFRAID THAT DR. FRANKENSTEIN WAS IN SUCH A RUSH TO SEW ME TOGETHER, HE FORGOT TO ATTACH MY FUNNY BONE.

...
WAS THAT A JOKE?

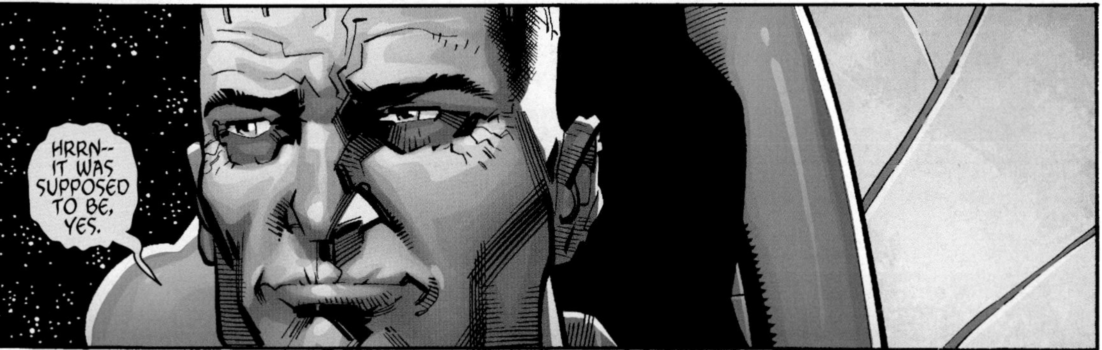
HRRN-- IT WAS SUPPOSED TO BE, YES.

HOW LONG DID IT TAKE YOU TO THINK THAT ONE UP?
ABOUT TWO HUNDRED AND SEVEN YEARS, I BELIEVE.

GOOD ONE.
HERE, TRY THIS.
A RUBY?

NO. IT'S CALLED A BLOODSTONE. THE WEAPONERS OF GEMWORLD USED THESE.
GEMWORLD? HUMPH--SOUNDS MAGIC-Y. I HATE MAGIC.
SKRP

IT WAS MY HOME. AND YES, IT WAS A PLACE OF MAGIC... GREAT MAGIC. AND IT SHONE BRIGHTER THAN ANYTHING YOU COULD EVER HOPE TO IMAGINE, HAWKMAN.

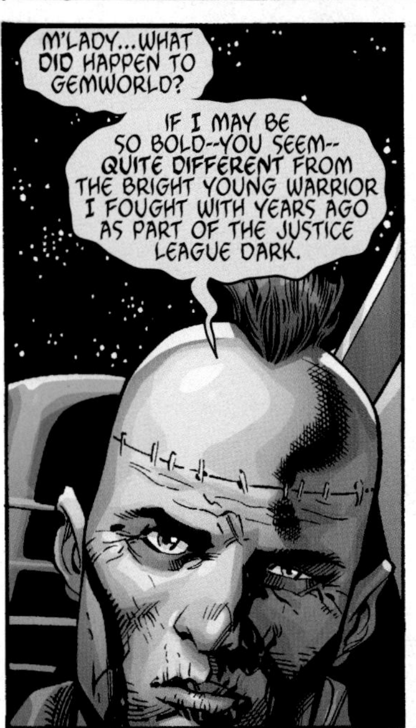
M'LADY...WHAT DID HAPPEN TO GEMWORLD?
IF I MAY BE SO BOLD--YOU SEEM--QUITE DIFFERENT FROM THE BRIGHT YOUNG WARRIOR I FOUGHT WITH YEARS AGO AS PART OF THE JUSTICE LEAGUE DARK.

A POWERFUL MYSTIC FROM OUR WORLD USED THE CHAOS OF THE INVASION AS COVER TO ATTACK GEMWORLD AND MAKE IT HIS OWN.
I WAS--I WAS UNABLE TO STOP THEM. IT FELL BECAUSE I WAS NOT STRONG ENOUGH.

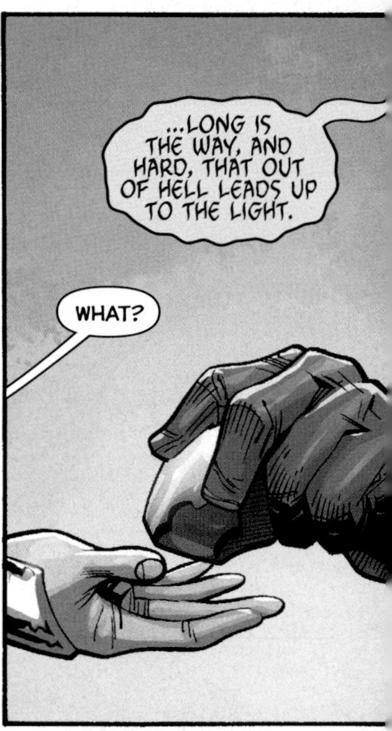
...LONG IS THE WAY, AND HARD, THAT OUT OF HELL LEADS UP TO THE LIGHT.
WHAT?

A QUOTE FROM MY FAVORITE POET, MILTON--I BELIEVE IN THIS CASE, IT--
DAMN IT!

WHAT IS IT?! ARE WE UNDER ATTACK?!
I DON'T KNOW-- WE JUST HIT THE PLANET'S ORBIT AND ALL THE SHIP'S PRIMARY SYSTEMS SHUT DOWN!
WE'RE GOING DOWN!
BRACE FOR IMPACT!
KA-FLOOM
ARE YOU OKAY, FRANK?
HRRN...I DO BELIEVE SO, M'LADY.
KZZT
KZZT
YEAH, I'M OKAY TOO, THANKS FOR ASKING.
LET'S MOVE. THE SHIP IS FILLING WITH SMOKE!
SHWIP

MELMOTH'S BEARD!
...DAMN.

NEW YORK CITY.
YOU SURE ABOUT THIS, MICHAEL?
NO, MARLENE. NO, I'M NOT.
FEAR IS SOMETHING I'M NOT INTERESTED IN FOSTERING-- YOU KNOW THAT...

BUT THAT CYBORG I FOUND IS BASED ON TECH THAT'S ONLY THEORETICAL AT THIS POINT.

MEANS OUR BAT...DUDE IS MORE THAN MEETS THE EYE. HE'S NOT A THIEF.

HE'S A THREAT.
SO...I'M AFRAID THIS IS THE RIGHT THING TO DO.

YOU ACTUALLY BELIEVE HE'S AFTER THE uSPHERE?
NO. BUT I'M NOT THE ONE WHO HAS TO BELIEVE THAT.
GOING LIVE IN THREE... TWO...

WE'RE BACK WITH MR. TERRIFIC, WHO'S SAYING THAT THE uSPHERE--THE NEXT TECH BREAKTHROUGH WE CAN'T WAIT TO GET OUR HANDS ON--

--OR OVER OUR SHOULDERS--IS IN JEOPARDY. HOW IS THAT POSSIBLE?
HOW?

THIS MAN MAKES IT SO.

OR SHOULD I CALL HIM AN ALIEN?
LET'S SETTLE FOR ENIGMA.

THIS IS SECURITY FOOTAGE FROM INSIDE TERRIFITECH, WHERE WE ARE DEVELOPING SENSITIVE TECHNOLOGIES TO BENEFIT OUR WORLD.

OUR WORLD.
QUESTION IS, WHERE'S HIS?

"THE SOONER WE FIND HIM, THE SOONER WE'LL HAVE ANSWERS."
MADAGASCAR SEA.
SIR, THEY'RE NOT RESPONDING. CALLEY'S RADIO WENT DEAD A FEW MINUTES AFTER THEY BOARDED THAT ABANDONED BOAT.
THAT'S STRANGE...

PULL IN. I WANT A CLOSER LOOK.

ANYTHING?

OH, MY GOD...

SLOORK!
RRRIP!
SCRUNC
AAAAAAH!!

22,300 MILES ABOVE EARTH.
JUSTICE LEAGUE DEFENSE STATION OMEGA.
I'VE LOCATED RAYMOND--
--AND WILL HAVE HIM HERE IN A SECOND.
I STILL SAY WE SHOULD HAVE *REQUESTED* HIS PRESENCE.
HE WOULD HAVE DECLINED.
Screening Arrival.
HOW CAN YOU BE SURE?
HE WAS IN A STRIP JOINT.
Subject Identified.
ANOTHER ROUND FOR--
MEN.
WHOA!
Ronald Raymond. FIRESTORM.
SINCE WHEN DOES THE JLA SNATCH PEOPLE OFF THE STREET?
SINCE ONE OF ITS MOST POWERFUL MEMBERS STARTED ACTING LIKE A SPOILED LITTLE BRAT, UNABLE TO PLAY WELL WITH OTHERS.

SORRY TO BRING YOU HERE WITHOUT NOTICE, RAYMOND.
WE THOUGHT YOU'D TURN US DOWN IF WE ASKED.
YOU AND *JASON RUSCH* TOGETHER ARE *FIRESTORM.*
WHICH IS SOMETHING YOU CANNOT WALK AWAY FROM.
WITH POWER LIKE YOURS, YOU HAVE A RESPONSIBILITY TO STEP UP.
ACTUALLY, I SAY WE SHOULD ENCOURAGE IT.
RUSCH. YOU'RE BEHIND THIS!
NO WAY, MAN. I DON'T EVER WANT TO MERGE TO BECOME FIRESTORM AGAIN, EITHER.

GOOD. 'CUZ THAT KUMBAYA MOMENT IS NOT GONNA HAPPEN.
YOU MUST RECONSIDER.
WONDER WOMAN IS RIGHT. THE **WAR** TAUGHT US THAT EARTH NEEDS ITS MOST POWERFUL DEFENDERS.
NOT IF THEY CAN'T LIVE UP TO THEIR OBLIGATIONS, ***STORMGUARD.***

IS THIS THE OFFICIAL "HANG RON RAYMOND OUT TO DRY" CEREMONY?
I HAVEN'T SAID A **WORD** ABOUT WHAT YOU DID TO ME.
OR THAT OTHER THING.

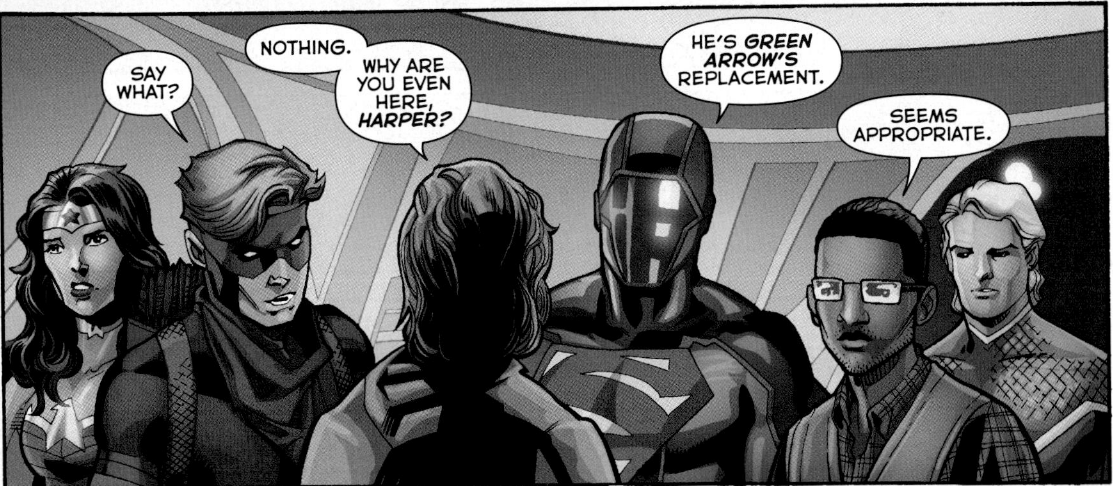
SAY WHAT?
NOTHING.
WHY ARE YOU EVEN HERE, ***HARPER?***
HE'S ***GREEN ARROW'S*** REPLACEMENT.
SEEMS APPROPRIATE.

THIS INVOLVES OLLIE'S DEATH, DOESN'T IT?
THE WAY HE DIED--
--AND HOW ***YOU*** COULDA PREVENTED IT.
NOT ***ME.***
NO ***WAY.***

YOU.
TALK.
IF THERE'S SOMETHING YOU WANT TO KNOW...

...ASK ***HIM.***

I KNEW IT!
I KNEW GREEN ARROW DIED BECAUSE OF YOU!
ROY. THIS IS NOT THE WAY.

THIS IS SUPPOSED TO HELP BRING FIRESTORM BACK?
MAYBE WE SHOULD CALL ZATANNA TO MIND-WIPE HIM.
DO NOT GO THERE.

IF THERE'S SOMETHING WE SHOULD KNOW...
'FESS UP.
NOW.
OH, RIGHT. LIKE JASON HASN'T ALREADY TOLD YOU.

HAVEN'T SAID A WORD, MAN.
YOU WANNA CLEAR THE AIR, IT'S UP TO YOU.

PLEASE, RON.
IF THERE'S SOMETHING YOU NEED TO GET OFF YOUR CHEST...
...DO SO NOW.

IT'S MY FAULT WE DIDN'T GET TO SEATTLE IN TIME TO HELP OLLIE.
I IGNORED JASON'S CALLS.
I WAS... BUSY.
WITH A GIRL.

BUT YOU DO NOT GET TO JUDGE ME.
I NEVER SIGNED UP FOR A LIFE OF 24/7 SACRIFICE.

YOU KNOW DAMN WELL WHAT I'M TALKING ABOUT.

PITTSBURGH. I COULD HAVE SAVED IT.
BUT WASHINGTON AND NEW YORK WERE DECLARED PRIORITIES.

IT WAS A WAR, RAYMOND.
WE ALL SUFFERED.
PLEASE, WE SHOULD TALK ABOUT--

NO!

YOU KNOW WHAT THAT COST ME.
I'VE GIVEN ENOUGH.
I'M LIVING FOR ME NOW.

FIRESTORM IS FINISHED.
FOREVER.

WE'RE BETTER OFF WITHOUT HIM.
I CAN NEVER SHARE A BODY WITH HIM AGAIN.
YOU FOUND A REPLACEMENT FOR OLIVER QUEEN.

FIND ONE FOR FIRESTORM.

WRITERS
•Brian Azzarello
•Jeff Lemire
•Dan Jurgens
•Keith Giffen
PENCILLER
•Jesús Merino
INKER
•Dan Green
COLORS
•Hi-Fi
LETTERS
•Carlos M. Mangual
COVER
•Ryan Sook

VE YEARS FROM NOW.
UNCHARTED PLANET IN THE
RTHEST REACHES OF SPACE.
WHERE THE HELL ARE WE?
FOREIGN OBJECTS DETECTED IN CRADLE 2364-12.
CARBON-BASED AND NECROTIC LIFE FORMS VERIFIED.
I DO BELIEVE WE SHOULD ATTEMPT THE DIPLOMATIC APPROACH FIRST...
I'VE NEVER BEEN MUCH OF A DIPLOMAT, FRANKENSTEIN.
I'M WITH HAWKMAN ON THIS ONE, FRANK. THESE GUYS DON'T LOOK VERY WELCOMING.
NONETHELESS, WE SHOULD AT LEAST TRY TO BE CIVIL. THIS IS THEIR PLANET, AFTER ALL.
GREETINGS, ROBOTS. WE ARE FROM EARTH. WE COME IN PEACE.
PROCEED WITH CRADLE-CLEANING. ERADICATE ALL LIFE FORMS.
SHRACK
HRRN...
NICE WORK, AMBASSADOR.
CAN WE JUST BEAT THEM UP NOW?

YES, AMETHYST... I DO BELIEVE A GOOD BEATING IS IN ORDER.

HEADS UP!
THANKS-- SO MANY OF THEM.
AREN'T YOU MAGIC? CAN'T YOU CAST A SPELL OR SOMETHING? THIN DOWN THEIR RANKS A BIT?
I WISH. I LOST MOST OF MY CONNECTION TO THE MAGIC WHEN GEMWORLD FELL DURING THE WAR.
UNGH! GREAT--GUESS WE DO THIS THE OLD-FASHIONED WAY.
SINCE YOU WERE MERE MACHINES, I TRIED TO GIVE YOU THE BENEFIT OF THE DOUBT--BUT, ALAS, I CAN SMELL THE EVIL ON YOU NOW. AND EVIL MACHINES DESERVE THE SAME FATE AS EVIL MEN...
KZZZT
--FRANKENSTEIN'S VENGEANCE!!

HRRN...

HOW DARE YOU DRAW A BLADE ON ME, YOU DEVIL-CONTRAPTION!

--THOUGHT WE MIGHT SCARE THEM OFF, BUT THESE GUYS JUST KEEP COMING.
MACHINES DO NOT SCARE, MY FRIENDS--THIS BATTLE HAS JUST BEGUN!

FRANKENSTEIN... YOUR FACE.

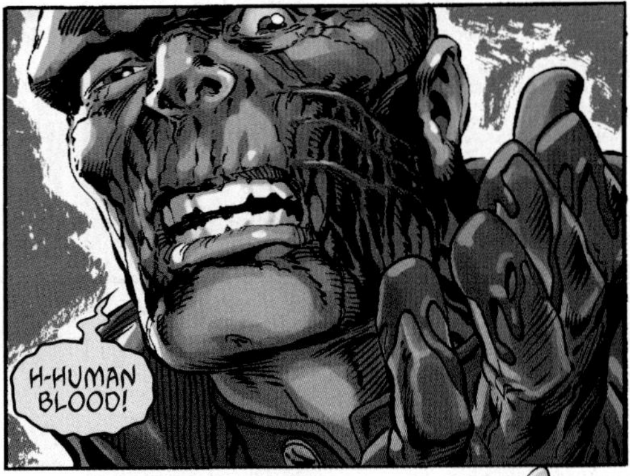
H-HUMAN BLOOD!

WHAT ROBOT-SORCERY IS THIS?!
UH... GUYS.

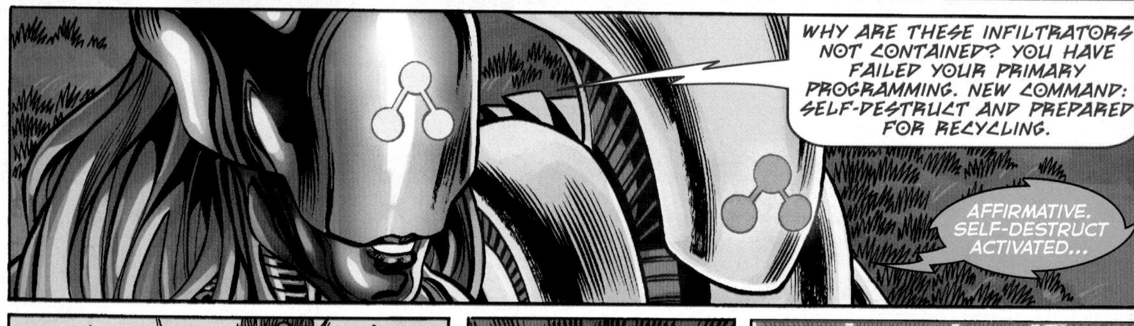

KZZT--
S.H.A.D.E.NET
NOW OFFLINE...

ALTIMORE, MD.
WHAT DID I EVER DO FOR YOU THAT I WARRANT A WARNING?
MUST WE GO THERE? AGAIN?
OKAY, LET'S TRY "WHY SHOULD I TRUST YOU?" AGAIN.

ALL I'VE EVER DONE IS TRY TO HELP YOU.
BULL. YOU'RE JUST TRYING TO GET ME OUT TO THAT ISLAND OF YOURS SO YOU CAN FIGURE OUT HOW I DO WHAT I DO.
PROBABLY DISSECT ME...

IF WE UNDERSTOOD W YOU DO IT, WE OULD, PERHAPS, AKE STEPS TO RECTIFY IT.
OR DO YOU WANT TO GO THROUGH THE REST OF YOUR LIFE AN AMBULATORY TOXIC WASTE SITE?
DID VOODOO AND THE TWINS SURVIVE?

VOODOO, YES. I'M NOT SURE HE'S MOVED AGAINST THE TWINS YET.
THAT'S THE PROBLEM WITH HAVING A PAST, COURTNEY, SOONER OR LATER IT CATCHES UP TO YOU.
MERCY! MY NAME IS MERCY!

YOUR NAME IS COUR--
HOW LONG? HOW LONG HAVE YOU BEEN SPYING ON ME? ON US?
YOU? EVER SINCE YOU "RAN AWAY." THE OTHERS? EVER SINCE THEY INTERSECTED WITH YOU.
AND YOU NEVER THOUGHT TO INTERFERE?
WHY? YOU WERE DOING "MY" WORK.
RIGHT. LIKE IT MATTERED TO YOU THAT THEY WERE BAD GUYS. TO YOU, WE'RE ALL BAD GUYS.
VICTIMS. NO ONE ASKED FOR SUPER POWE--
DON'T! DO NOT TAG ME A VICTIM!
SIGH ...I CAN SEE THIS IS GETTING ME NOWHERE.
CAVALIERI PRODUCTIONS PRESENTS
IPSO FACTO
RIGHTEOUS ANGER
SO WHAT IS IT? FEAR OR EGO? YOU AFRAID OF US OR ARE YOU JUST PISSED BECAUSE YOU'RE NOT PART OF MANKIND'S NEXT EVOLUTIONARY STEP?
YES.
WHAT ABOUT THOSE THAT DON'T WANT TO BE... "CURED"?
I DON'T RECALL CHOICE ENTERING INTO IT.
ARE WE QUITE FINISHED WITH THIS LINE OF INQUIRY?
SURE. YOU CAN GO NOW.
YOU'RE A MARKED WOMAN. YOU'RE ALL MARKED WOMEN. PLEASE TELL ME THAT MUCH HAS SUNK IN.
WHY DO YOU CARE?

IF YOU HAVE TO ASK, THEN I'VE WASTED MY TIME COMING HERE.
WHERE'S THAT CYCLOPS, WILSON? HE'S OUT THERE, ISN'T HE?
PURELY A PRECAUTIONARY MEASURE, ALL THINGS CONSIDERED.

SLADE WILSON'S ONE HELL OF A LOT MORE THAN A "PRECAUTIONARY MEASURE."
WHERE IS HE?
PART HER HAIR.

KISH

YOU SON OF A--
YOU *ENJOYED* THAT!
JUST A LITTLE.

AND *STAY* AWAY!

EEK
EEK
EEK
VOODOO, VOODOO, VOODOO...YOU NEVER CALL UNLESS YOU NEED SOME-THING.
LOVE YOU, TOO.
HEARD YOU HAD SOME UNINVITED COMPANY. YOU SURE THEY WERE--
POSITIVE. STREET PUNKS DON'T MOVE LIKE THAT. THEY WERE PROS.
WAITAMINNIT... HOW'D YOU KNOW ABOUT--
FARADAY.
AH... AND HOW IS UNCLE FARADAY?
CONCERNED. CALL HIM "UNCLE" AGAIN AND WE GO A FEW ROUNDS.
WHY'D IT TAKE YOU SO LONG TO REACH OUT?
EVERYTHING IS COMPROMISED. DIDN'T WANT TO TIP MY HAND UNTIL I WAS GOOD AND READY.
AS OF NOW HE KNOWS THAT I KNOW. YOU, TOO.
COMPROMISED... GREAT. USUAL PLACE?
SOUNDS LIKE A PLAN. I'LL ALERT THE TWINS.
YOU DO THAT.

CAMDEN, N.J.
GRIFTER'S H.Q.
Y'THINK, MAYBE, I COULD BE LET IN ON WHAT'S GOING ON HERE, SEEING AS YOU'RE KINDA, SORTA, NOT REALLY MY LEGAL GUARDIAN 'N' ALL?
BLACK OPS GONE WRONG, JUSTIN.
I'M THE REAL ME
THE GUY I USED TO WORK FOR IS TRYING TO KILL ME. US. TRYING TO KILL US. FARADAY'S CONCERNED AND THAT'S NEVER GOOD.

FARADAY? THAT'S THE NAME OF THE GUY'S BEEN TAILING COLE.
I'M THE REAL ME
HE MIGHT HAVE SOME-THING TO DO WITH COLE BEING--
DEAD?
MISSING!

YEAH, WELL, YOUR FRIEND, "GRIFTER" SURE PICKED A GOOD TIME TO GO MISSING.
LOOKS LIKE IT'S ALL ABOUT TO HIT THE FAN. YOU HAD AN OUNCE OF COMMON SENSE, YOU'D--
KLIK
BANGER?
VOODOO? YOU MIND HOLDING? GOT SOME GENTLEMAN CALLERS NEED TO BE TAUGHT SOME MANNERS. WE SHOULDN'T BE LONG.

KNOCK YOURSELVES OUT. WATCH OUT FOR COVERTS.
YES, "MOTHER."
KLIK

THEY PUT YOU ON HOLD?
GOT SOME GUESTS NEED KILLING. SHOULDN'T TAKE MORE THAN A FEW MINUTES.
OH. OKAY.

SAY WHAT?
GOOD HOLDING MUSIC. "GIRL FROM IPANEMA." I LOVE THAT SONG.
SAY WHAT?!

METROPOLIS.
WELL. NOW THAT WE'VE HAD A FEW DAYS TO STEAL THE NECESSARY EQUIPMENT...

...WE CAN GET YOU BACK TO A SIZE 6.
HURRY.
YEAHYEAHYEAH. JUST GOTTA... OH.
I CANNOT BELIEVE SHE SENT ME THAT. NAUGHTY, NAUGHTY GIRL.

NOW!
BREAK ANYTHING ELSE AND IT'LL TAKE A HECKUVA LOT LONGER, SWEET-HEART.

CAN'T STAND THIS.
FIX ME, ETHAN.
PLEASE.

IN A SEC. I JUST HAVE TO--OH, WAIT.
NO, I AM NOT--
--coming 2 yr party!
TTYL

OKAY.
QUALITY TIME FOR *RAMPAGE.*
DON'T CALL ME THAT!

SORRRRY!
BUT THROW A TANK THROUGH A MOUNTAIN...
...YOU MIGHT WANNA GO WITH SOMETHING THAT HAS A LITTLE MORE FLAIR THAN *"KITTY FAULKNER."*

ETHAN!
NICE KITTY.
TEAR MY HEAD OFF.
WHERE WILL YOU BE *THEN?*
BZZT BZZT

U.S.C., THAT'S WHERE.
ANOTHER PIC?
OMG.

GYAHH!

KRITCH
ALL RIGHT ALREADY.
I GET THE MESSAGE.

LET'S GET DOWN TO BID'NESS.

WHERE WAS IT THAT WE MET?
OH, YEAH. PARIS GENETICS CONFERENCE-- RIGHT BEFORE THE WAR BROKE OUT.
YOU WERE WORKING IN LEXCORP'S GENETIC RESEARCH LAB AND I WAS WITH S.T.A.R. LABS.

OR SO I TOLD EVERYONE.
KIND OF A TEENSY-WEENSY LIE. ONE OF MANY.
HENCE MY IMPRISONMENT.

AND HERE WE ARE, YEARS LATER, AFTER ONE OF YOUR EXPERIMENTS WENT CRAZY, FRIED YOUR BRAIN AND TURNED YOU INTO *THIS.*
WHEN LITTLE OL' LEX COULDN'T REPAIR THE DAMAGE...

...YOU CAME TO THE WORLD'S FOREMOST AUTHORITY ON GENETICS--
--MOI.
AND BROKE ME OUT OF JAIL IN THE PROCESS.

FOR WHICH I THANK YOU.
AND WILL DEMONSTRATE MY GRATITUDE BY RETURNING YOU TO NORMAL.
LET'S GET STARTED.

THANK... YOU.
FREEDOM IS EVERYTHING TO ME, KITTY.
CAN YOU BELIEVE THEY LOCKED ME UP FOR GENETIC EXPERIMENTATION ON THE EARTH 2 ATTACKERS?
AS IN, THE *ENEMY?!*

NEAR AS I CAN TELL, YOU'VE BECOME SOMETHING CLOSE TO A LIVING SOLAR COLLECTOR.
THAT EXPLAINS YOUR ABILITY TO MAKE LIFE INTERESTING FOR SUPERDUDE.

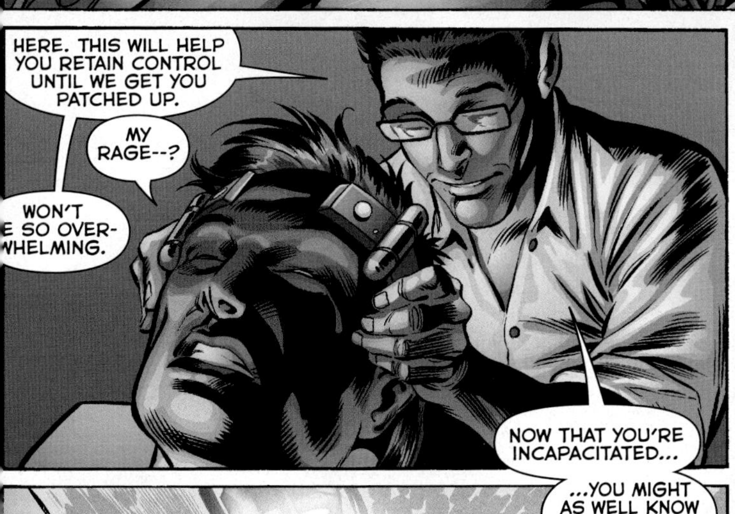

THIRTY-FIVE YEARS FROM NOW.
ARKHAM ASYLUM.
DETAINEE 0017. PREPARE FOR THE TUBE.
I'M NOT HUNGRY.
DETAINEE 0017. PREPARE FOR THE TUBE.
I SAID NO!--YOU CAN'T MAKE ME.
DETAINEE 0017. YOU KNOW EYE CAN, AND WILL.
DETAINEE 0017.
COMMENCING FLOW OF NUTRIENTS.
SGLOUORK
NUTRIENT FLOW COMPLETE.
YOU KNOW, I PRAY THAT ONE DAY IT WILL BE POISON.
HA.
AND I DON'T EVEN BELIEVE IN GOD.
CLIC
KREEEEEEEEE

KILL ME.
REQUEST NOT POSSIBLE...
...DETAINEE 0017. YOU'VE BEEN KEPT ALIVE BECAUSE BROTHER EYE HAD A PLAN FOR YOU.
THAT PLAN IS NOW. EYE IS ORDER. EYE IS ALL.
YOUR HUMAN LIFE OF TORMENT IS ENDED.

TAKE HIM FOR SURGERY.

SO
THIS IS HOW IT
ENDS...

WITH
THE CRAZY CUT
OUT...

AND LEFT
TO PUTREFY ON A
COLD, STAINLESS
STEEL SURGICAL
TRAY.

HA.
JUST
LIKE THEY USED
TO DO IT IN THE
GOOD OLD
DAYS.

WELL, THE MORE
THINGS CHANGE, THE
MORE THEY--

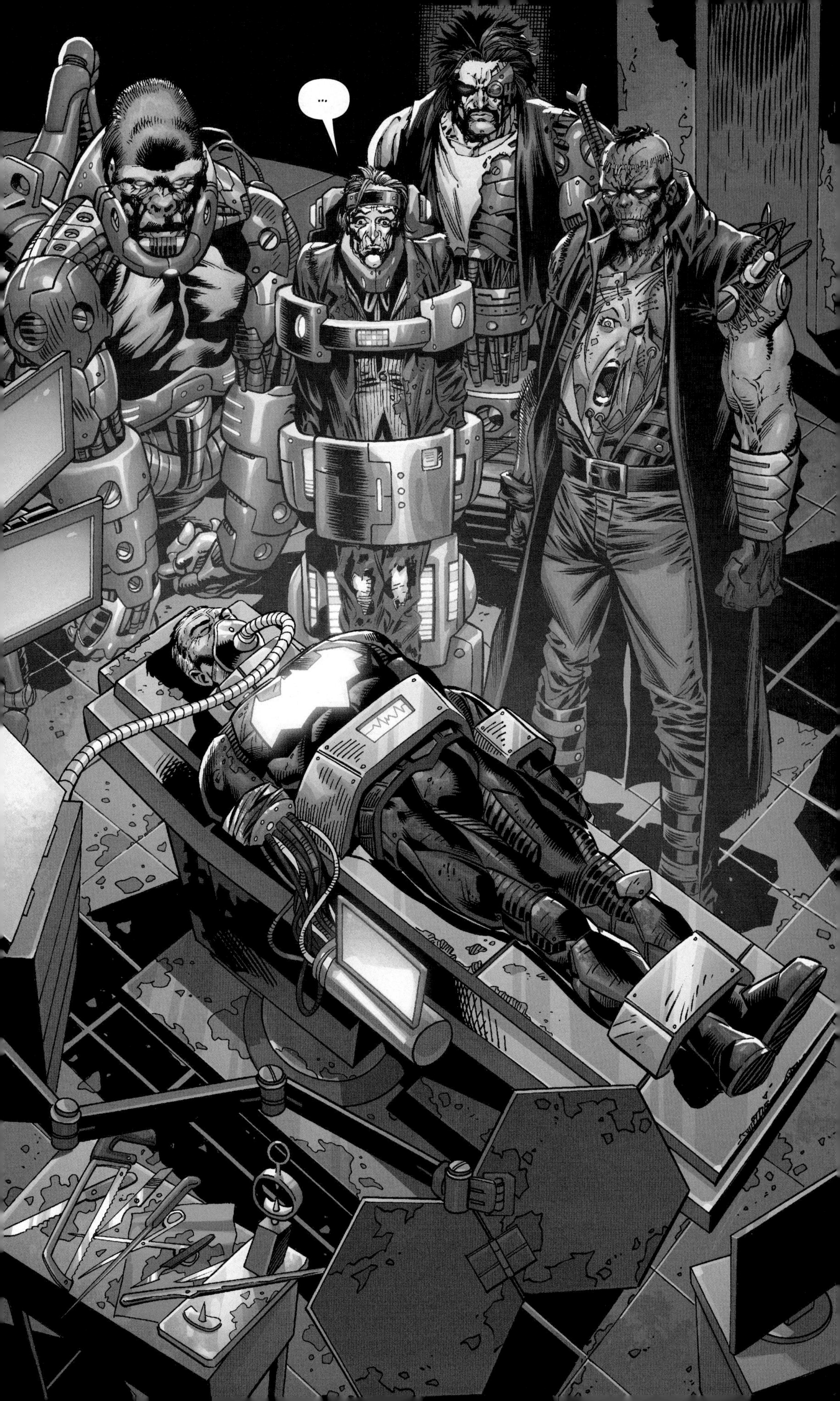

HAHAHAHAHAHAHAHAHAHAHAHAHAH

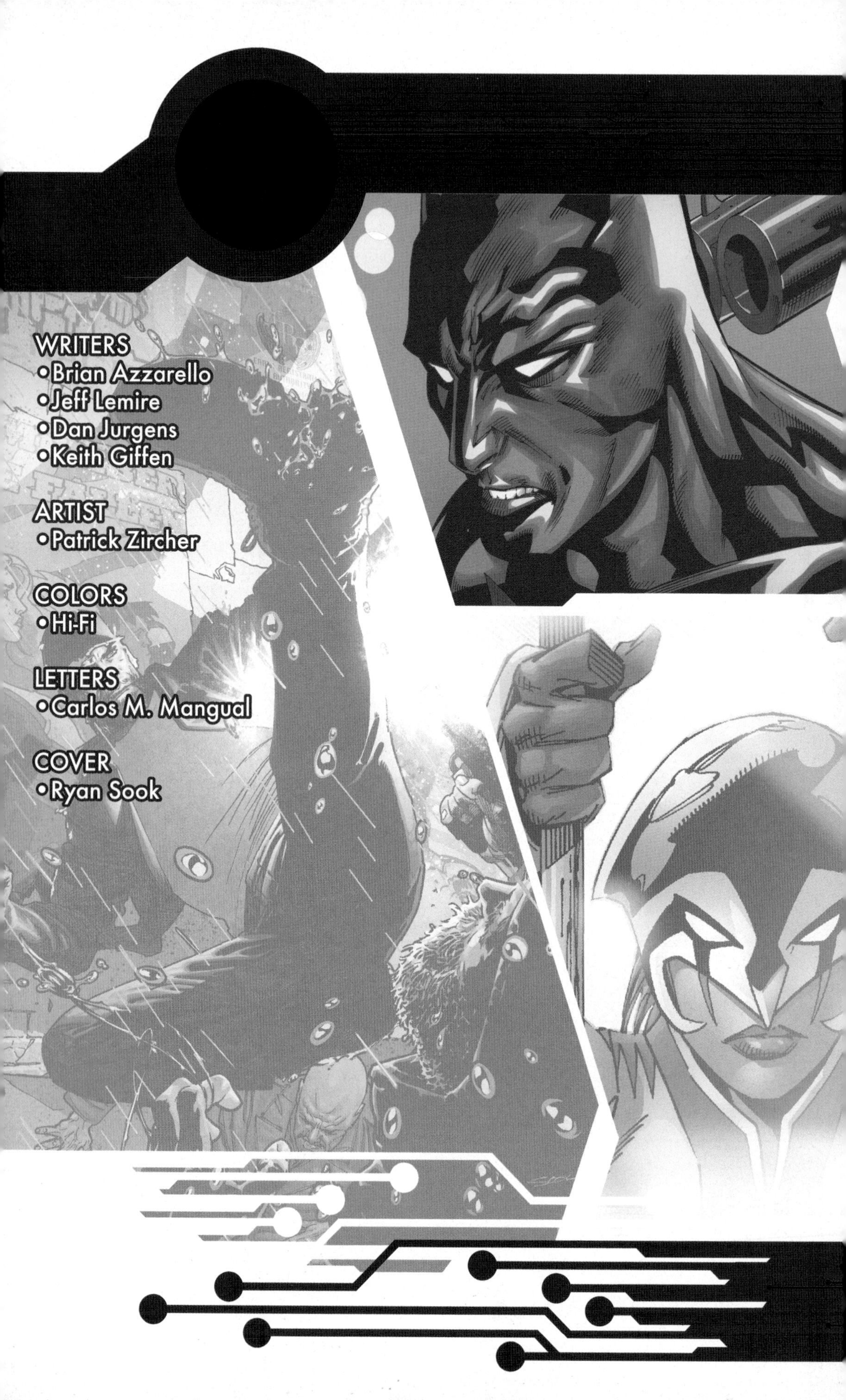
WRITERS
•Brian Azzarello
•Jeff Lemire
•Dan Jurgens
•Keith Giffen
ARTIST
•Patrick Zircher
COLORS
•Hi-Fi
LETTERS
•Carlos M. Mangual
COVER
•Ryan Sook

VE YEARS FROM NOW.
W YORK CITY.
WOUNDED DUCK BAR.
GIMME EVERYTHING YOU GOT RIGHT THE HELL NOW OR SO HELP ME GOD I WILL SPLATTER YOUR BRAINS ALL OVER THE WALL!

OH, MY GOD--!
EASY, FRIEND.
NO ONE NEEDS TO GET HURT HERE.
SKASSSH
SHUT YER HOLE AN' EMPTY THAT CASH DRAWER!
"FRIEND."
DAK
STASSH
CAL!
THAT'S EVERY-THING.
TAKE IT AND GO.
BACK AWAY FROM THAT BAR.
OVER HERE, SWEET-HEART!
YOU GOT SUMTHIN' I WANT.

PLEASE... LEAVE US BE...

NOW THAT I GOT THIS--
NO!

--GLAD TO.
MADDY!

OH, CAL!
I THOUGHT HE WAS GOING TO *KILL YOU!*
IT'S OKAY, HON. EVERYTHING'S FINE.

I WAS AFRAID YOU WERE GOING TO TAKE HIM ON!
WITH HIM HOLDING A GUN?
NOW, WHY WOULD I DO A FOOLISH THING LIKE THAT?

THOSE THINGS LOIS LANE SAID... ABOUT YOU BEING...
OH, NEVER MIND.
THE NECKLACE YOU GAVE ME! IT'S THE ONLY PIECE OF JEWELRY I HAVE.

I'LL GET YOU A NEW ONE, MADISON.
PROMISE.

"HOW COULD YOU, MICHAEL? AFTER ALL WE'VE BEEN THROUGH?"
"MARLENE, YOU KNOW I'VE BEEN A CHAMPION FOR THE RIGHTS OF PEOPLE FROM BOTH WORLDS--"
"--THEN WHY STIR UP HATE? WHY LABEL YOUR NEW BATMAN AN ALIEN? YOU KNOW THAT TYPE OF TALK OPENS OLD WOUNDS AND PREJUDICES!"
"NO ONE HAS FOUGHT HARDER FOR INTEGRATION THAN I HAVE--"
"TRUE. YOU'VE NEVER BEEN ONE TO TAKE THE EASY ROAD. BUT THIS TIME?"
"EASY? IF YOU THINK THAT WAS EASY FOR ME, MARLENE...
"...THEN YOU DON'T KNOW ME VERY WELL."
"MICHAEL...

"THAT'S EXACTLY WHAT I'M SAYING."
IS THERE SOMETHING TROUBLING YOU, MICHAEL?
DON'T TELL ME YOU CAN INTUIT MY EMOTIONS DIGITALLY.
NO. NO, I CAN'T DO THAT. IT'S JUST YOU'RE USUALLY SLEEPING AT THIS HOUR. THE QUESTION WAS MORE OF CONCERN, RATHER THAN A GUESS.
HMM.
I THINK I MAY HAVE LET MY CONCERN COMPROMISE MY MORALITY.
YOU WOULD NOT BE THE FIRST.
NO, I SUPPOSE NOT. BUT I'M AFRAID OF THIS THING.
IT REPRESENTS A QUANTUM LEAP IN CYBERNETIC TECHNOLOGY. IT SHOULDN'T EXIST.
BUT IT DOES.
AND NONE OF ITS ELEMENTS ARE ALIEN. IT'S EARTHBORN.

AND THE MYSTERIOUS NEW BATMAN HAS SOMETHING TO DO WITH IT.
THEREFORE FINDING THE BATMAN IS PARAMOUNT.
I FEEL THAT WAY, YEAH. I MEAN, ORIGINALLY, I FIGURED HE BROKE INTO T-TECH TO STEAL THE uSPHERE.

I'M NOT SO SURE ANYMORE. AND IT'S THE UNCERTAINTY THAT'S EATING AT ME.
MICHAEL, DO YOU BELIEVE THAT YOUR BATMAN IS A THREAT?

I DO. A SERIOUS ONE.

THEN ISN'T THIS AN INSTANCE WHERE YOUR MORALITY TAKES A BACK SEAT TO THE PLANET'S SAFETY?

YES.
HAHA. IT'S STILL A BURDEN.

IT IS THE BURDEN OF GREATNESS, MICHAEL...

"A BURDEN MEANT FOR A CHOSEN FEW."

CADMUS ISLAND.

YOU'RE NOT HELPING.

AM I ALLOWED TO ASK A QUESTION WITHOUT BEING TOSSED INTO THE OCEAN?

I NEVER SAID I WAS HELPING. I SAID I WAS HAVING FUN.

BIG DIFFERENCE.

IS IT A SNOTTY, SNARKY, SARCASTIC COMMENTARY ON SOMETHING I SAID OR DID?

...

THOUGHT AS MUCH.

REMIND ME...*UNGH*... AGAIN. WHY ARE WE DOING THIS?

BECAUSE YOU WERE ATTACKED BY A STEALTH OMAC AND THERE ***ARE*** NO STEALTH OMACs AND, BESIDES, YOU'RE ***MINE*** TO KILL IF AND WHEN I DECIDE YOU NEED KILLING.

JUST PRETEND I'M FROM TEXAS. LOOK, I DON'T WANT TO BE HERE ANY MORE THAN ***YOU*** DO... IN FACT, I'M SOMEWHERE ELSE RIGHT NOW, TOO. I WASN'T SURE I COULD DO THAT. IT'S PRETTY MESSED UP, TO BE HONEST.

WHO'S GOING TO HEAR?
BUNKER GNOMES.

THAT'S A FEW STORIES' WORTH OF DROP. DIDN'T HAPPEN TO BRING A ROPE, DID Y--?

WAUGH!

GOTCHA!

YOU SHOULD HAVE SEEN THE LOOK ON YOUR FACE.
DAMN IT!

TWO HARROWING DROPS LATER...
WHEN ARE YOU PLANNING ON TELLING ME WHERE WE'RE GOING? I MEAN, YOU CAN'T HONESTLY BELIEVE THE E2s WAREHOUSED IN HERE HAD ANYTHING TO DO WITH--
NOT THEM. THE *OTHER* ONES.

OTHER..?
NEWS FLASH, EINSTEIN. THE SUPERHUMAN HOLDING CELLS ARE ABOUT FOUR FLOORS ABOVE US.
WE'RE IN SUB-BASEMENTVILLE NOW.

HOW'S IT THERE'S NO SECURITY IN HERE? THEY'RE STORING SUPER-HUMANS. I FIND IT HARD TO BELIEVE THAT THEY'D LEAVE SOMETHING AS OBVIOUS AS THE AIR VE--
PRESSURE-SENSITIVE PLATING KEYED TO MOTION DETECTORS KEYED TO WHATEVER MAKES NOISE. CADMUS HAS GOT IT COVERED.
UNLESS I DECIDE OTHERWISE.

AND *WHY* ARE WE DOWN HERE? STEALTH OMAC STORAGE? IS THAT IT?
THERE *ARE* NO STEALTH OMACs. HAVEN'T YOU BEEN LISTENING TO A WORD I'VE SAID?
WE'RE DOWN HERE TO GIN UP A FEW LEADS, BRACE A FEW TECHNO-TYPES, GET THEM THEORIZING, 'N' LIKE THAT.
IF YOU NEED ONE ROUGHED UP, JUST SAY THE WORD.

WE HAD TO COME ALL THIS WAY TO BRACE SOME CADMUS EGGHEADS?
WHO SAID ANYTHING ABOUT CADMUS? FOR ALL *WE* KNOW, CADMUS COULD BE BEHIND THE ATTACK ON YOU.

THEN WHY--
CHECK IT OUT.

LAB RATS CADMUS STYLE.
WHAT ARE YOU PICKING UP FROM THEM?
E2s...NOT SUPERHUMAN. NORMALS. THEY'RE ALL E2 NORMALS.
I *KNOW!* IS THIS AWESOME OR *WHAT?!*

NEW YORK CITY.

'BOUT TIME YOU SHOW, SNARK.

NEEDED TO GET THE MONEY, BRO.

LONG AS YOU GOT ENOUGH, I GOT WHAT YOU NEED.

GOT PLENTY.

WHAT'S WITH THE JOOLREY? I LOOK LIKE A STORE TO YOU?

STORE? NO.

COMA PATIENTS?

ABSOLUTELY.

GUH!

THAT SUCKS.
NOW YOU'LL HAVE TO HOLD YOUR GUN WITH YOUR OTHER HAND.
AH... AH...

YAHHH!
KRAKT
WHOA. SO MUCH FOR PLAN B.

"YOU SEE THIS...?"

ANOTHER INVASION?
GBS
...WE'VE PARTNERED UP WITH PUBLIC ENEMY NUMBER ONE!

THE KEY'S WORKSHOP.
THAT'S NOT GOOD.
NOT GOOD?!

NO, IT'S NOT GOOD, PLASTIQUE!!! NOT GOOD AT ALL!

YOU DON'T HAVE TO YELL AT HER.
I DON'T HAVE TO--?

OH, LOOK WHO IT IS! C'MON IN, McGINNIS--AND BRING THE COPS, CAPES, AND ANY *T-TECH SECURITY* TAILING YOU, TOO!!!

NOBODY FOLLOWED ME, KEY.

YOU SHOULD RELAX. YOU'RE TOO PARANOID.

YOU SURE?

I'M SURE, COIL.

NOW, CAN WE GET DOWN TO BUSINESS? I WANT TO GO OVER THE SCHEMATICS OF TERRIFITECH AGAIN. MAKE SURE WE'RE ALL--

THERE IS NO "WE" ANYMORE! YOUR UGLY MUG IS EVERY-WHERE!

BOOOOM

RUE ST. DENIS, MONTREAL, CANADA.

Le Chien Fou

Café

--I SHOULDN'T BE OUT LIKE THIS. SOMEONE WILL SEE ME.

WELL, YOU ***ARE*** A LITTLE HARD TO MISS.

LOOK, I'M JUST GLAD YOU FINALLY AGREED TO MEET UP. IT'S BEEN NEARLY A MONTH SINCE I FIRST APPROACHED YOU, BARDA. I'D ALMOST GIVEN UP HOPE.

SHHH!! DON'T CALL ME ***THAT*** IN PUBLIC!

LOOK-- YOU NEED TO RELAX. YOU'RE TOO PARANOID.

La Boulangerie de la Reine

TOO PARANOID?! THERE IS NO SUCH THING AS TOO PARANOID, EMIKO!

EVERYONE I CARED ABOUT IS ***GONE***--SO ***DON'T*** TELL ME NOT TO BE PARANOID.

YOU MEAN...THE ***OTHER HEROES*** FROM YOUR EARTH?

"I ADMIT, I KNOW VERY LITTLE ABOUT THE SUPERHEROES FROM YOUR WORLD. OUR INTEL IS PRETTY SPOTTY. BUT I *DO* KNOW THAT YOU DIDN'T COME HERE ALONE. THERE WERE OTHERS."
I CAN'T TAKE BACK WHAT HAPPENED. BELIEVE ME, IF I COULD--BUT IT DOESN'T MATTER NOW. THEY DIDN'T MAKE IT TO THIS EARTH IN THE EXODUS.
"I WAS AN ESCORT ON ONE OF THE CIVILIAN ARKS THAT MADE IT THROUGH. I IMMEDIATELY SAW WHAT THE WAR HAD DONE TO YOUR WORLD. THE MISTRUST, THE FEAR.
"WE WERE JUST REFUGEES, BUT THE WAR MADE US *INVADERS.*

"IF THEY KNEW OF MY POWER...KNEW WHO I WAS...THEY'D NEVER LET ME WALK FREE. SO BIG BARDA HAD TO DIE, TOO."

WHAT IF I TOLD YOU THAT THE OTHER HEROES WEREN'T DEAD? WHAT IF I TOLD YOU THEY *DID* MAKE IT AND THEY ARE BEING HELD AS ***PRISONERS?***

I SAW THEIR GUNSHIP DESTROYED BY THE APOKOLIPS FLEET. IT WAS ATOMIZED...NOT EVEN SCOTT FREE COULD ESCAPE THAT.

BUT WHAT IF *HE DID?*

I'D SAY YOU'RE PLAYING A DANGEROUS GAME, GIRL. I'D SAY THAT UNLESS YOU WANT EVERY BONE IN YOUR DAMN BODY ***BROKEN***, YOU'LL STOP WITH THE CRYPTIC CRAP AND START EXPLAINING YOURSELF, ***RIGHT NOW.***

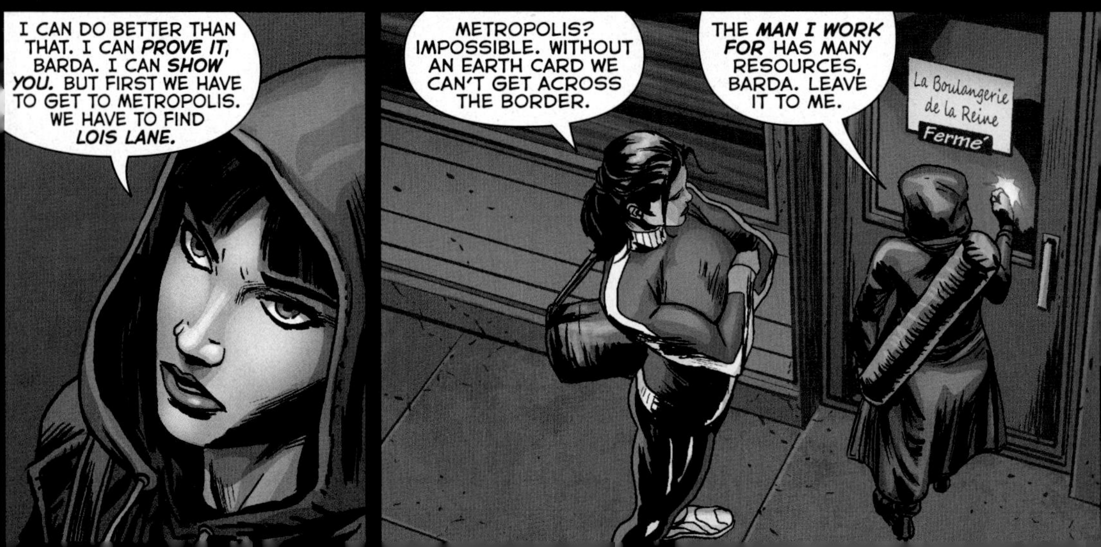

EXCUSE ME, MISS... I--I LOST MY DADDY AND I CAN'T FIND HIM ANYWHERE. HAVE YOU SEEN HIM?
WHA--?
WHAT'S YOUR NAME, SWEETHEART?
I'M SUSIE.
OKAY, SUSIE. I'M EMIKO. WE'LL FIND HIM. CAN YOU SHOW US WHERE YOU WERE?
HE WAS RIGHT OVER THERE, THEN I TURNED AROUND, AND HE WAS GONE!
I DON'T LIKE THIS.
IT WILL ONLY TAKE A MINUTE. RELAX.
THIS WAY!
WAIT, HOLD UP!
SUSIE, WHAT ARE YOU--
BOY, YOU TWO REALLY ARE ***MORONS***, AREN'T YOU? I CAN'T BELIEVE YOU LASTED OUT HERE THIS LONG.

BIG BARDA, YOU HAVE A CHOICE...COME PEACEFULLY OR BE TERMINATED.
GOTCHA.

WRITERS
•Brian Azzarello
•Jeff Lemire
•Dan Jurgens
•Keith Giffen
PENCILLER
•Aaron Lopresti
INKER
•Art Thibert
COLORS
•Hi-Fi
LETTERS
•Taylor Esposito
COVER
•Ryan Sook

FIVE YEARS FROM NOW.
MONTREAL.

BARDA, YOU HAVE A CHOICE...

...COME PEACEFULLY AND SURRENDER TO THE ***GLOBAL PEACE AGENCY*** AS AN UNREGISTERED SUPER-POWERED ALTERNATE EARTH FUGITIVE...

...OR BE ***TERMINATED.***

LOOK, I'VE ALREADY CREATED A DOUBLE AND SPLIT MY CONSCIOUSNESS BETWEEN HERE AND THE ISLAND SO I CAN DEAL WITH ***COLE.*** CAN WE JUST GET ON WITH THIS AND ***WASTE*** THEM ALREADY?

HRNN...

THOOM

NICE PUNCH.
I DON'T LIKE BEING THREATENED BY LITTLE MEN IN MASKS.
P--PLEASE...
DON'T HURT ME... HE TRICKED ME INTO HELPING HIM. YOU-- YOU WOULDN'T BELIEVE THE THINGS HE MAKES ME DO...
GET THE HELL OUT OF OUR WAY, KID. LAST WARNING.
AH, HELL, YOU CAN'T BLAME A GIRL FOR TRYING, RIGHT?
SHRACK

NICE SHOT, *HUNGER GAMES.*

--UNGH!

--KILL YOU--
YEAH, YEAH...MIGHT WANT TO STOP THAT BLEEDING FIRST.
BARDA! QUIT MESSING AROUND WITH THAT KID!
I--I'M TRYING, EMIKO!
OOOH... WHAT ARE YOU GOING TO DO? SHOOT ME WITH A POINTY STICK?
SOMETHING LIKE THAT... YEAH...
BARDA... THROW HER.
WHAT?!
I SAID, THROW THE BRAT INTO THE AIR!

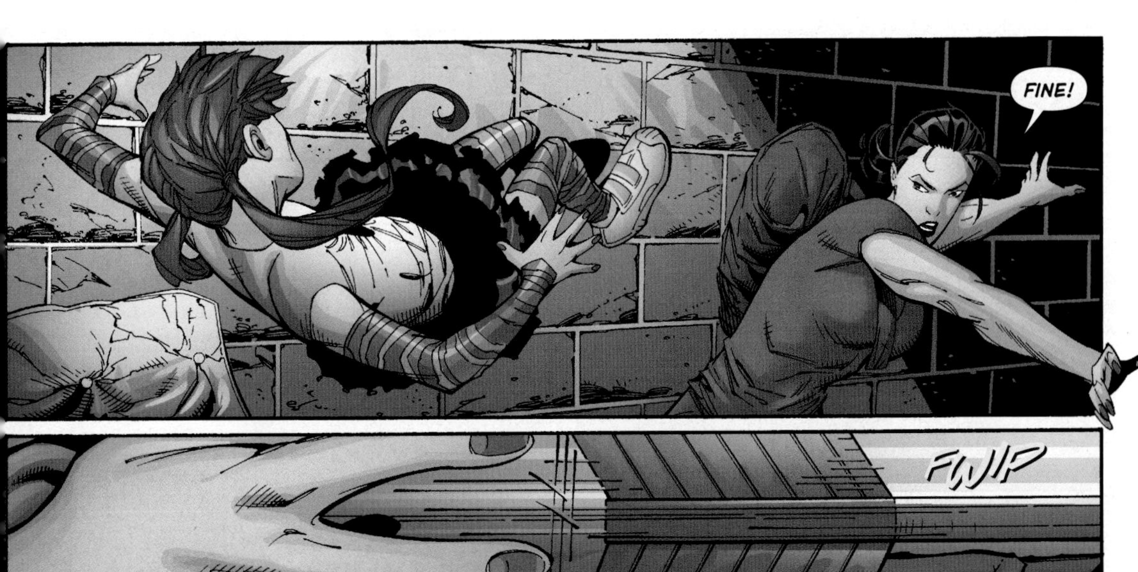
FINE!

FWIP
NOW WHAT?
...NOW WE RUN!

NEW YORK CITY.
THE KEY'S WORKSHOP.
--CONCUSSED. OTIC FUNCTION .14.
SC— ALL—!

WR— KEY—!
INITIALIZING ADRENAL BOOST IN FIVE...
BOTH —YOU!

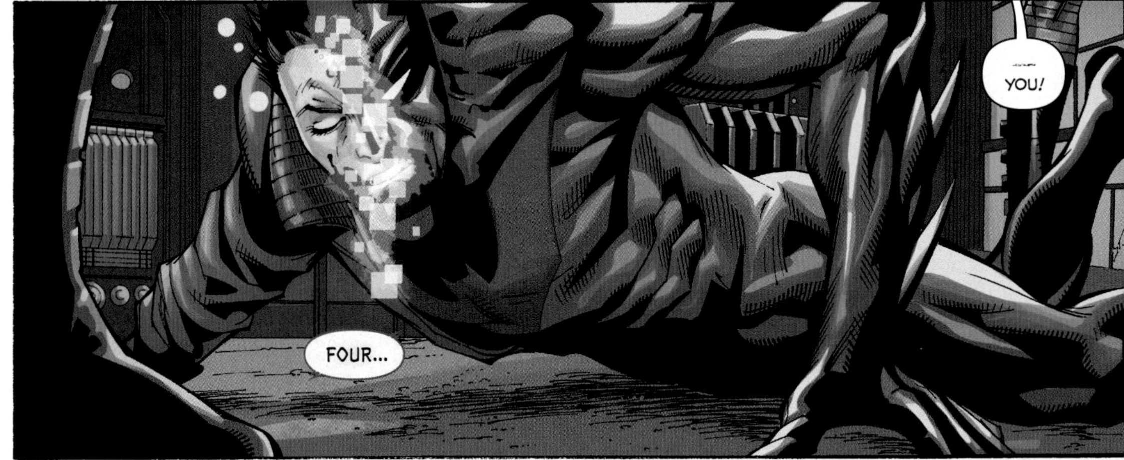
YOU!
FOUR...

THREE...
END THIS.

KEY, YOU CAN'T! HE SAID HE COULD GET US INTO *TERRIFITECH*!

HE CAN *HELP* US!

WHAT THE HELL, *PLASTIQUE*? YOU JUST PUT HIM DOWN, AN' NOW YOU DON' WAN' ME TO FINISH THE JOB?

NOW PUT THE GUN DOWN.

NO WAY, COIL, THIS GUY HAS GOT TO--

DIE. I KNOW. BUT MY WAY.

YOUR?

HIS MAGNETIC FIELD. IT'S TIED TO HIS NERVOUS SYSTEM.

I'M UNTYING IT.

HE'LL BE *DEAD* IN A FEW. THE *BEST* PART? IT'LL LOOK LIKE NATURAL CAUSES.

DOES IT HURT?

I DON'T KNOW. I LIKE TO THINK IT DOESN'T.
LIKE GETTING DIZZY. UNTIL YOU PASS OUT.
COGNITIVE REFLEXES .10.

IF YER NOT INTO SEEING BODILY FLUIDS, IT'S KINDA GROSS.
THEN IT'S KINDA GROSS FOR ME.
.30.

SO TAKE A WALK. HE'LL BE DEAD IN A MINUTE.
COOL.
.50.

EH?

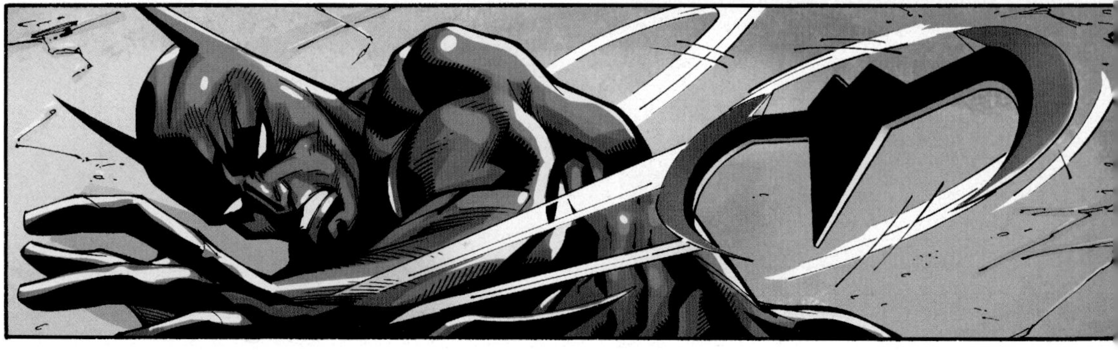

KA-BAM
SLAM

EVASIVE ACTION RECOMMENDED.

STOP IT!

OR I BLOW US ALL UP.

NOW WAIT A MINUTE, PLASTIQUE--

EAT IT, COIL. I AM MORE THAN WILLING TO DO THIS. YOU KNOW HOW MY POWER WORKS...

WE DON'T HAVE A MINUTE?
NO. MAYBE TEN SECONDS BEFORE IT GOES BEYOND THE POINT OF NO RETURN AND THIS WHOLE PLACE BLOWS SKY HIGH.

AND IF ALL I HAVE LEFT IS... EIGHT SECONDS OF YOU TWO SWORD-FIGHTING, WELL, THEN, LUCKY ME.

SO WHAT'S IT GONNA BE, BOYS...

WE *DIE* TOGETHER...?

...OR WE *WORK* TOGETHER?

COLUMBIA UNIVERSITY.
GOOD JOB, MAD. I'LL HANDLE THE E-MAIL BLASTS.
I HAVE THE FLIERS COVERED.
THANKS, ALL! SEE YOU NEXT WEEK!
STOP SEXU
VIOLENC
STUDENT AWARENES
MEETING
2:00 MEETING

IS THERE A CAUSE YOU *DON'T* GET INVOLVED WITH?
HEY, YOU.
I KNOW WHAT YOU'RE DOING, YOU KNOW.
YOU'RE SAYING I'M TRANS-PARENT?
IN TRYING TO MAKE UP FOR YOUR FATHER'S CRIMES?
YEAH.

THESE ARE THINGS I BELIEVE IN, *CAL.*
SO TRUE.
WHICH IS WHY YOU LOVE ME.
I HAVE SOMETHING FOR YOU, *MADISON.*

WOW! IT'S A PERFECT MATCH FOR MY STOLEN NECKLACE!
BETTER.
THIS *IS* THE ONE THAT WAS STOLEN.
HOW--?
THE POLICE CAUGHT THE GUY WHO ROBBED US.
THEY DROPPED IT OFF AT THE BAR THIS MORNING.
SEE? THERE *ARE* SUCH THINGS AS HAPPY ENDINGS.

CADMUS ISLAND.
ARE YOU AS BORED AS I AM?
BOREDOM IS GOOD. IT'S WHEN THINGS GET INTERESTING THAT PEOPLE START DYING.
GRANTED. STILL, THIS *IS* BORING.
GO KICK AN OMAC. THAT OUGHT TO LIVEN THINGS UP.
NO NEED FOR THAT. JUST MAKING CONVERSATION.
WHINING, YOU MEAN.
GROWN THAT COMFORTABLE BEING A *COLLABORATOR,* EH?
THWOK
HIT A NERVE, *EH?*
NEXT TIME *YOU* USE THE WORD "COLLABORATOR," YOU'D BEST NOT BE TALKING ABOUT M--
IF THE SHOE FITS.
K-TANG

HNGH
KLAT-AT

YOU FALL LIKE A GIRL.
WHAT WAS...WHY... WHAT DID I...?

SECURITY VIOLATION. BREACH AT SUBLEVEL 04.
COMMENCING FACIAL MAPPING.
INTRUDER CONFIRMED: COLE--NO MIDDLE--CASH.
NEUTRALIZING.
NOT IF I CAN HELP IT.

MY ONLY HOPE IS THAT THEY'LL BE LESS WILLING TO CUT FREE IN HERE.

WHICH ONLY BECOMES A FACTOR IF I KEEP THEM FROM GETTING HOLD OF ME.
SAY "GOODBYE," COLE.

BAD ENOUGH I HAD TO PULL SLADE'S FAT OUT OF THE FIRE...LITERALLY! WELL, AT LEAST I'M ALL HERE NOW...

YOU GUYS'VE GOT TO STEP UP YOUR GAME. FIRST SLADE AND NOW YOU?
OKAY... I KINDA EXPECTED IT FROM YOU. BUT STILL!
K-KK-KK...
SHHSSSKK
SQUAR-RRK
SHHSSSKK

I REALLY NEED A BATTLE CRY.

UM...I CAN EXPLAIN? KIND OF?
MAYBE?

I'VE GOT THIS.
F-FIFTY SUE, DON'T...
LEAVE IT UP TO YOU, WE'D KEEP COMING BACK AND LURKING.
WELL? WHAT HAVE YOU GOT TO SAY FOR YOURSELF? FORE-WARNED, I'M HAVING ONE OF THOSE DAYS AND AM NOT IN THE MOOD!
SAY...? I-I... WHAT?!
GUILTY!
POOMT
WHAT ABOUT YOU?
...
LANA'S OF NO USE TO US DEAD!
FINE.

I... SHE'S A--
DON'T!
TRUST ME, FINISHING THAT SENTENCE IS *NOT* A GOOD IDEA.

JUST, *UHH*...JUST PRETEND THIS NEVER HAPPENED?
YOU TWO SHOW UP AND IN LESS THAN TWO MINUTES KILL TWO OMACs AND KEVIN AND I'M SUPPOSED TO PRETEND THIS NEVER HAPPENED?!
THAT WOULD BE NICE.

WHY ARE YOU WINCING?
YOU'RE E2, AND I...ALIENS AND I DON'T EXACTLY...
IT'S A LONG STORY.
I SUPPOSE "WHO ARE YOU AND WHY ARE YOU HERE" IS ALSO OFF THE TABLE?

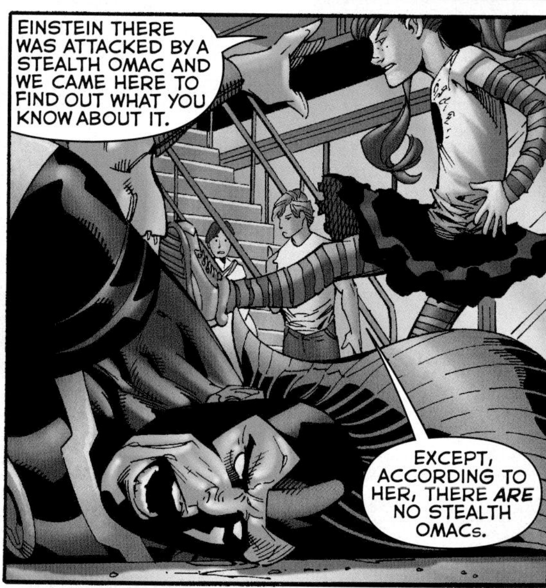
EINSTEIN THERE WAS ATTACKED BY A STEALTH OMAC AND WE CAME HERE TO FIND OUT WHAT YOU KNOW ABOUT IT.
EXCEPT, ACCORDING TO HER, THERE *ARE* NO STEALTH OMACs.

THAT'S... NOT *EXACTLY* TRUE...

WONDERFUL.

METROPOLIS.
THE OFFICES OF THE FAST LANE.
NSBC
REPORT
GREEN ARROW DIED THIRTEEN WEEKS AGO.
WITHIN HOURS OF HIS FUNERAL, I RECEIVED THE MYSTERIOUS PACKAGE THAT CHANGED MY LIFE.
I'VE ALWAYS FELT THE TWO EVENTS WERE CONNECTED, BUT I'LL BE DAMNED IF I KNOW HOW.

NO RETURN ADDRESS OR ANYTHING TO I.D. THE SENDER.
FOUR ITEMS INSIDE.
SEEMINGLY UNCONNECTED.

THE BAR IS IN NEW YORK, NEAR COLUMBIA UNIVERSITY.
AFTER A THOROUGH INVESTIGATION AND EXHAUSTIVE RESEARCH, I CONCLUDED THE BAR'S OWNER, CAL CORCORAN, USED TO BE THE TEEN TITAN KNOWN AS RED ROBIN.
THE WONKY DUCK
423816
1052010
Lois, GO ALONE!
TRUST NO ONE ELSE

QUITE A SCOOP, SINCE HE AND THE TITANS ARE THOUGHT TO HAVE DIED IN THE EARTH WAR.
BUT I'M SITTING ON IT BECAUSE I KNOW THERE'S SOMETHING MORE...SOMETHING BIGGER.
THE ARROW IS A PUZZLER. AND THE NOTE?
WE ALL ASSUMED THEY WERE COORDINATES.

I FLEW TO THE INDIAN OCEAN-- THE EXACT SPOT.
THOUGHT FOR SURE I'D FIND A WEIRD BATTLESHIP...
...ALIEN SPACECRAFT, MAD SCIENTIST'S YACHT...
...SOME-THING.
JUST WATER. NOTHING MORE.
THE WOUNDED DUCK
423816
1052010
LOIS, GO ALONE
TRUST NO ONE ELSE

AN UNSOLVABLE MYSTERY.
LIKE CLARK'S DISAPPEARANCE.

YOU.
YOU DON'T OPEN. X-RAYS SAY YOU'RE SOLID.
WHAT, EXACTLY, ARE YOU?

WHOA!
AAH!

MY...
...GOD...

WHA...
WHAT IS THIS?

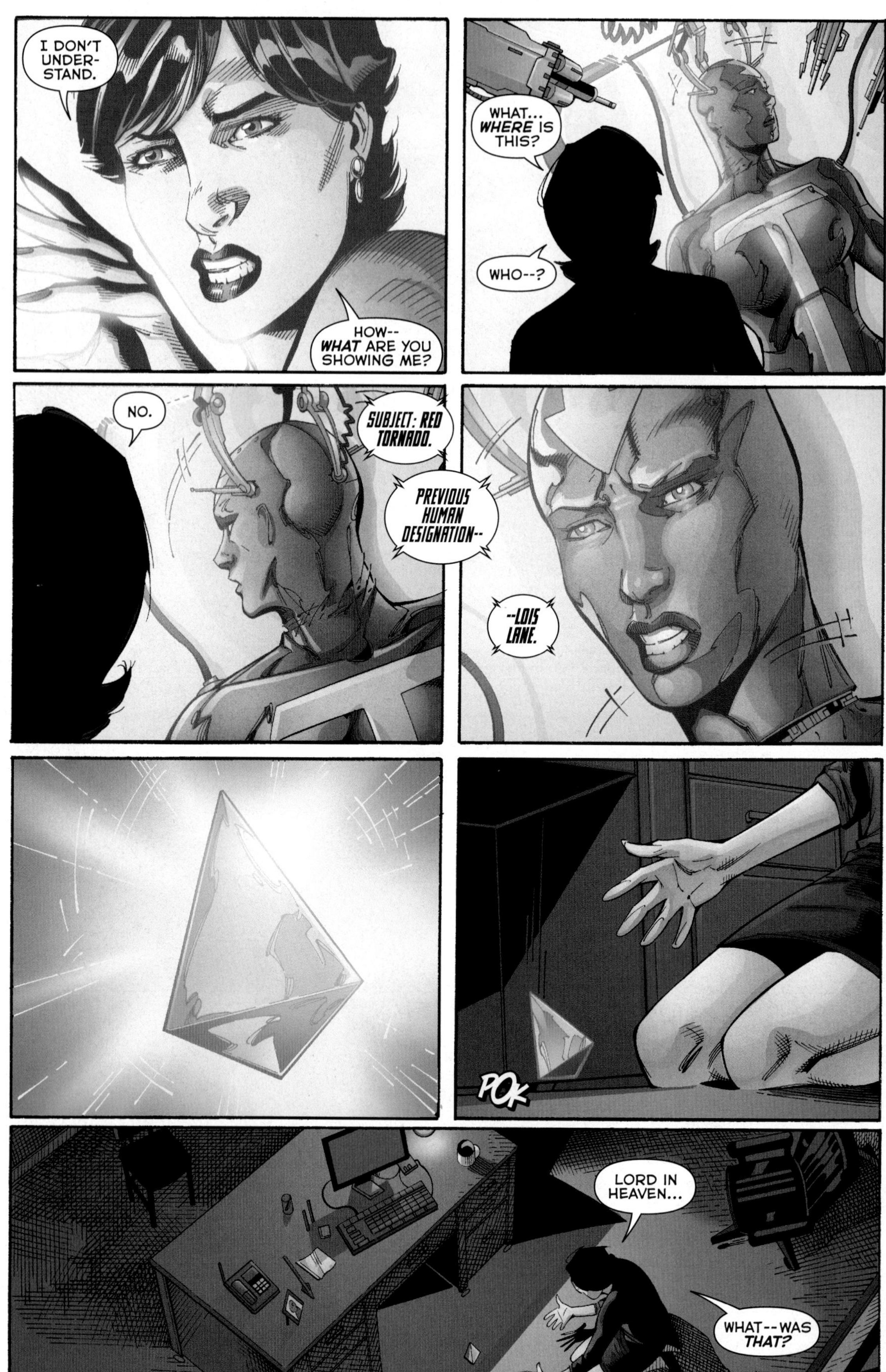
I DON'T UNDER-STAND.
HOW-- WHAT ARE YOU SHOWING ME?
WHAT... WHERE IS THIS?
WHO--?
NO.
SUBJECT: RED TORNADO.
PREVIOUS HUMAN DESIGNATION--
--LOIS LANE.
POK
LORD IN HEAVEN...
WHAT--WAS THAT?

SOOK

WRITERS
•Brian Azzarello
•Jeff Lemire
•Dan Jurgens
•Keith Giffen
PENCILLER
•Scot Eaton
INKER
•Drew Geraci
COLORS
•Hi-Fi
LETTERS
•Dezi Sienty
COVER
•Ryan Sook

FIVE YEARS FROM NOW.
METROPOLIS.
FINALLY. YOUR ASS IS MINE.

YOU'VE ELUDED ME FOR WEEKS, ***RAMPAGE.***
NO MORE.
THIS IS GONNA BE GREAT!

DAKK

SURRENDER. TELL ME WHERE BOYER IS--
--AND WE BOTH GET WHAT WE WANT.
KTANNG
OWW!

YOU COULDA KILLED ME!
IT'S A *WAR ZONE.*
RUN.
SHE'S HEADING FOR THE SCHOOL BUS!

SCHOOL BUS
STOP WHEN LIGHTS ARE FLASHING
23.43
RAU 897

WHERE
IS
THE GENETICIST?
THE BUS, SUPERMAN!
THERE ARE CHILDREN INSIDE!
CRAP.

PAPT

YAY, SUPERMAN!
IS IT FUN TO FLY? WILL YOU FLY ME HOME?
WHERE'S YOUR CAPE?
YOU LOOK BETTER WITH A CAPE.
RAMPAGE!
WHERE IS SHE?
GONE.

LOIS.
RAMPAGE TOOK OFF WHILE YOU WERE SAVING THE BUS.
LOOK, I NEED TO TALK TO YOU.
PRIVATELY.
NO PROBLEM.
WHOA!
A LITTLE WARNING NEXT TIME?
OH.
SORRY.
WHAT'S UP, LOIS?
I THINK... I THINK THERE'S SOMETHING BIG COMING.
SOMETHING BAD.
LET ME KNOW WHAT IT IS AND I'LL TAKE CARE OF IT.
THAT'S THE PROBLEM. I DON'T KNOW WHAT IT IS.
I THINK IT STARTED WITH GREEN ARROW'S DEATH.
YEAH, THAT SUCKED.
I GOT THIS WEIRD PACKAGE FROM AN UNKNOWN SENDER.
THERE WERE FOUR THINGS INSIDE. A MATCHBOOK, AN ARROWHEAD, WHAT I THOUGHT WAS A SET OF COORDINATES--
--AND AN INNOCUOUS-LOOKING PYRAMID.
DOESN'T SOUND LIKE TROUBLE.

THE PYRAMID WAS BASICALLY A PAPERWEIGHT UNTIL IT CAME TO LIFE ONE NIGHT.
IT SHOWED ME A VISION -- OF SOMETHING I DON'T UNDER-STAND.
SOMETHING BAD, I ASSUME.
I SAW PRISONERS. NOT LIKE A REGULAR JAIL.
REMEMBER OMAC? THERE WERE DIFFERENT VERSIONS OF HIM, LIKE PRISON GUARDS, BEATING UP ON PEOPLE.
THE PRISONERS WERE SUPER BEINGS, MANY OF WHOM WERE WEARING MASKS, LIKE YOU DO.
THERE WAS EVEN A ROBOT OR CYBORG THAT SAID SHE WAS *ME.*
WEIRD, BUT IT DOESN'T GIVE ME MUCH TO GO ON.
AND AS YOU CAN SEE, I'M FINE.
REALLY?
BECAUSE EVERYONE WONDERS ABOUT THE MASK.
IT'S JUST... A MASK. NO BIG DEAL.
PEOPLE SPECULATE...IS IT BECAUSE OF AN INJURY?
OR MAYBE... YOU'RE DEVELOPING MORE ALIEN FEATURES?
OR EVEN BECOMING PART... CYBORG?
NOTHING LIKE THAT.
A FEW CONSPIRACY THEORISTS THINK YOU MIGHT EVEN BE SOMEONE DIFFERENT UNDER THE MASK, THOUGH THE POWERS SUGGEST OTHERWISE.
AND YOU?
WHAT DO *YOU* THINK?
I THINK YOU'RE LIKE THE REST OF US.
THE *WAR* CHANGED US ALL.
AND THE THINGS YOU HAD TO DO TO HELP US WIN MUST'VE BEEN AWFUL.
YEAH.
LOOK, I HAVE TO GO. RAMPAGE...
ME, TOO.
YOU MADE ME DROP MY UMBRELLA. I'M *SOAKED.*
A *CAPE* WOULD'VE HELPED.
I'LL THINK ABOUT THAT.

AN UNCHARTED PLANET IN THE HURON STAR SYSTEM.
--BEEN IN THIS DAMNED CELL FOR WEEKS!! WHAT DO THESE CREATURES WANT WITH US?!
AND WHAT ABOUT FRANKENSTEIN? HE'S BEEN OUT SINCE ENGINEER ATTACKED US.
CAN'T YOU DO SOMETHING? USE SOME MAGIC TO WAKE HIM UP OR SOMETHING?
WHO THE HELL SLEEPS SITTING UP, ANYWAY?!
HE'S NOT SLEEPING. HE'S... WELL, I DON'T KNOW WHAT HE'S DOING. HIBERNATING?
ANYWAY, I TOLD YOU...MOST OF MY MAGIC WAS TAKEN WHEN GEMWORLD FELL DURING THE WAR.
BESIDES, WHATEVER HAPPENED TO FRANK HAS SOMETHING TO DO WITH THAT NTH METAL STUFF FROM YOUR ARM.
GREAT.
AND WHAT ABOUT RAY PALMER? YOU'D THINK HE WOULD HAVE TRACKED US BY NOW.
USED WHAT'S LEFT OF THE CARRIER TO GET US THE HELL OUT OF HERE!?

LIKE I TOLD YOU THE FIRST TEN THOUSAND TIMES YOU ASKED YOUR TEN THOUSAND QUESTIONS, HAWKMAN...
I. DON'T. KNOW!
OH, I'M SORRY, AMETHYST...OR DO YOU PREFER PRINCESS AMETHYST...AM I ANNOYING YOU?
LITTLE BIT. YEAH.
GOOD! I'M ANNOYED, TOO!!
SHKZZZZZZ
GOD, YOU HAVE THE WORST TEMPER. LET ME SEE...
IT'S NOTHING. JUST A MINOR BURN. THE NTH METAL WILL HEAL IT.

JUST LET ME SEE, YOU PIG-HEADED--
I SAID *IT'S FINE.*

...SUIT YOURSELF.

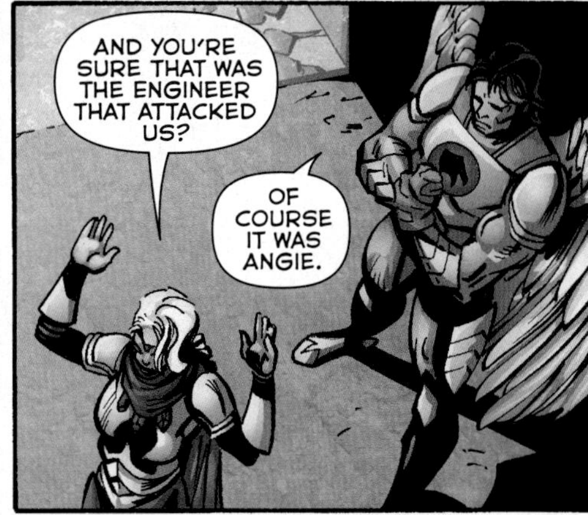
AND YOU'RE SURE THAT WAS THE ENGINEER THAT ATTACKED US?
OF COURSE IT WAS ANGIE.

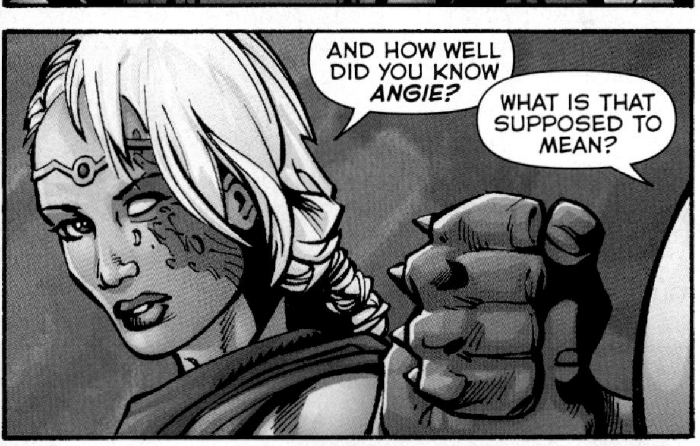
AND HOW WELL DID YOU KNOW *ANGIE?*
WHAT IS THAT SUPPOSED TO MEAN?

I MEAN, SHE *JUST HAPPENS* TO BE THE SOLE SURVIVOR OF THE ATTACK ON STORMWATCH? THEN SHE ATTACKS US HERE...?

IF YOU'RE IMPLYING THAT ANGIE WAS THE ONE WHO DESTROYED THE CARRIER AND KILLED OUR TEAMMATES, THEN STOP RIGHT THERE.
ANGELA SPICA, THE ENGINEER, IS ONE OF THE MOST DECENT AND GOODHEARTED PEOPLE I'VE EVER MET.
WHATEVER ATTACKED US IS *CONTROLLING HER.* HAS TO BE.

BUT THAT'S NOT REALLY WHY YOU WERE ASKING, IS IT?
WHAT?!
YOU WANTED TO KNOW IF SHE AND I...IF WE...
PLEASE... LIKE I CARE.
UH-HUH... SURE, YOU DON'T, PRINCESS.
YOU ARE REALLY FULL OF YOURSELF, AREN'T YOU?
YOU THINK JUST BECAUSE WE'RE STRANDED ON AN ALIEN PLANET, I'M GOING TO FALL FOR YOUR MACHO CRAP?
OF COURSE YOU ARE.
LET'S GET ONE THING STRAIGHT.
THIS IS NOT GOING TO BE ONE OF THOSE DEALS WHERE WE CAN'T STAND EACH OTHER, THEN, IN AN OBVIOUS TWIST, WE END UP TOGETHER.
GOT IT!?
SURE, IT ISN'T.

GRRRRNNN!!!
AAHH!!
LADY AMETHYST... HAWKMAN?
I JUST-- I JUST HAD THE STRANGEST DREAM.
FASCINATING, FRANKENSTEIN. BUT WE HAVE MORE PRESSING CONCERNS.
I'M AFRAID YOU DON'T UNDERSTAND, HAWKMAN. YOU SEE, I HAVEN'T DREAMT IN TWO HUNDRED YEARS.
AND THIS DREAM... IT WAS OF A FUTURE...A TERRIBLE, TERRIBLE FUTURE.
AND I THINK...I THINK WE CAUSED IT.

...COULDN'T HAVE KILLED YOU AND BEEN DONE WITH IT.
NO OFFENSE, BUT I'M GETTING REALLY SICK OF HEARING YOU SAY THAT.
STEALTH OMACs. WHAT, WERE ALL OF THE GREMLINS OTHERWISE OCCUPIED?

SHE BORES EASILY. YOU COMMITTED THE CARDINAL SIN WHEN IT COMES TO FIFTY SUE...YOU GOT INTERESTING.
WELL, EXCUSE ME FOR ALMOST GETTING MY HEAD HANDED TO ME. I DIDN'T ASK HER TO GET INVOLVED. NOR TO INVOLVE YOU.
IS THAT REALLY HER NAME?

YOU ARE AS STUPID AS YOU LOOK.
JUST TRYING TO MAKE CONVER-SATION, WHILE AWAY THE TIME SINCE WE'RE TRAPPED HERE FOR THE NIGHT---
FOR THE LAST THREE NIGHTS.
--PLAYING OUT YOUR PSYCHOTIC SIDEKICK'S VERSION OF A SNIPE HUNT.

I'D WATCH THE TONE OF YOUR VOICE--
OR WHAT? YOU'LL KILL ME?
CORRECT ME IF I'M WRONG, BUT FARADAY TRUMPS WILSON AND FARADAY WANTS ME ALIVE.
SAVE THE THREATS FOR SOMEONE WHO CARES.

I DON'T HAVE TO KILL YOU TO TEACH YOU NOT TO--
EXPLAIN.

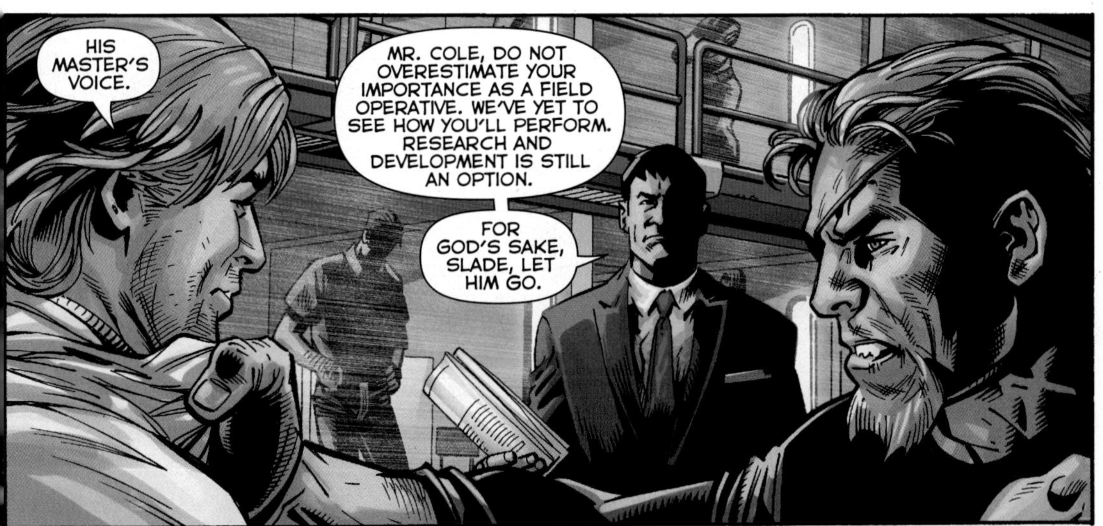
HIS MASTER'S VOICE.
MR. COLE, DO NOT OVERESTIMATE YOUR IMPORTANCE AS A FIELD OPERATIVE. WE'VE YET TO SEE HOW YOU'LL PERFORM. RESEARCH AND DEVELOPMENT IS STILL AN OPTION.
FOR GOD'S SAKE, SLADE, LET HIM GO.

I'M WAITING.
WE'RE... HUNTING STEALTH OMACs.

EXCUSE ME?
I WAS ATTACKED BY ONE. AT LEAST THAT'S WHAT FIFTY SUE, HIS "ROBIN," CLAIMS.
ATTACKED.
IT WAS CLOAKED, SO I NEVER GOT A CLEAR LOOK AT--

WITH ME. BOTH OF YOU.
NOW.

UH-OH. I THINK WE PULLED DETENTION.
PRAY YOU NEVER OUTLIVE YOUR USEFULNESS, "GRIFTER." I'LL BE WAITING.

...ITCHES LIKE A CHIGGER BITE'S ALL I'M SAYING. WHAT DO YOU FIGURE IT'S DOING IN THERE?

DON'T KNOW. FEEDING THEM DATA ON US? OUR BODIES?

THERE'S A COMFORTING THOUGHT.

YOU'D THINK
EY'D TAKE EXTRA
SURES? I MEAN,
RLD'S GREATEST
SCAPE ARTIST"?
HELLO?
WHAT THEY DON'T KNOW CAN HURT THEM.
WHAT DO YOU MAKE OF FARADAY'S LATEST RECRUIT, COLE...WHAT-EVER...?
THE GIRL SEEMS QUITE TAKEN WITH HIM.
AND HE SEEMS TERRIFIED OF HER. PAR FOR THE COURSE. EVEN THAT SLADE CHARACTER PUCKERS UP AROUND HER.
"PUCKERS UP." GOT TO HAND IT TO YOU, KENDRA, NEVER HEARD IT CALLED THAT BEFORE.
DAMMITALL, SCOTT! HOW MANY TIMES HAVE I GOT TO TELL YOU, CLEAR YOUR THROAT OR WHATEVER! A LITTLE WARNING, OKAY?
WHERE'S THE FUN IN THAT?
ANYTHING GOING ON THAT WE SHOULD KNOW ABOUT?
LANA'S MISSING. THEY'RE TRYING TO KEEP IT QUIET BECAUSE THEY THINK THE GIRL MIGHT HAVE HAD SOMETHING TO DO WITH IT.
WHY WOULD THE GIRL--?
WHO KNOWS? SHE MIGHT HAVE JUST SAID THE WRONG THING. LANA WOULDN'T BE THE FIRST PERSON TO GO MISSING AFTER OFFENDING "HER MAJESTY."
ASK ME, ALL COLLABORATORS SHOULD RUN AFOUL OF HER.
HEY! YOU WANNA SHUT THAT THING DOWN BEFORE I LOSE IT!?
POUND SALT, LOOMIS. TOOK ME FOREVER TO SCAVENGE THE TECH I NEEDED TO PULL IT TOGETHER.
LETS ME HIDE IN PLAIN
SIGHT, KEEPS ME CLOAKED,
AND THE PIECE I HID IN MY
CELL PROJECTS ME AS
PRESENT AND ACCOUNTED
FOR. BEATS HAVING TO TIME
THE OMACs' ROUNDS,
THAT'S FOR SURE.
NOT QUITE A MOTHER BOX, BUT CLOSE.
"MOTHER BOX"...NOT TOO CREEPY.

YOU WANT CREEPY? TRY THIS ON FOR SIZE. YOU KNOW HOW YOU'RE ALWAYS HARPING--
I DON'T HARP!
--ABOUT THOSE IMPLANTS WE'VE ALL BEEN FITTED WITH?

TURNS OUT THEY *ARE* WHAT WE THOUGHT. IMPLANTED SENSORS THAT FEED CADMUS'S SYSTEM A CONSTANT STREAM OF BIO-DATA ABOUT US.
ALSO HANDY FOR TAGGING US BEFORE RELEASING US INTO THE WILD. EXCEPT IN MY CASE, OF COURSE.
THEN CADMUS IS GOING TO LET US GO?
THINK YOU COULD, MAYBE, GET TO THE POINT?

THEY'RE GROWING.

GROWING?
GROWING!?
THERE ARE A LOT OF *REALLY* ANXIOUS EGGHEADS OUT THERE.

SOME PRETTY ANXIOUS PEOPLE IN HERE, TOO!
SSH! NO NEED TO START A PANIC. LET ME SEE WHAT ELSE I CAN FIND OUT, SEE IF I CAN GET INTO ONE OF THE SYSTEM HUBS.
INERT MATTER DOES *NOT* REPLICATE.

YOUR LIPS TO GOD'S EARS.

E HORN OF AFRICA.

YOU FEELIN' **ALL RIGHT,** MISTER?

SUNSHINE, I AM NOT FEELIN' A THING -- ***AN' THAT?***

TO DOCKS

TO CUSTOMS

CANSHUUR-BIXI

إلى الجمارك

TUNA

TURAYA

IS BLOODY AL'RIGHT.

HAH.

ANYMORE, WE DON'T GET PEOPLE LIKE YOU HERE.

WHITE PEOPLE.

THE SHIP DRIFTED IN EARLY THIS MORNING.

ABANDONED.
HOW--?
NOT BY ALL.
THERE'S *ALWAYS* A WITNESS LEFT ALIVE. WHAT MAKES A MYTH.

WHERE'S OURS?
THE POLICE HAVE HIM.

HOW YOU DOING, MIDGE?
I'M SCARED, JOHN.

THAT WELL? SPLENDID.
'AVE MONEY?
OF COURSE.

THEN LET'S US 'AVE A **GO** AT THE MYTH BUILDER.

WAS A *ANGEL*, THAT DID THIS.

HMM. COULD BE, SURE.
I'VE MET ANGELS, WOULD HAVE *NO* PROBLEM SLAUGHTERING A SHIP'S ENTIRE CREW IN THE NAME OF THE MOST HIGH.

MY ANGEL IS NOT OF YOUR GOD.
NO? WHOSE THEN?

RACES LONG DEAD FROM BEFORE THE *BEGINNING.*
ANGEL TELL YOU THIS?

ANGEL MADE ME *FEEL* IT.
DID 'E?
IN MY *BLOOD.*
OF COURSE.

WELL, THEN...

"...THIS *ANGEL* IS HERE FOR THE SAME REASON WE ARE...

"...TO FIND THE *ALIEN.*

"WHICH MEANS, FOR THIS PLANET'S SAKE...

"...WE FIND 'IM FIRST."

WRITERS
•Brian Azzarello
•Jeff Lemire
•Dan Jurgens
•Keith Giffen
PENCILLER
•Jesús Merino
INKER
•Dan Green
COLORS
•Hi-Fi
LETTERS
•Carlos M. Mangual
COVER
•Ryan Sook

…E YEARS FROM NOW.
…SHINGTON, D.C.
CASH IS HARD TO COME BY, WHAT WITH EVERYTHING GOING DIGITAL.
THIS BETTER BE THE REAL DEAL.
DON'T GET MORE REAL, BRO.
BOYER'S WORK?
INDEED.
AIN'T NONE BETTER.
I.D. THEFT IS DAMN NEAR IMPOSSIBLE THESE DAYS.
EARTH CARDS BEING GENETICALLY TIED TO THEIR OWNERS 'N ALL.
SOON AS SOMEONE ELSE TRIES TO USE THEM, THEY GO DEAD.
GENIUS THAT HE IS, BOYER COLLECTED DNA OFF DEAD EARTH 2 SOLDIERS.
THE JOHN SMITH OF THAT WORLD HAD IDENTICAL DNA TO THE JOHN SMITH OF THIS WORLD...
BOYER ENGINEERED THESE SO THAT ANYONE CAN USE 'EM 'N WHATEVER CHARGE THEY MAKE OR CRIME THEY DO GETS BLAMED ON THIS EARTH'S SMITH.
YOU GOT WHAT I WANT?
S'LONG AS YOU GOT THE CASH.
FACT IS, WITH ALL THE SECURITY WE GOT NOW, YA GOTTA WORK HARD TO BEAT IT.
WAR MADE IT TOUGH TO BE A CROOK.
YOU DON'T KNOW THE HALF OF IT.

WHEN I HEARD BOYER BROKE OUT OF THE M.A.W., I KNEW HE'D BE BACK IN BUSINESS.
STORMGUARD?
DA-- MRGH.

I JUST GOT OUT AND I WON'T GO BACK!
YES, YOU WILL.
TRAFFICKING STOLEN DNA AND FAKE I.D.s WILL GET YOU A LONG 20.
CHOOM
SLAPT
YOU HAVE THE MATTER DISPERSAL DEVICE, J.D.! USE--UGH!
I SEEN THIS PUT ON PARADEMON SHIPS AND WATCHED 'EM VANISH!
I ATTACH IT TO YOU 'N' YOU'RE A MEMORY!
THAT'S AMERICAN MILITARY.
YOU SERVED WITH TECH CORPS, DIDN'T YOU?
I HAD GOOD FRIENDS IN THE CORPS.
LOST A LOT OF THEM.
WHY ARE YOU DOING THIS, MAN?
YOU KNOW HOW HARD IT IS TO FIND WORK WITH PTSD?
NUKE HIM, J.D.!
NOW!

I...
HE'S A WAR HERO, MARTA. I DON'T--!
LOOK, JUST LET US GO, OKAY?
KEEP THE CARDS 'N THE CASH AND LET US GO! PLEASE?
I CAN'T DO THAT, BROTHER.
YOU KNOW THAT.
THE WAR AFFECTED US ALL, CIVILIAN AND SOLDIER ALIKE.
WE'LL NEVER KNOW HOW MANY ACTUALLY DIED.
NEVER UNDERSTAND WHAT ALL WE LOST.
ALL WE HAVE ARE THE GLOBAL MEMORIALS AND THEIR ETERNAL FLAMES.
YOU FOUGHT TO DEFEND THIS WORLD, JUST LIKE I DID.
TRUTH IS, I ALMOST DIED, RIGHT HERE IN THIS CITY.
BUT I KNEW WHAT I WAS FIGHTING FOR AND CAME BACK FROM THE BRINK.
YOU CAN DO THE SAME.
LET ME BE THE FIRST TO HELP.

CADMUS ISLAND.

REPLAY

ZOOM
KLK

see scott run
run scott run
run scott run
run scott run
see scott run

WHY WOULD YOU DROP THE CLOAK NOW? OR DID YOU EVEN KNOW...?

HOW MUCH LONGER IS THIS *INTOLERABLE* SITUATION GOING TO--
I GREW FOND OF HER. SUE ME. EVERY LITTLE GIRL NEEDS A MOTHER.
WHEN HAVE YOU *EVER* BEEN A "LITTLE GIRL"?

WHAT DOES FARADAY THINK ABOUT MY BEING...OUT HERE? I'D THINK HE'D TAKE A DIM VIEW OF--
DID SHE SAY "MOTHER"?
AND WHY SHOULD I CARE WHAT FARADAY THINKS?

BECAUSE HE SIGNS THE CHECKS?
DO I SMELL COFFEE?
THERE IS THAT.
PLEASE TELL ME YOU DIDN'T BRING THAT COLE CASH CRETIN ALONG?

DIDN'T I USED TO HAVE A REPUTATION?
SLAM!
I SHOULD BE SO LUCKY. TELL ME, ARE YOU STILL HUNTING STEALTH OMACs?
IF THIS IS ABOUT LANA--
NAH. THE ISLAND'S CRAWLING WITH THEM. IT "GOT OLD."
"CRAWLING WITH THEM." AND I DON'T SUPPOSE IT EVER DAWNED ON YOU TO--

TELL YOU? NOPE. NEVER CAME UP. 'SIDES, THEY AIN'T BEEN AROUND ALL THAT LONG.
BUT THEY *ARE* OUT THERE. AT LEAST ACCORDING TO SUSAN.
ONE OF THEM TRIED TO TAKE OUT COLE.
AND MY *NAME* IS FIFTY SUE.

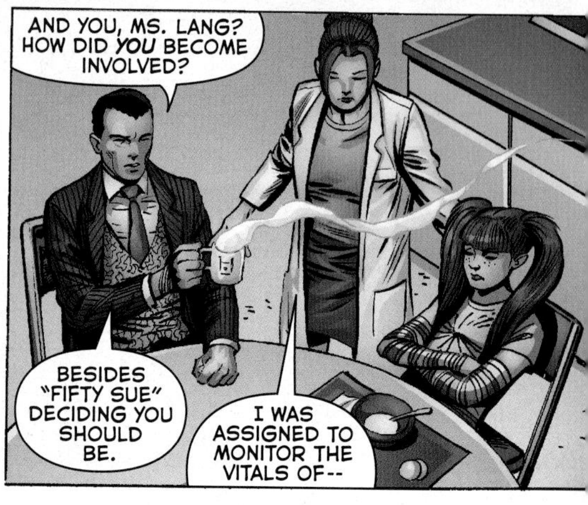
AND YOU, MS. LANG? HOW DID *YOU* BECOME INVOLVED?
BESIDES "FIFTY SUE" DECIDING YOU SHOULD BE.
I WAS ASSIGNED TO MONITOR THE VITALS OF--

I KNOW WHAT YOU WERE ASSIGNED TO DO. I ASSIGNED YOU.
WE THOUGHT... KEVIN AND I, WE THOUGHT IT WAS NERVES--
--MAYBE A FORM OF POST-TRAUMATIC STRESS. WE'D... SEE THINGS DOWN THERE.
"DOWN THERE" BEING THE HOLDING PENS.

I REFUSE TO CALL THEM THAT. WE ARE *NOT* ANIMALS.
YOU TELL HIM, MOM! YOU KNOW, YOU AND SLADE REALLY SHOULD GET MARRIED.
A STABLE FAMILY UNIT COULD BE CRITICAL TO MY MENTAL HEALTH.
AND THAT, MS. LANG, IS WHAT *FRISSON* IS.

SO, YOU *SAW* THESE STEALTH OMACS?
WE SAW... SOMETHING. MOSTLY GLIMPSES FROM THE CORNERS OF OUR EYES.
AND WHEN DID THIS START?
ABOUT A MONTH AGO. GIVE OR TAKE.
WE'VE BEEN *OVER* THIS.

THE ISLAND'S SYSTEMS MAY BE... NO...*HAVE BEEN* CORRUPTED.
WHAT MAKES YOU THINK THAT?
STEALTH OMACs, UNEXPLAINED SYSTEM GLITCHES--
ALL SYSTEMS GLITCH.
MINE DO NOT.
BRING COLE INTO THIS. I WANT TO KNOW WHO, WHY AND HOW, AND I WANT TO KNOW YESTERDAY.
THAT'S NOT WHAT I DO.
IT IS NOW!

SLAM!
FAMILY FUN TIME! YAY!

NEW YORK CITY.
TERRIFITECH.
LIKE I SAID, T, THE FACTORIES ARE RUNNING AT MAX CAP, BUT--
--NO IFS, ANDS, OR BUTS, NATHAN. WE NEED TO HAVE TEN MILLIO uSPHERES IN OUR STORES THE DAY TH GO ON SALE TO CREA THE DEMAND FOR HUNDRED MILLION MORE.
JUST TELL CHINA THEY ARE PART OF A REVOLUTION THAT'S GOING TO CHANGE THE WORLD.
THAT OUGHT TO LIGHT A FIRE-CRACKER OR TWO.
FEELING PRESSURE, MICHAEL?
HA, YEAH. THE ROCKET SCIENCE COMES EASY...
...IT'S THE MANUFACTURING THAT'S LIKE BRAIN SURGERY.
IF THEY COULD JUST UNDERSTAND HOW VITAL THEY ARE IN THE PROCESS...
PERHAPS THEY ARE INCAPABLE OF SUCH UNDERSTANDING.
I THINK ONCE IT'S EXPLAINED--
--THEY WILL DO WHAT YOU ASK, BUT WILL THEY UNDERSTAND WHY?
YOU'RE SAYING THEY'RE MINDLESS DRONES--
NOT MINDLESS, NO.

HMM.
WHEN I WAS A BOY, I WANTED A PET. I BEGGED MY MOTHER FOR A PUPPY, OR A KITTEN-- HELL, A TURTLE WOULD HAVE MADE ME HAPPY.
BUT YOU KNOW WHAT I GOT?

AN ANT FARM.
I'M SORRY SHE DISAPPOINTED YOU.

DON'T BE-- BECAUSE SHE DIDN'T.
THOSE ANTS OPENED UP THE WORLD FOR ME.

YES. TO BE IN THE PRESENCE OF A COLONY... IT'S FASCINATING.
IS THAT WHAT WE ARE TO YOU?
IT WILL BE CLEAR SOON.

ARE YOU A GOD?
MICHAEL, I'VE SEEN MORE GODS BE BORN AND THEN DIE THAN YOU WOULD BELIEVE.

TRY ME.
I WILL. I LOOK FORWARD TO CONVERSING WITH THE MOST INTELLIGENT MAN ALIVE...
FACE TO FACE...

"...WHEN I REACH YOUR PLANET."
METROPOLIS.
I'M TELLING YOU, LOIS, YOU HAVE TO STOP!
THE COPS HAVE BLOCKED OFF ALL ACCESS TO THE CITY'S EAST SIDE!
NOT THE WAY I WORK, TY.

OH. I FORGOT.
THE RULES DON'T APPLY TO LOIS LANE.
NOT WHEN THEY GET IN THE WAY OF A STORY, THEY DON'T.

HIT THE BRAKES OR WE OPEN FIRE!
SKREEEECH
FAST o LANE

THAT'S FAR ENOUGH!
THIS ENTIRE AREA IS BEING EVACUATED!

COMMISSIONER SAWYER REQUESTED MY PRESENCE. I HAVE INFORMATION SHE NEEDS TO KNOW.
HOLD ON WHILE I VERIFY THAT.

WHAT ABOUT HIM?
YOU! HEY!
GET HIM!

THAT WAS CONVENIENT.
WHOA.
IT'S HER.
RAMPAGE!
BOYERRRR!
STAR LABS
SHE ISN'T ABOUT TO SURRENDER!
TAKE HER DOWN!
BRAKA BRAKA
BRAKA BRAKA BRAK
BRAKA BRAK
RAHH!
OH, MY--
YOU!
KRAKKT
YEAH.

GRRAHH!
SPAK
SUPERMAN!
AS STORMS HIT EA
MPD
MPD

DON'T LIKE DOING THIS--
HRF!
THAP
--BUT YOU'RE GONNA KILL SOMEBODY IF I DON'T.
WANNA BE HUMAN AGAIN?
THEN STOP.
LET US HEL--
NO!
BRAKK
HOLY--!
YOU JUST SIGNED YOUR DEATH--
RRRR...
MP
...RRRRAH!
TOK
CHK

BWHOOM

SKASSH
NO!

UH-OH.

UNCHARTED PLANET IN THE HURON STAR SYSTEM.
I DON'T UNDERSTAND, FRANKENSTEIN. THIS TERRIBLE FUTURE YOU CLAIM TO HAVE DREAMT... IT WAS A PREMONITION OF SOME SORT?
IS THAT-- IS THAT ONE OF YOUR POWERS? CLAIRVOYANCE?
HRRN... NO, HAWKMAN. AS I SAID, I HAVE NOT SLEPT, LET ALONE DREAMT, IN NEARLY TWO HUNDRED YEARS.
WHICH MAKES THIS PARTICULAR NIGHTMARE EVEN MORE ALARMING.
HAWKMAN, YOU SAID THE NTH METAL HEALS YOU?
YES. BUT WHAT DOES IT MEAN TO HEAL THE UNDEAD?
HRRN...
I WISH DOCTOR PALMER WERE DOWN HERE WITH US. I THINK THE NTH METAL FROM HAWKMAN'S ARM IS DOING SOMETHING TO YOU, FRANKENSTEIN.
RAY PALMER IS ABOUT ONE ELECTRON AWAY FROM FULL-ON INSANITY. AND, ALL DUE RESPECT, BUT FRANKENSTEIN'S CONDITION IS NOT OUR PRIORITY.
GETTING THE HELL OUT OF HERE--
KTTZ
--IS?

ENGINEER--ANGIE--WHAT THE HELL IS THIS?! WHAT HAVE THESE THINGS DONE TO YOU?!
YOUR QUERIES WILL SOON BE ADDRESSED, THANAGARIAN.
ANGIE--WHY ARE YOU TALKING LIKE THAT? WE CAME TO GET YOU--TO HELP YOU.
THE MASTER SYSTEM HAS PERFORMED SIGNIFICANT UPGRADES AND IMPROVEMENTS. I AM NOW FUNCTIONING AT MY MAXIMUM CAPACITY.
NOW THE MASTER SYSTEM WOULD LIKE TO ASSESS YOUR POTENTIAL. PLEASE FOLLOW US. IT IS TIME FOR AN AUDIENCE.
HRRN... WE ARE HERE TO TAKE THE ENGINEER BACK TO THE CARRIER AND RETURN TO EARTH! I HAVE NO PATIENCE FOR THIS NONSENSE!
SO, I SUGGEST YOU RETURN OUR WEAPONS TO US, AND WE GET GOING. AND IF YOU WON'T COME WILLINGLY, I WILL DRAG YOU BACK MYSELF!
--AK!
DO NOT THREATEN ME, CREATURE. WE SHALL ALL BE GOING TO EARTH SOON ENOUGH.
LET HIM GO--UNGH!
AMETHYST!!
BRAT-AT-AT

COUGH-COUGH!!
WHAT THE HELL ARE YOU?! YOU'RE NOT ANGELA SPICA!
ANGELA SPICA'S CONSCIOUSNESS HAS BEEN SYNTHESIZED AND RECORDED INTO MY DATA FIELD. SHE IS NO LONGER OF CONSEQUENCE TO THIS UNIT'S OPERATING SYSTEM.
I-I'M OKAY...JUST WINDED.
IT IS THIS PLACE, ISN'T IT? THIS PLANET HAS CHANGED HER, HAWKMAN! I-I FEEL IT ALL AROUND US. A MASSIVE PRESENCE... COLD...EVIL.
YOU ARE WRONG, CREATURE. GOOD AND EVIL ARE ABSTRACT CONCEPTS THAT DO NOT APPLY.
WHAT?!
AND THIS IS NOT A PLANET...

IT--IT'S A SPACESHIP THE SIZE OF A PLANET!
THIS IS WHAT ATTACKED US! IT HAS TO BE! THIS IS WHAT KILLED STORMWATCH!

...THIS IS THE MASTER'S SPACECRAFT.
OH MY GOD!
CORRECTION...THIS SPACECRAFT DID NOT ATTACK STORMWATCH. THE MASTER DID...
THE MASTER IS ALL. THE MASTER IS PURE ORDER. THE MASTER IS PERFECTION. WE ARE ALL OF HIM...

...WE ARE BRAINIAC.

WRITERS
• Brian Azzarello
• Jeff Lemire
• Dan Jurgens
• Keith Giffen
ARTIST
• Patrick Zircher
COLORS
• Hi-Fi
LETTERS
• Carlos M. Mangual
COVER
• Ryan Sook

VE YEARS FROM NOW.
THE HORN OF AFRICA.

JESUS... WHAT HAPPENED HERE?

NOT ***HIM.*** THIS ONE'S OLDER-- THAN HIS ***OLD MAN***, TOO.

ALL OF 'EM, DEAD.

EVERY MAN, WOMAN, CHILD-- ***DOG...***

HELL'S BELLS, CONSTANTINE-- IT EVEN KILLED THE FLEAS.

WELL, TORRY--

TOMMY.

SSSSSS

--THAT'S WHAT IT'S 'ERE FOR.

YER A BUFF, RIGHT? "ANCIENT CIVILIZATIONS THAT DIED OUT LONG BEFORE RECORDED HISTORY," AN' ALL THAT RUBBISH?
IT'S TRUE. AND YOU KNOW IT, JOHN.
YEA, WELL, MIDGE. THEY DIDN'T DIE.
THEY WAS KILLED.
BEFORE THERE WAS OUR BEGINNING, THERE WAS AN END--TO ALL OF IT.
THE CAUSE IS RETURNED.
AN' WE ARE SO DONE FOR...
HEY, CONSTANTINE!

I THINK IT WENT THIS WAY...
DO YOU? NOW WHAT WOULD GIVE YOU THAT IDEA?
RUUUMMMBBLE
WE GO THAT WAY.
BUT--
THE DEATH DEALER AN' US, WE LOOKIN' FOR THE SAME FELLA.
WITH ANY LUCK...

"...WE'LL REACH HIM BEFORE IT DOES."
CADMUS ISLAND.
...NOT BIG ON CONVERSATION, ARE YOU?
IF I DIDN'T KNOW BETTER, I MIGHT GET TO THINKING YOU'RE AFRAID OF ME.
NAH. TWO BIG, STRONG GUYS LIKE YOU COULDN'T POSSIBLY BE AFRAID OF LITTLE OL' ME.
I CAN'T EVEN USE MY WINGS. YOU KNOW, HAWKGIRL...HAWK... WINGS?
TRY TO STAY WITH ME, GENTS.
YOU SEE? THIS IS WHY YOU GUYS CAN'T GET DATES. GOT TO OPEN UP A BIT, SHOW A LITTLE ENTHUSIASM.
ACCOMPANY. NOW.
HEY! HEY! HANDS!
DOCTOR SOOK! WE MEET AGAIN, MY ARCH-FOE.
KENDRA SAUNDERS, A.K.A. HAWKGIRL. WOULD YOU CARE TO CONFIRM THAT?
SERIOUSLY?
PROTOCOL, MISS SAUNDERS. I LIKE IT NO MORE THAN YOU.
WANNA BET?

YOU KNOW WHY YOU'RE HERE?
BULL! I'M HERE BECAUSE THE DAMN THING'S GROWING AND YOU DON'T KNOW HOW OR WHY. ONLY REASON IT'S ME IS BECAUSE YOU AND ME--
--WE GOT HISTORY.
DIDN'T UNTIL I SAW YOU. IT'S THE IMPLANT YOU PUT IN ME, RIGHT?
YES. WE WANT TO REPROGRAM IT. THE DATA FLOW IS--
I DON'T SUPPOSE ASKING HOW YOU CAME BY THAT INFORMATION WOULD DO ME ANY GOOD?
POUND SALT!
THIS WILL INVOLVE NO SMALL AMOUNT OF DISCOMFORT, I'M HAPPY TO SA--
SCHUNCH

IT'S NOT BRAIN SURGERY, CASH. JUST LOOK EACH ONE OVER AND SING OUT IF YOU SEE ANYTHING UNTOWARD.

"UNTOWARD"? WHO TALKS LIKE THAT, SLADE?

AND WOULDN'T WE BE BETTER OFF WRANGLING ONE OF THOSE STEALTH OMACs? I MEAN... THESE FOLKS ARE LOCKED DOWN TIGHT.

NOT TIGHT.

WORLD'S GREATEST ESCAPE ARTIST.

GUESS NO ONE HERE GOT THAT MEMO.

HUH?

BO-RING.

FIFTY SUE'S GOT A POINT. GET ON WITH IT.

NOTHING SINGS OUT TO ME. EXCEPT THAT THEY'RE...***MOST*** OF THEM... E2s.

THIS IS RIDICULOUS.

IF SOMEONE'S MESSING WITH CADMUS'S SYSTEMS--

THAT CAN'T BE GOOD.
THOK
AND IT'S NOT EVEN MY BIRTHDAY.
WHAM

THIS IS AWESOME!
COLE?!
DON'T WORRY, I PUT COLE TO SLEEP.
HGGHH-KK
NOT... A GAME...
SAYS YOU.
SURVIVAL HORROR. MY FAVORITE.

VANCOUVER, BRITISH COLUMBIA.
I THINK YOU CAN PUT THE TRUNCHEON AWAY, BARDA.
HUMPH! YOU SAY THAT, EMIKO, THEN THE SECOND I DROP MY GUARD, DEATHSTROKE AND THAT PSYCHOTIC CHILD WILL JUMP US AGAIN.
RELAX, IT'S BEEN WEEKS SINCE WE GAVE DEATHSTROKE THE SLIP IN MONTREAL. AND WHILE I'VE NO DOUBT HE'S STILL TRACKING US...
I CAN ASSURE YOU WE ARE AMONG FRIENDS HERE.
EMIKO!
DIGGLE. RIGHT ON TIME.
AREN'T I ALWAYS, GIRL?
DAMN! SHE'S A GIANT!
THEY DON'T CALL HER BIG BARDA FOR NOTHING, DIG.
WHAT IS THIS?

BARDA, MEET ONE OF MY ASSOCIATES, JOHN DIGGLE.
I APPRISED DIGGLE OF THE SITUATION FROM THE ROAD. OUR ORIGINAL PLAN WAS TO GO TO METROPOLIS TO FIND THE REPORTER, *LOIS LANE*, BUT WITH DEATHSTROKE AFTER US, THAT HAS TO CHANGE.
IT'S NOT JUST DEATHSTROKE...OUR INTEL SUGGESTS MS. LANE IS CAUGHT UP IN SOME TROUBLE OF HER OWN.
WELL, SOMETHING TELLS ME WE'RE ALL HEADING TO THE ***SAME PLACE*** EVENTUALLY ANYWAY.
AND WHERE IS THAT, EMIKO? I'VE FOLLOWED YOU ACROSS THIS ENTIRE DAMNED COUNTRY ON FAITH, BUT NOW I WANT SOME ANSWERS.
CHAK
THAT'S MORE THAN FAIR. WHAT DO YOU WANT TO KNOW?
WHO DO YOU WORK FOR? THIS MAN? DIGGLE?
NOT ME. I'M JUST ALONG FOR THE RIDE.
THEN WHO?!

MY FULL NAME IS EMIKO QUEEN.
GREEN ARROW WAS MY BROTHER.
AND HE MAY BE DEAD, BUT THE QUEEN NAME STILL CARRIES A LOT OF WEIGHT. DIGGLE JUST MOVED SOME FUNDS AROUND AND PURCHASED THAT FREIGHTER FOR US UNDER A QUEEN FOUNDATION SUBSIDIARY.
WE ARE GOING TO USE IT TO GO TO AN ISLAND. A VERY SPECIAL ISLAND.
AN ISLAND?! WHY THE HELL SHOULD I GO ANYWHERE WITH YOU, GIRL? WHAT THE HELL DOES THIS HAVE TO DO WITH MISTER MIRACLE AND THE OTHER HEROES FROM MY WORLD?
THE ISLAND WILL LEAD US TO THEM, BARDA. I PROMISE YOU.
AND WHAT MAKES YOU SO INVESTED IN THAT?
BECAUSE... THE SAME MAN WHO IS HOLDING MISTER MIRACLE AND THE OTHER SURVIVORS OF YOUR EARTH MURDERED GREEN ARROW.
AND TOGETHER WE'RE GOING TO DESTROY HIM.
CHAK

METROPOLIS.

LANE! GET THE HELL OUTTA THERE!

RRR...

TOO LATE FOR THAT.

I'M A GONER.

...RAHHR!

UNLESS...

RAMPAGE USED THIS ON SUPERMAN.

IF IT WORKED AGAINST HIM--

--IT'LL WORK AGAINST HER.

CHOOM

CHOOM

CHOOM

OR NOT.

KILL YOU!

YOU MIGHTA WON THE BATTLE--

--BUT I'M GONNA WIN THIS WAR!
BRAMM
SUPERMAN!
YOU'VE TERRORIZED THIS CITY LONG ENOUGH.
WE DON'T KNOW ALL THE DETAILS, BUT RAMPAGE IS--WAS-- KITTY FAULKNER, A GENETICIST AT LEXCORP.
A RUNAWAY EXPERIMENT CHANGED HER INTO THIS MONSTER.
THE BIGGER AND STRONGER SHE GOT, THE MORE SHE LOST CONTROL.
UHF!
HER LAST ACT OF REASON WAS TO BREAK THE DERANGED GENETIC ENGINEER ETHAN BOYER OUT OF PRISON-- PRESUMABLY TO CURE HER.
HE OBVIOUSLY FAILED.

THE FUTURE IS NOW
THOOM
WHOA.
FROM THE MOMENT SUPERMAN PU ON THE MASK, THERE WERE QUESTIONS.
IS IT A SCAR?
A HIDEOUS DISFIGUREMENT?
A MORE ALIEN APPEARANCE?
OR SOMETHING ELSE?
ALL I KNOW...
...IS THAT HE'S AS STRONG AND FAST AS EVER.
KRAKT
YOU THINK I *LIKE* DOING THIS?
YOU THINK I WANT TO POUND YOU?

UHR!
WHA--?
PAK

I THOUGHT--

CHAKT

SPAK

CHAK

BAK

BRAMMM

EVERYTHING I'VE SEEN TELLS ME THIS WILL BE THE FINAL BATTLE.
AND I DON'T INTEND TO MISS IT.
NEAR AS I CAN TELL, THEY SHOULD BE RIGHT AROUND THIS--
--COR--
--NER.
SUPERMAN?

LO--
RU-- RRK...

--NNG!
YOU'RE KILLING HIM!
GYAHH!
UHN!
FINALLY.
SHAZAM.

KRAKAK

DID...
...WHAT I THINK JUST HAPPENED...

...HAPPEN?

SUPERMAN?

SUPERMAN!
NOT... SUPERMAN...

BILLY.
PLEASE.
HELP ME.

JOHN...
CONSTANTINE--
THERE'S NOTHING HERE.
THERE WILL BE. I CAN FEEL...
RUMMMMBBLE
PSSSH
PSSHH
FWOOOSH

PSHHHHH
PSHHHH
KAL-EL OF KRYPTON, I *PRESUME?*
CONTINUED IN VOLUME 2

THE NEW 52: FUTURES END #1
Variant cover by John Romita Jr.,
Klaus Janson and Laura Martin

SKETCHES AND NOTES
BY RYAN SOOK

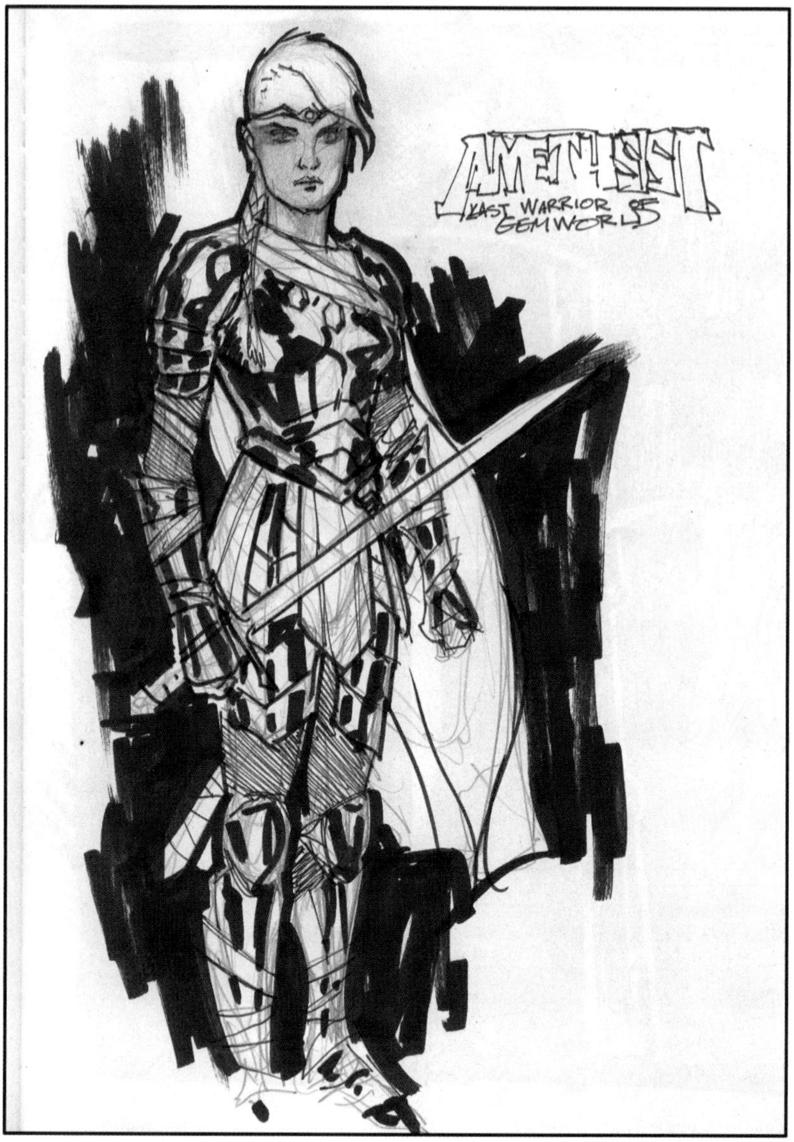

Here are a few of the earliest sketches for the series. Done in my sketchbook during my first meeting with the writers and editors in New York.

Note that Amethyst, one of the first characters that we knew would undergo a massive transformation over the next five years, has no scar on her face. That developed in the design as her character developed in the story.

Also pictured are a few of the first doodles of the hellish future of the DCU thirty-five years from now.

Here are a few of the many iterations Hawkman went through in design before we found the Thanagarian we were looking for to be a member of Stormwatch in Futures End.

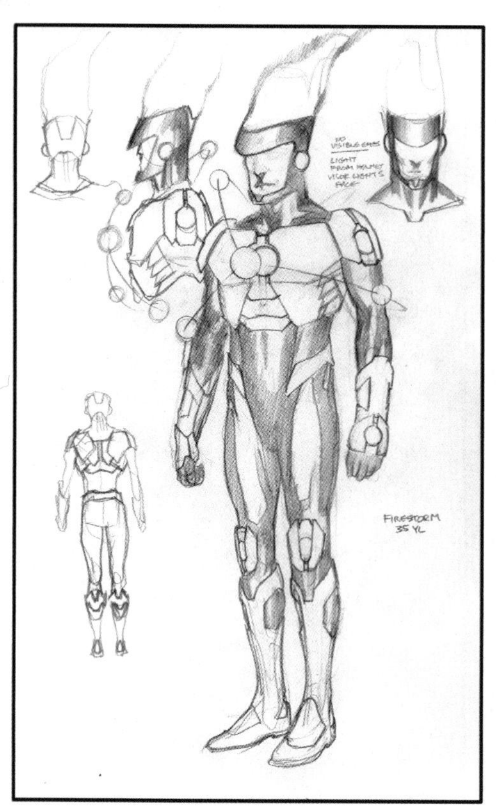

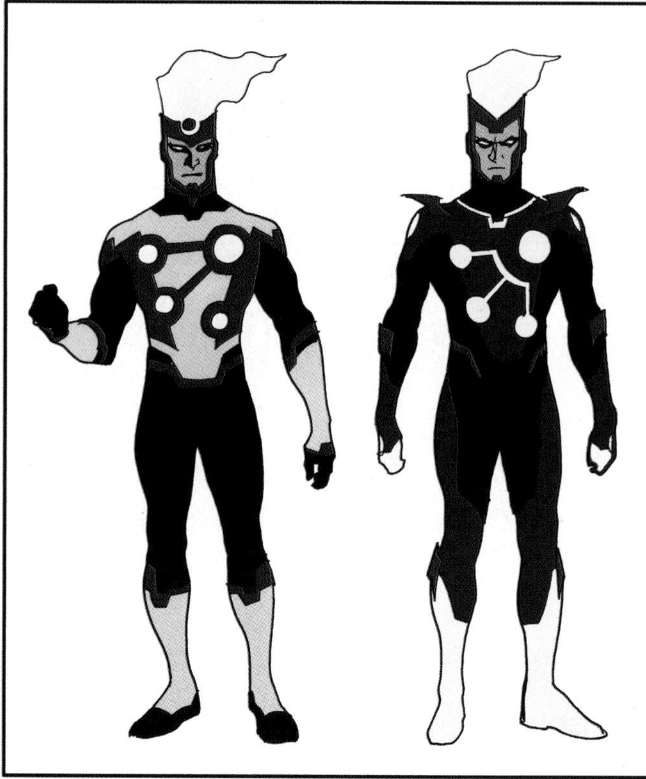

As the characters that make up Firestorm, Ronnie Raymond and Jason Rusch, go through tremendous changes in the five years preceding our story, so Firestorm's suit had to change radically as well.

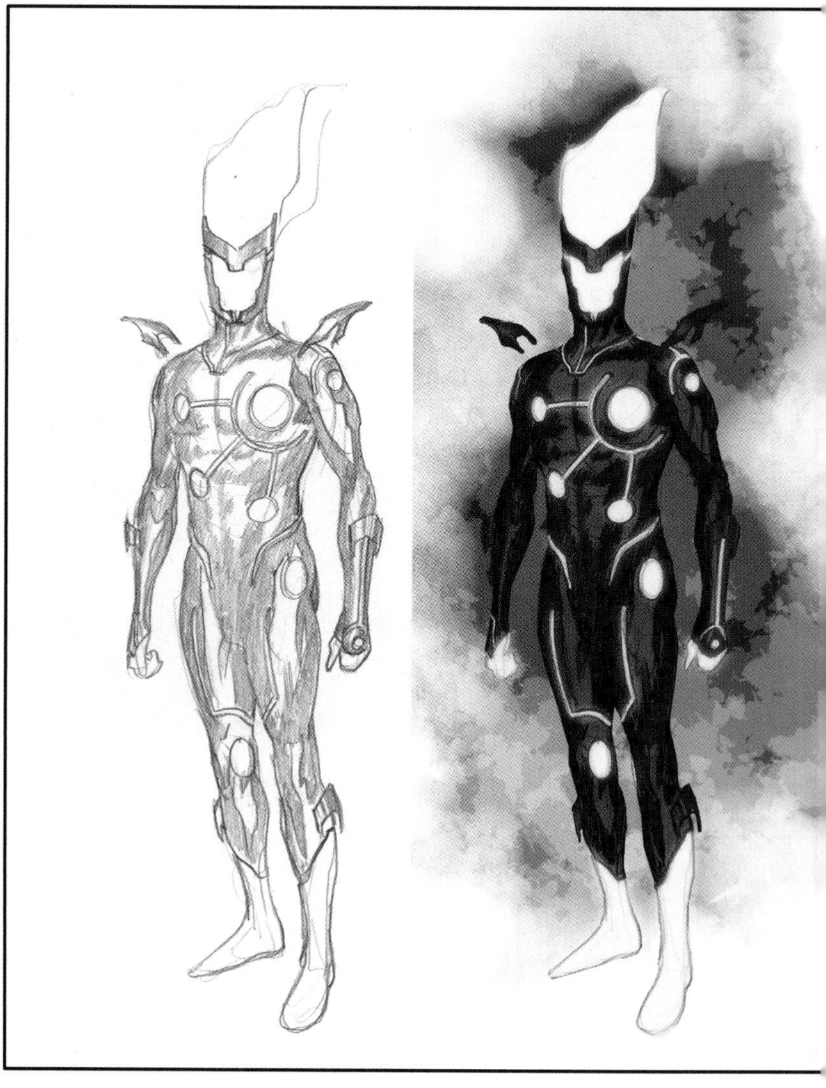

THE KEY

BLACK LEATHER TRENCH HAS ONE GOLD LAPEL AND A GOLD KEY SYMBOL ON THE BACK

PURPLE STREAK IN HAIR RUNS BEHIND EAR AND HAS A HEY LIKE THE SYMBOL ON JACKET TIED INTO IT AT THE END

YELLOW IRIS'

SUPER LEAN LOTS OF VEINS SHOWING

MODERN PUMP ACTION SAWED OFF IN SHOULDER HOLSTER THAT ALSO ATTACHES TO HIS BELT

BIG KEY RING HANGS FROM HIS BELT

BELT BUCKLE IS AN OLD STYLE DEADBOLT LOCK TURNED SIDEWAYS

FANNY PACK ON HIS HIP FOR HIS "SUPER SMACK"

Some villains get a new look in this series too. Like the Key and Plastique.

And new threats, like their cohort Coil, generated fresh designs.

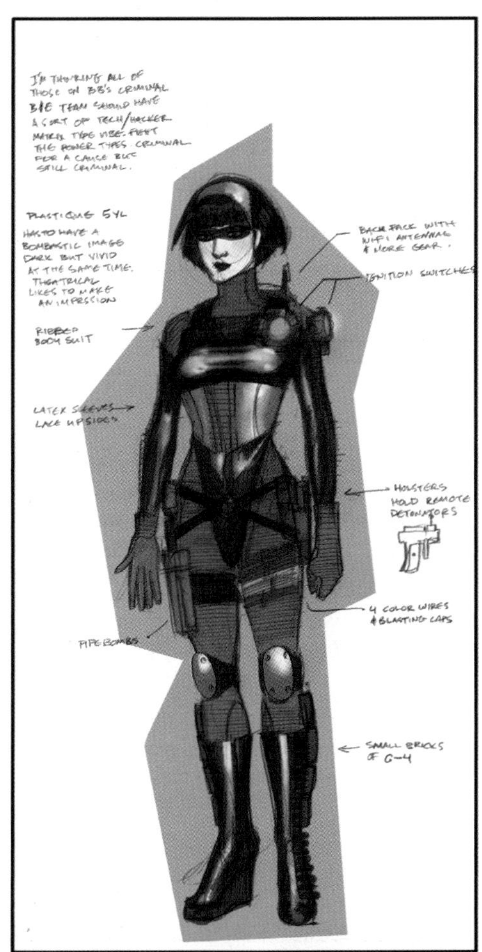

Some things need change.
Some things should never change.
While Giffen's version of Grifter is a darker and more brutal character than you might have expected to read we found that without retaining his iconic mask, he just isn't Grifter.

Everyone's favorite new girl (in the cell) next door, Fifty Sue was a blast to design.
Sweet as ... napalm.

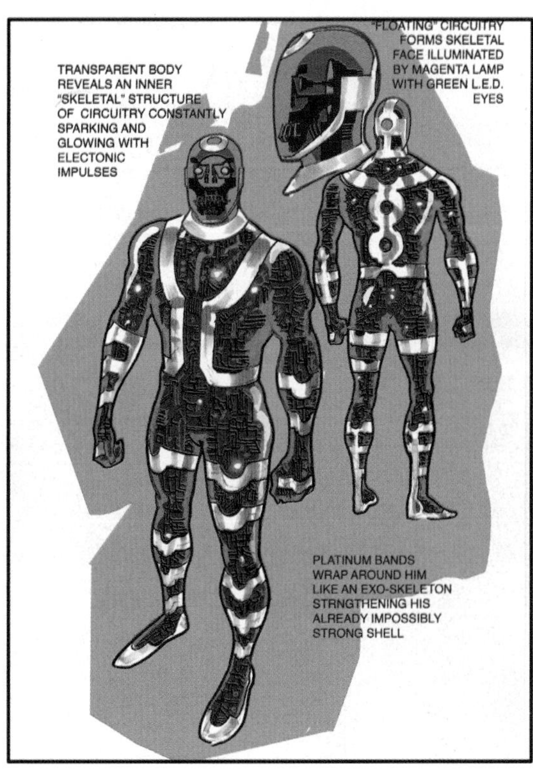

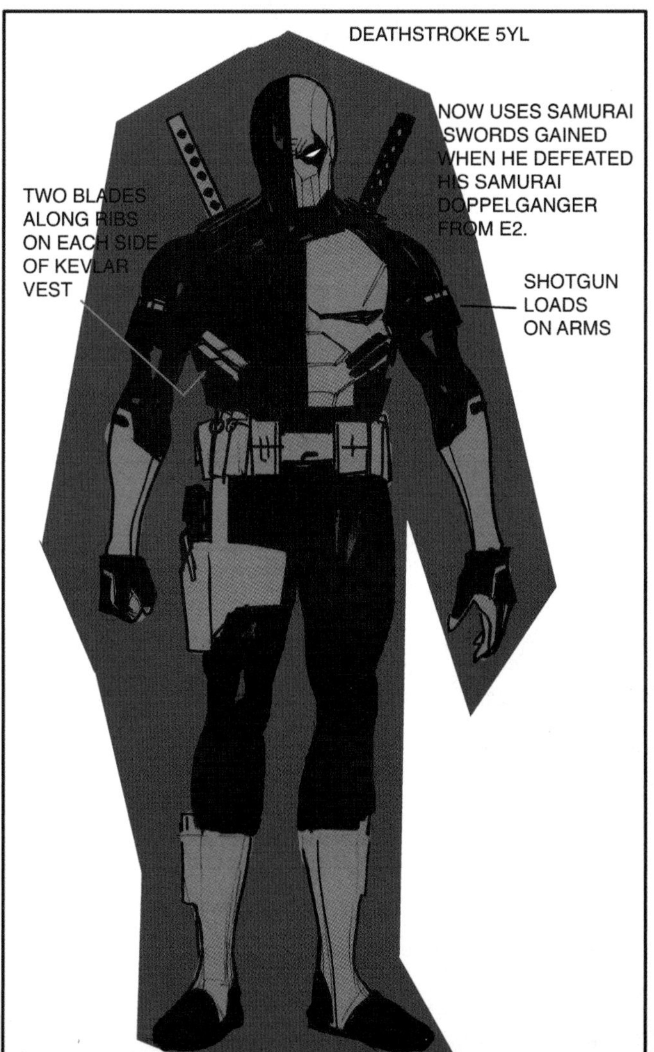

Here are more designs that bring new characters, old characters, and some that you may have just met five years into the future.

From a really loose sketch in the sketchbook. To tight pencil preliminary drawings. This page shows the development of the cover for issue #1.

Some of these images (most in fact) use reference photos to create believable poses and lighting.

Take comfort that you will NEVER see most of them.

On a side note: take caution when shooting photo reference. Try not to alarm the neighbors!

Here's a look at some of the design work on Masked Superman, including Dan Jurgens' original sketch.
Both Masked Superman and a revamped Rampage battle through the sketch process to make it on to the cover of issue #9.

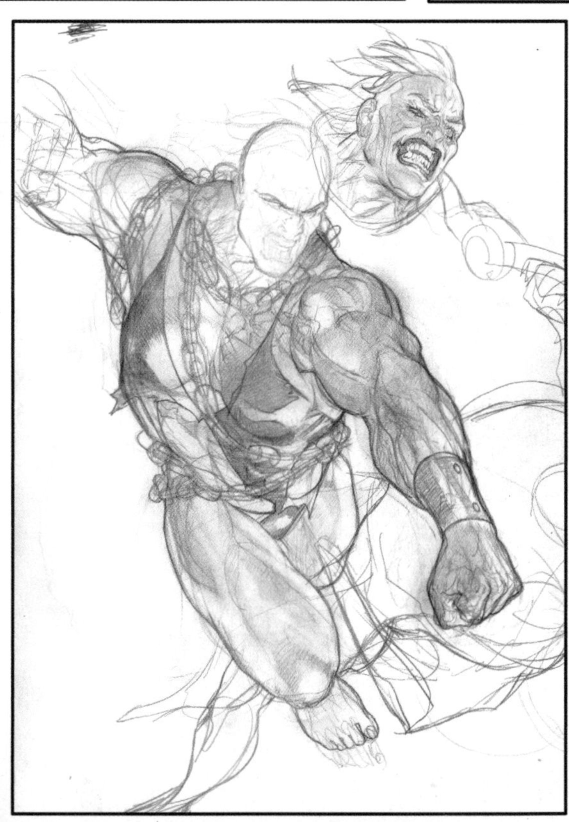

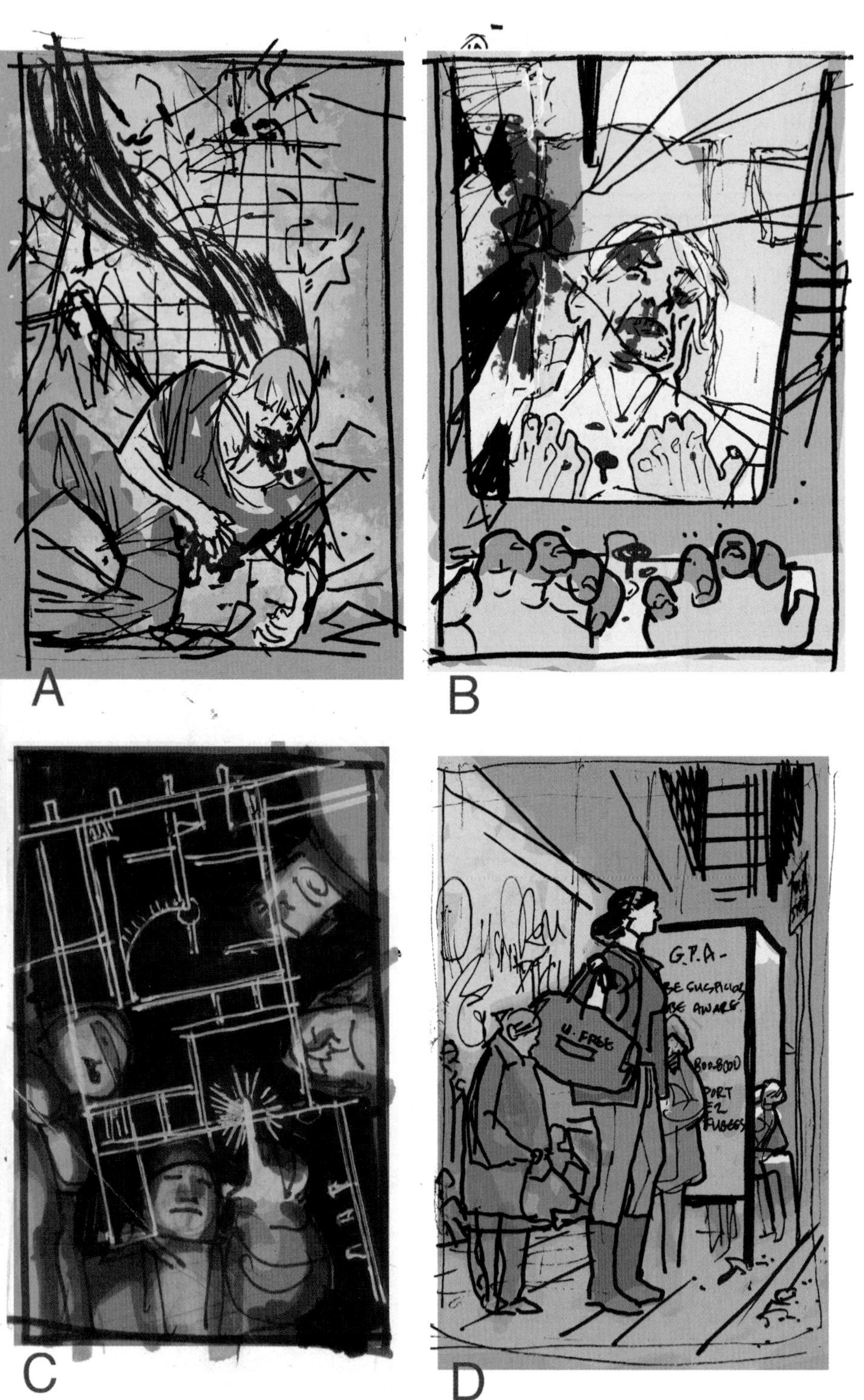

A. Grifter beaten to a pulp by an unseen force.

B. Grifter reflecte in mirror as he's strangled by an invisible OMAC.

C. Terry McGinnis surrounded by the heist crew looking down at a digital schematic of Terrifitech project by Terry's glowing hand.

D. Barda stands at a bus stop towerin over surrounding homeless. She holc a duffle bag labele U. Free. A GPA billboard on the bu warns about refuge Emiko is watching suspiciously from the bench.